Music and Dance in Eastern Africa

Current Research in Humanities and Social Sciences

Editors: Kahithe Kiiru & Maina wa Mũtonya

All rights reserved. No part of this publication may be reproduced or utilized in any form or by any means, electronic or mechanical, including photocopying, recording, or by any information storage and retrieval system, without permission in writing from the publisher.

© Copyright IFRA 2018

Published in 2018 by:
Twaweza Communications Ltd.
P.O. Box 66872 - 00800 Westlands
Twaweza House, Parklands Road
Mpesi Lane, Nairobi Kenya
website: www.twawezacommunications.org
Tel: +(254) 020 269 4409

Design and Layout: Catherine Bosire
Cover Design: Steve '64' Kivutia

ISBN: 978-9966-028-75-4

Printed by: Don Bosco Printing Press
PO Box 158, 01020 Makuyu, Kenya.

Contents

Notes on Contributors — 5

Foreword — 7
Kīmani Njogu & Marie-Emmanuelle Pommerolle

Introduction: Music, Dance and Social Change in Eastern Africa — 8
Maina wa Mũtonya & Kahithe Kiiru

PART I: Dance and the Forming of a Nation in Colonial Kenya

Colonial Choreography: How the British Administration Shaped Dance Heritage in Kenya — 16
Kahithe Kiiru

"Dancing is Part and Parcel of Someone who is Cultured":
Ballroom Dancing and the Spaces of Urban Identity in 1950s Nairobi — 32
Bettina Ng'weno

PART II: The Performance of Local Politics and National Identities

Pan-Somalist Discourse and New Modes of Nationalist Expression in the Somali Horn: From Somali Poetic Resistance to Djibouti's *Gacan Macaan* — 48
Kenedid A. Hassan

The Symbolism of *Gada* in Local Political Campaign Songs among the Boran of Marsabit County in Northern Kenya — 63
Hassan H. Kochore

PART III: Music and the Politics of Love and Gender

Singing Love in(to) Somaliland: Love Songs, "Heritage Preservation", and the Shaping of Post-War Publics — 76
Christina J. Woolner

Dancing to the Marriage Beat(ing): The Gender Debate in a Gīkūyū Popular Music Discourse — 91
Maina wa Mũtonya

Engendering Music: Changing Trends of Music Performance and Dance in Luo Nyanza — 103
Gordon Onyango Omenya

PART IV: Music and Dance in Life Writing

Representing Performance: Memories of Song, Music and Dance in the
Autobiographical Writing of Ngũgĩ and Wainaina   120
Inge Brinkman

Index   135

Notes on Contributors

Inge Brinkman is professor of African Studies at the Department of African Languages and Cultures at Ghent University (Belgium). She studied History and African Studies and received a Ph.D. degree from Leiden University (The Netherlands) with a thesis on oral and written literature, identity and gender in Central Kenya. Her fields of research include: African literature, African popular culture, and African history. The themes of her research engage African literature, performance, popular culture, narrative, literacy and books in the wider context of communication and public debate in terms of cultural history.

Kenedid A. Hassan is Associate Professor at Mount Kenya University (MKU) and the director of the Centre for Frankincense, Environmental and Social Studies (CFESS). He is currently involved in several ongoing research projects focusing on the Horn of Africa: the international frankincense trade, journalism and democracy in Somaliland, and the development of nationalist discourses in relation to poetic and musical expressions in Djibouti, Somaliland and Somalia. Kenedid holds a PhD in Sociology from the Université du Québec à Montréal (UQAM).

Kahithe Kiiru is a PhD candidate in Anthropology at the University Paris Nanterre, attached to the Centre for Ethnology and Comparative Sociology (LESC). She got her master's degree (MPhil) at the same university, with a specialization in Ethnomusicology and Dance anthropology. She is also a dancer, dance educator and choreographer. Since 2011, she has been doing research on traditional dances in Kenya and is currently writing her PhD dissertation. In her research, she examines the constitution of dance heritage in Kenya from the perspective of continuous circulation of individual and institutional actors, choreographic and identity strategies, and dance forms and vocabularies between the local and the national level.

Hassan H. Kochore is a PhD candidate at Max Plank Institute for Social Anthropology in Halle, Germany. His research interests include: pastoralist identities, ethnic and national identity politics, socio-economic and religious change. His PhD project draws on the disciplines of Anthropology, Demography and African Studies to critically explore the impacts of socio-economic change on traditional age/generation structuring system in an East African Age-set Society – the Boran of Northern Kenya.

Maina wa Mũtonya, a senior lecturer in Pwani University holds a Ph.D. in African Literature from University of the Witwatersrand in South Africa. He writes largely on literature, popular culture and politics in Africa. He has taught in Mexico, South Africa and Kenya. His research interests include the performance of power in post-independence Africa and identity formation in popular culture in Africa and the African Diaspora. His latest book, *La Política de la Vida Cotidiana en la Música Popular Gĩkũyũ de Kenia* (2017) talks about the interaction between culture, politics and popular music in postcolonial Kenya. Mũtonya is currently working on migration in Africa and the Caribbean as well as the Afromexican identities and representation of blackness in Mexico.

Bettina Ng'weno is associate professor in African American and African Studies at the University of California, Davis. Trained as an anthropologist she works on issues of space, property, identity, social justice, citizenship and states within Latin America, Africa and the Indian Ocean region. She received her PhD in Anthropology from Johns Hopkins University and her Master's degree also in anthropology from Stanford University. At the moment, she is writing a book on Nairobi that focuses on long-term residents, and the time and space of the city.

Gordon Onyango Omenya obtained his PhD in History from Université de Pau in France. He is currently a lecturer in the Department of History, Archaeology and Political Studies at Kenyatta University, Nairobi Kenya. His areas of interest include race relations, gender history, global history, popular culture and history of international relations.

Christina Woolner is a PhD candidate in Social Anthropology at the University of Cambridge (King's College), where she is completing a dissertation on the social and political lives of love songs in contemporary Hargeysa. Building on a long-standing interest in the role of narrative and storytelling in war and peace-building processes, her current research explores issues of voice and voicing, the mediation of experiences of intimacy, and the intersection of the personal and the political. She holds an MPhil in Social Anthropology (Cambridge) and an MA in International Peace Studies (Notre Dame), and has worked as a lecturer in peace studies at various universities in Canada and Somaliland.

Foreword

Of all the cultural forms, music and dance are the most fluid when it comes to cultural expressions. Music and dance find themselves in this paradox that oscillates between their fluidity and the fixity of some of the traditions that they express. In this view, music and dance provide a research minefield to interrogate and engage with varying themes within the Eastern African region.

The chapters of this book provide a template onto where other socio-political and cultural issues in Eastern African could be discussed. This project is a mosaic of research interests including and not limited to urban and gender identities, the colonial imagination of the colonized through music, dance and performance, as well as the representation of the same in literary works. There is an emphasis on performances in the Horn of Africa, a region that has suffered from the vagaries of war but which has not impacted on a people's attachment to the beat and rhythm of their music and dances. Topics that emanate from the parlance of everyday life in the Eastern African region form part of the research too.

Drawing scholars from diverse disciplines and academic backgrounds to collaborate in this project not only underlines the interdisciplinary ethos in which to approach music and dance, but also calls for new and emergent ways of enhancing an intellectual discourse on the same. Research on music and dance is transgressing boundaries set by the rigid disciplines and charting a new trajectory of its own.

IFRA and Twaweza Communications have been important partners in creating synergies between conducting research and archiving knowledge in Eastern Africa. This book comes exactly ten years after *Songs and Politics in East Africa* (2007), an initiative by IFRA. The book pronounced itself well on the issue of music, politics and performance of power.

These peer-reviewed chapters herein formed part of the presentations at the Music and Dance Research in Eastern Africa conference organized by IFRA Nairobi and the Technical University of Kenya (TUK), with the support of Alliance Française in Nairobi and the African Music Development Programme. The publication of the conference proceedings in this book offers a platform for discussions on innovative research topics and new trends in the Eastern African academic community. It is our hope that the book, alongside others will spur further research in music and dance within the region and the continent.

Kĩmani Njogu
Twaweza Communications

Marie-Emmanuelle Pommerolle
IFRA-Nairobi

Introduction

Music, Dance and Social Change in Eastern Africa

Maina wa Mũtonya & Kahithe Kiiru

Societies are always in a continuous mode of change, from all aspects that define life. The Eastern African region is a community in flux, and has always been. With some countries emerging from internal strife, others have continually engaged in a search for a national identity that is complicated by competing ethnic interests. Historically, whether it's the colonial government dictating and inscribing meaning onto natives' performances, or the constant dialogue in attempt to understand the post-colonial nation and its complexities, or negotiating the question of gender, music and dance have been instrumental. As Barber is wont to remind us, it is "under conditions of pervasive political and economic change that music continues to play a crucial role as a medium of symbolic transaction and a means of forging and defending communities" (1987: 4). Music and dance have thus become avenues of confronting such socio-political realities.

In this way, music and dance provide us with a crucial template for "processes through which identities are (per)formed both at personal and collective levels" (Connell and Gibson 2003: 117). As Wade (2000: 2) argues, "the way people think about identity and music is tied to the way they think about places". This book therefore explores new avenues of rethinking the eastern African region through music and dance as well as understanding "ways in which music [and dance] can be used as a means of transcending the limitations of our own place in the world, of constructing trajectories rather than boundaries across space" (Stokes 1994: 4).

Undoubtedly, the fact that music and dance form part of our everyday experience is justification for engaging in research that revolves around these variables. If Mbiti (1969) characterized Africans as "notoriously religious", it also becomes important to underline that music and its performance is the "most widely appreciated art form in the continent" (Allen 2004: 1). Whereas this book project does not tackle the theme of religion, it emphasizes the notion that the study of music and dance explores different paths of approaching other thematic concerns. Agawu (2001: 8) has averred that African music and dance can be designated as text because the varieties 'constitute complex messages rooted in specific cultural practices'. But because of its fluid nature, 'music refuses to provide a uniform or static text to manipulate or deconstruct' (Connell and Gibson 2003: 3).

In a wider context, adjectives such as universal, essential and social are used to describe music and dance and their place within the human experience. These words attest to the awareness of the relevance of structured sound and movement in human societies across geo-cultural contexts. Although the establishment of separate disciplines with exclusive focus on music and dance within social and cultural studies can be dated to mid-20th century, their symbolic, interpretive and permeable nature has appealed to scholars since the late 19th century.

Early anthropologists and historians examined music and dance as cultural expressions in relation to their ability to translate, into composition and into performance, the values, mores, principles and predominant social relations of a given society. From the idea of a "comparative musicology" studying elements and structures of non-Western musics and the establishment of folklore studies in the late 19th century Europe; through Merriam's emphasis on the anthropological component of music (1964) and Blacking's theory on the nature of musicality (1973); to linguistics and phenomenology inspired analysis of both sound and movement, music and dance have in the 21st century overcome disciplinary barriers and been integrated in a large variety of thematic concerns of contemporary social sciences and humanities.

Regardless of disciplinary labels, scholars today agree on one major point - music and dance not only reflect but also shape historical and contemporary realities of our diverse communities. This is true in Africa as much as it is elsewhere. This important role of musical and dance practices cannot be overemphasized. As Allen (2004) argues, music, through its creation, performance or consumption potentially provides a revealing window into Africa people's experiences.

Having established the important place that music and dance occupy in the everyday lives of Africans, the development of a solid academic and research community on the topic in Africa still presents major challenges. Whereas there is a growing number of scholars dedicated to the study of music and dance in Africa, most of this research is undertaken in Western institutions. On the continent, few universities have incorporated disciplines of ethnomusicology, anthropology of dance and cultural studies in their academic programs.

This collection of articles stresses the importance of research projects and publications giving space to music and dance studies conducted by researchers on the continent, regardless of the discipline they stem from. However, it is important to note that there is a precedent of studies in this domain done on the eastern African region.

While acknowledging the colonial root of ethnography and its attendant baggage, there is a deliberate attempt to exclude from this brief historical overview the early writings on music and dance in the region by British administrators and missionaries with ethnographic ambitions. Therefore, the historically pioneering work becomes undoubtedly that of Terence Ranger (1975) who first drew attention to competitive dance practices in East Africa and defined the coastal *Beni Ngoma* ensembles as musical and social products of cultural contact. In 1985, Paul Spencer edited the first collective book in British anthropology devoted entirely to dance. In his unique analysis of Samburu rites, Spencer (1985) interprets dance as a channel for expression of discontent with social inequalities, an antithesis to predominant discourse expressed in the ritual setting. These two books are seminal works that opened avenues for future research in the region.

Thus, several authors pursued and developed the topic of East African competitive music traditions, e.g. Gearhart (1998), some of which was brought together in *Mashindano!*, edited by Gunderson & Barz in 2000. The subject of competitions and its impact on musical practices within the modern East African context continues to nourish contemporary research; Nannyonga-Tamusuza (2003) studies competitions in Uganda, Gearhart (2005) in Tanzania and Kiiru (2017) in Kenya.

Another important focus has been that of music in relation to nation building and creation of national identity. Kelly Askew (2002) explores the relations between musical practice, political ideology, and economic change in Tanzania. In their book *Songs and Politics in Eastern Africa,*

Njogu & Maupeu (2007) focus on instances where music and performing artists contested, supported or countered power structures in the Eastern African region.

Early ethnomusicology classics giving an overview of traditional music genres and instruments (Hyslop 1958; Kubik 1967; Wachsmann, 1971; Senoga-Zake, 1986) have spurred further research on different traditional music and dance expressions, for example in Darkwa (1991) and Nyakiti (1997), as well as more recent research focusing on the invented and dynamic character of these traditions e.g. Wanyama (2012), Kiiru (2014) and Bushidi (2015).

Religious music and its fusion with elements of various traditional sounds has equally attracted research interest. Publications by Kidula (2010, 2013) and Katuli (2013) in Kenya; and Cooke (2000) and Ssempijja (2012) in Uganda are some of the examples that handle the aspect of gospel music.

There have been studies dedicated to the issues of gender in music and dance performances, notably Fair (1996) who studied dances of female initiation rituals in Zanzibar and their power to mediate ethnic and cultural boundaries between different segments of the island's Muslim populations; and Nannyonga-Tamasuza (2005) who did an historical, theoretical and spatial analysis of gender construction and performance in Bakisimba traditional music of the Buganda community in Uganda.

Recently, in popular culture studies, we have seen a number of oeuvres on popular and urban music and dance genres of East Africa. Nyairo & Ogude (2003; 2005) analyze a popular Kenyan song in relation to the first multi-party general elections in the country, a recurrent theme in their subsequent publications, Nyairo (2004) and Ogude (2012). Other examples include Barz's (2001) analysis of the meaning in *benga* music of Western Kenya; Mũtonya's (2013; 2014) work on Gĩkũyũ popular music in Central Kenya; as well as several diverse analyses of hip hop music in the region e.g. Ntarangwi's (2009) and Eisenberg (2012), and Sanga's (2013) approach to Tanzanian *bongo fleva* genre. Rosenberg's (2011) research is a comparative effort that looks at the relationship between songs and the literatures in the Eastern African region.

Others include Gunderson's (2010) research on Sukuma labour songs in Tanzania; Edmondson's (2001) analysis of the eroticization of traditional *ngoma* in the same country; Mwangi's (2006) retracing of music censorship in colonial and post-colonial Kenya; and Marmone's (2017) recently published analysis of social change in the Samburu community of Northern Kenya through music.

These are just some of the works dedicated to the topic of music and dance in the eastern African region. The references above are by no means exhaustive. As a resurgent practice both in the academia and among other stakeholders, it has become clear that there is growing interest in studies on music and dance and this publication is just an addition to the growing list. Connell and Gibson (2001) argue that the academic world has, in many respects, shifted in ways that make it possible to take music and dance seriously. "The move away from the rigid theories of society and economy towards studies of social diversity and heterogeneity has illuminated the complexities of how members of communities create meanings and identities for themselves". (Connell and Gibson 2001: 2)

This book is a product of a regional conference on Music and Dance Research in East Africa organized in October 2016 by The French Institute for Research in Africa (IFRA, Nairobi) and the Technical University of Kenya (TUK), with the support of the African Music Development Program (IMC & EU). The general framework for the conference was the inclusion of music and/or dance in the widely studied topics in social sciences, such as the construction of the state, national and ethnic identities, political and social activism, heritage creation and preservation, cultural tourism and development studies, gender and generational issues, etc. The chapters of this book are reviewed papers presented at the 2016 conference, which had assembled researchers from the region and beyond, critically interrogating issues concerning creation, tradition, innovation, and appropriation in music and dance.

With this project, the French Institute for Research in Africa (IFRA, Nairobi) asserts its commitment to assisting and advocating for research enquiry into music and dance in the regional academic landscape, as seen in an earlier publication mentioned above by Njogu & Maupeu (2007) that centered on the relationship between music and politics.

The first two sections of this book resonate with the theme of politics, whether in view of the shaping of music for and through historically diverse political agendas or the contestation of power structures in place via musical performance. The historical background of the first part is set in late colonial Kenya, where the political and social friction between the settler and the native communities is reflected in both rural and urban musical and dance expressions. As the British colonial administration regulates native dances and translates them into commercial performance scenarios (Kiiru), the African dwellers of rapidly expanding Nairobi town engage in ballroom dancing competitions and use dance as means for creating an urban identity (Ng'weno).

While considering the performance of local politics and national identities, the second part of the book begins by exploring the evolution of nationalist discourses in the Somali Horn (Hassan), through the artistic expression of several actors, notably Somali musicians, poets and a Djiboutian band. The emphasis here is on the transnational circulation of sounds and ideas and their impact on local historical developments. In the succeeding chapter Kochore, looks at the ways in which the Boran community of Marsabit in Northern Kenya use the reference to their traditional institution *gada* in contemporary political campaign songs in order to make sense of the Kenyan political system and position themselves in it.

The third part of the book assembles the themes of gender and gender relations. The live performance of love songs in a unique venue in Hargeysa, Somaliland is implicated in the shaping of post-war publics (Woolner), who celebrate "traditional" Somali identity, while simultaneously pushing the limits of everyday social conventions between genders. In the Kenyan context, Mũtonya unravels the stereotypes derived from the intricate power play in marital relationships and their echo in Gĩkũyũ popular songs, while Omenya interrogates the changing trends of gender participation in Luo music.

In part four, Brinkman offers a unique approach to the study of music through literature, more specifically looking at memories of music and representation of performance in autobiographical writing of Ngũgĩ wa Thiong'o and Binyavanga Wainaina. This intertextual reference points to how music and other disciplines constantly talk to each other.

Finally, the collection of articles presented here tackle a large number of themes and cover different historical periods, as authors approach music and dance from an interdisciplinary perspective. It is hoped that it shall provide innovative insights and make a relevant contribution to the recurrent dialogue towards emphasizing the relevance of music and dance studies in the larger context of humanities and social sciences.

Bibliography

Agawu, K. 2001. African Music as Text. *Research in African Literatures* 32(2) 8-16

Allen, L. 2004. Music and Politics in Africa. *Social Dynamics* 30(2) 1-19

Askew, K. 2002. *Performing the Nation, Swahili Music and Cultural Politics in Tanzania*. Chicago, University of Chicago Press.

Barber, K. 1987. Popular Arts in Africa, *African Studies Review* 30(3) 1-78

Barz, G. 2001. Meaning in *Benga* Music of Western Kenya. *British Journal of Ethnomusicology* 10 (1): 107-115.

Barz, G. 2004. *Music in East Africa: Experiencing Music, Expressing Culture*. New York, Oxford University Press.

Blacking, J. 1973. *How Musical is Man?* Seattle, University of Washington Press.

Bushidi, C. 2015. Reflections on the fabrication of musical folklore in Kenya from the early 1920s to the late 1970s. *Les Cahiers d'Afrique de l'Est* 50: 8-21.

Connell, J. and Gibson C. 2003. *Sound Tracks: Popular Music, Identity and Place*. London, New York, Routledge.

Cooke, P. 2000. Appeasing the Spirits: Music, Possession, Divination and Healing in Busoga, Eastern Uganda. In Ralls-MacLeod K. & Graham Harvey G. (eds) *Indigenous Religious Musics*. London, Routledge: 102-121.

Darkwa, A. 1984. Traditional Music and Dance Practices of the Iteso of Kenya. *The Cambridge Journal of Anthropology* 9 (1): 68-76.

Darkwa, A. 1991. Sengenya Dance Music: Its Instrumental Resources and Performance. *African Music* 7 (1): 48-54.

Edmondson, L. 2001. National Erotica: The Politics of "Traditional" Dance in Tanzania. *The Drama Review* 45 (1): 153-170.

Eisenberg, A. 2012. Hip-Hop and Cultural Citizenship on Kenya's 'Swahili Coast'. *Africa* 82 (4): 556 – 578.

Fair, L. 1996. Identity, Difference, and Dance: Female Initiation in Zanzibar, 1890 to 1930. *Frontiers: A Journal of Women Studies* 17 (3) 146-172.

Gearhart, R. 1998. *Ngoma Memories: A History of Competitive Music and Dance Performance on the Kenya Coast*. Gainesville, University of Florida, unpublished PhD diss.

Gearhart, R. 2005. Ngoma Memories: How Ritual Music and Dance Shaped the Northern Kenya Coast. *African Studies Review* 48 (3): 21-47.

Gunderson, F. & Barz G. (eds) 2000. *Mashindano! Competitive Music Performance in East Africa*. Dar es Salaam, Mkuki na Nyota Publishers.

Gunderson, F. 2010. *Sukuma Labor Songs from Western Tanzania: 'We Never Sleep; We Dream of Farming'*. Leiden: Brill.

Gunderson, F. 2013. Expressive Bodies / Controlling Impulses: The Dance between Official Culture and Musical Resistance in Colonial Western Tanganyika. *Soundings* 96 (2): 145-169.

Hyslop G. 1958. African Musical Instruments in Kenya. *African Music* 2 (1): 31-36.

Katuli, J. 2013. Ethnic Music in Christian Worship: The Challenges of incorporating Traditional Music into the Liturgy of the Catholic Church in Ukambani, in Strumpf M. (ed) *Readings in Ethnomusicology: a collection of papers presented at Ethnomusicology Symposium*. Ar-es-Salaam, University of Dar-es-Salaam.

Kidula, J. 2010. "There Is Power": Contemporizing Old Music Traditions for New Gospel Audiences in Kenya. *Yearbook for Traditional Music* 42: 62-80.

Kidula, J. 2013. *Music in Kenyan Christianity: Logooli Religious Song*. Bloomington, Indiana University Press.

Kiiru, K. 2014. Bomas du Kenya: local dances put to the test of the national stage. *Mambo!* 12 (1).

Kiiru, K. 2017. National competitive festivals: formatting dance products and forging identities in Kenya. *Cultural Analysis* 15 (2): 1-28.

Kubik, G. 1967. The Traditional Music of Tanzania. *Afrika* 8 (2): 29–32.

Kubik, G. 1981. Neo-Traditional Popular Music in East Africa since 1945. *Popular Music* 1: 83-104.

Marmone, G. 2017. War and Predatory Economy in Northern-Kenya: How Ethnomusicology Can Explore Social Change. *Cahiers d'Histoire* 34(1): 157–186.

Mbiti, J. 1969. *African Religions & Philosophy*. Oxford: Heinemann.

Merriam, A. 1964. *The Anthropology of Music*. Evanston, Northwestern University Press.

Mũtonya, M. 2013. *The Politics of Everyday Life in Gikuyu Popular Musice of Kenya 1990-2000*. Nairobi, Twaweza Communications.

Mũtonya, M. 2014. Jogoo La Shambani Haliwiki Mjini: The Village and the Town in the *Mũgithi* and One-Man Guitar Performances in Kenya. *African Studies Quarterly* 14 (4): 1-16.

Mwangi, P. 2006. Silencing Musical Expressions in Colonial and Post-Colonial Kenya, in Cloonan M. & Drewett M. (eds) *Popular Music Censorship in Africa*. London, Routledge: 157-169.

Nannyonga-Tamusuza, S. 2003. Competitions in School Festivals: A Process of Re-inventing Baakisimba Music and Dance of the Baganda (Uganda). *The world of music* 45(1): 95 – 116.

Nannyonga-Tamusuza, S. 2005. *Baakisimba: Gender in Music and Dance of the Baganda People of Uganda*. London & New York, Routledge.

Njogu, K. & Maupeu, H. (eds) 2007. *Songs and Politics in Eastern Africa*. Dar-es-Salaam: Mkuki na Nyota Publishers.

Ntarangwi, M. 2009. *East African Hip Hop: Youth Culture and Globalization*. Chicago, University of Illinois Press.

Nyairo, J. & Ogude, J. 2003. Popular Music and the Negotiation of Contemporary Kenyan Identity: The Example of Nairobi City Ensemble. *Social Identities* 9 (3): 383-400.

Nyairo, J. & Ogude, J. 2005. Popular Music, Popular Politics: *Unbwogable* and the Idioms of Freedom in Kenyan Popular Music. *African Affairs* 104 (415): 225–249.

Nyairo, J. 2004. Reading the Referents': The Ghost of America in Contemporary Kenyan Popular Music. *Scrutiny* 29(1): 39–55.

Nyakiti, C. 1997. Seven Traditional Dances from Selected Ethnic Communities of Kenya, in Dagan E. (ed) *The Spirit's Dance in Africa, Evolution, Transformation and Continuity in Sub-Sahara*. Montréal, Galerie Amrad African Arts Publications.

Ogude, J. 2012. The Invention of Traditional Music in the City: Exploring History and Meaning in Urban Music in Contemporary Kenya. *Research in African Literatures* 43 (4): 147-165.

Ranger, T.O. 1975. *Dance and Society in Eastern Africa 1890 – 1970: The Beni Ngoma*. London, Heinemann Educational Books Ltd.

Rosenberg, A. 2011. *Eastern African Popular Songs: Verbal Art in States of Transformation*. Trenton, New Jersey, Africa World Press.

Sanga, I. 2013. Musical Figuring of Postcolonial Urban Segmentarity and Marginality in Selected "Bongo Fleva" Songs in Dar-es-Salaam, Tanzania. *International Review of the Aesthetics and Sociology of Music* 44 (2): 385-405.

Senoga – Zake, G. 1986. *Folk Music of Kenya*. Nairobi, Uzima Press.

Spencer, P. (ed) 1985. *Society and the Dance: the social anthropology of process and performance*. Cambridge, Cambridge University Press.

Ssempijja, N. 2012. Globalizing Catholicism in Uganda through Musical Performance: A case study of the Kampala Archdiocesan Schools' Music Festivals, in Nannyonga-Tamusuza S. & Solomon T. (eds) *Ethnomusicology in East Africa: Perspectives from Uganda and Beyond*. Kampala, Fountain Publishers.

Stokes, M. 1994. *Ethnicity, Identity and Music: The Musical Construction of Place*. Oxford, Berg.

Wachsmann, K. 1971. Musical Instruments in Kiganda tradition and their Place in the East African Scene. In Wachsmann K. (ed) *Essays on Music and History in Africa*. Evanston, Northwestern University Press: 93-134.

Wade, P. 2000. *Music, Race and Nation: Música Tropical in Colombia*. Chicago, University of Chicago Press.

Wanyama, M. 2012. Researching on Kenyan Traditional Music and Dance Today: Methodology and Ethical Issues Revisited. *Muziki – Journal of Music Research in Africa* 9 (2): 1-8.

Part I:

Dance and the Forming of a Nation in Colonial Kenya

Colonial Choreography: How the British Administration Shaped Dance Heritage in Kenya

Kahithe Kiiru

The study of progressive creation of dance heritage in Kenya reveals that the substrate of this set of practices originated in the colonial enterprises of staging and promoting communal dances of different communities, a process that began in the 1950s. Control over native populations was one of the main preoccupations of the British administration in the settler context of Kenya Colony. Yet, following a long period of restriction and prohibition, different forms of control over dance events and celebrations translated into a form of "choreography". This was a case of distinct use of folklorization as a tool of partial censorship.

In this chapter we discuss the processes and institutions put in place, intentionally or unconsciously, by the colonial administration in the "native dances" department, including the negotiation and disagreement inherent to their establishment. We also argue that some of these institutions were built on and around the nature of pre-colonial cultural practices and the dynamics between pre-colonial conflicts and social consensus.

Finally, examples from current research confirm that the impact of what I hereby call "colonial choreography" extends to the perception of "traditional" dance in Kenya, as it also resonates with relevant questions of valorisation and (self)representation.

Introduction

In the last few decades, the layeredness of dance has inspired numerous studies on the relationship and the dialogue between culture - body and movement – and politics. The simultaneous expression of power and of resistance, as well as the negotiation and creation of identities *through* and *by* dance is the theoretical rooting of the study from which this chapter stems. In line with Kirshenblatt-Gimblett (1995), we analyse dance heritage in contemporary Kenya in terms of processes rather than immutable products. These heritage making processes are thought as both ongoing and rooted in various historical developments. They are also observed from the perspective of continuous circulation between two interdependent levels - the local and the national.

Our dynamist approach to choreographic knowledge takes into account the historical and social evolution of "traditional" dance in Kenya and attempts to leave the academic burden of *the authentic* behind us. As we analyse transformations of dance vocabularies, of choreographic strategies, of dance imaginaries and representations, we do not perpetuate established "normative expectations" (Schechner 1990) for "unadulterated" traditional performances. On the contrary, we consider dance heritage to be a dialogue between tradition and historicity of practices on one hand and individual creativity and artistic input on the other.

In our attempt to respond to all of the above intentions, we have complemented data collected "in the field", through participant observation and a myriad of interviews, with archival research. This has proven to be both a challenging and a rewarding approach, as archives on "traditional" music and dance in Kenya are scarce and neglected. Yet, in this process, the colonial archive was possibly the most valuable source of information on the effects which external historical developments can have on dance. Our previous interest in this historical period was confirmed when, perhaps naively, we started our search by using the keyword "dance" and discovered that a large number of entries in the collection of the National Archives (NADS) headquarters in Nairobi dated from the pre-independence era. Since one of the most frequent terms associated with "dance" was that of a "permit", our follow-up focused on dating and analysing the various legislative measures concerning dance set in place by the British colonial administration in different historical periods.

Progressively, we have become aware of the complexity of those measures, as well as of the disagreements and negotiations they entailed. In order to gain access to different layers of British attitudes towards native dances in Kenya Colony, we enlarged our search and added to the formative legislative documents (such as minutes and orders), correspondence exchanged between administrators and other actors involved (missionaries, settlers), reports from meetings and anecdotes concerning dance events noted in different districts of the colony. The hypotheses presented in this chapter are a fruit of analysis of these documents. We introduce them with caution and remain aware of the possible defaults they may have, resulting from the difficulties in accessing colonial archives in Kenya and from the apparent fact of an important percentage of the archive being kept in the United Kingdom.

Before introducing the central argument of this chapter, we believe we owe the readership a clarification of the terminology they are about to encounter. In place of problematic prefixes of *traditional*, *indigenous* or *folk* dances, which all have a well-known history of contestation, we opt here for essentially two terms. The first one is that of "cultural dances of Kenya." This is synonymous to dance heritage and defined as a set of traditional practices reinvented and re-contextualized for a stage experience and a contemporary social use (Kiiru 2017). The term itself was reported from interviews with institution representatives as well as with artists and practitioners in the field. We have found it particularly relevant because of its reference to the notion of "culture", as opposed to "tradition". According to source informants, "culture" in this sense describes better the dynamic and evolving character of the practices in question (Kiiru 2014).

The second term used in this chapter is that of "native dances". This has been intentionally replicated from the colonial archives for mainly two reasons. Firstly, it creates a tangible connection to the legislative terminology and to the category of "Native Affairs" under which all laws, issues and discussions regarding the relationship the colonial government had to local African populations was filed. Secondly, it encompasses a double reference to birth right citizenship (*jus soli*) and to indigeneity defined in terms of specific rights based on a historical tie to the territory, both of which have paradoxical implications for the Kenyan settler colonial experience.

Thus, this chapter will focus on what we call "colonial choreography", a term which refers to the historical impact British colonial administration had on the progressive constitution of dance heritage in Kenya, as well as on its perception. It will entail an analysis of the evolution of colonial legislation and regulation towards native dances in Kenya Colony with a special focus on the orchestration and staging of native dances commenced in the late colonial period, notably the 1950s. Subsequently, we shall discuss the impact these legislative, normative and empirical procedures have had on dance perceptions, imaginaries and vocabularies in Kenya, using examples from the field.

The Colonial Experience in Kenya

Any researcher in social studies or humanities dealing with historical developments in Africa cannot avoid the question of "traditional Africa's" violent encounter with the Europeans, nor of the impact of repressive colonisation politics. This impact was especially significant in Kenya, because of the specific nature of the British rule. According to Ochieng:

> "The most important single element which was to determine the nature of Kenya's future political economy was the decision by the British Commissioner, Sir Charles Eliot, in 1902 to invite settlers to the country..." (Ochieng 1985: 219)

The occupation of natives' lands, which were declared void, unclaimed and economically neglected, was considered as inevitable as was the mission of their salvation from a primitive state of being. Hence, in order to protect British interests, in 1920 the territories of former East Africa Protectorate (also known as British East Africa) were annexed and the Colony and Protectorate of Kenya were officially established.[1]

European immigrants to the Colony were attracted by such real-life factors as fertile soil and good farming conditions, business prospects and investment speculations, as well as by a romantic idea of adventure and new beginnings, spread among others by the 'Kenya Novel' literary phenomenon (Duder 1991). Yet, White settlement in Kenya[2] did not elude controversy, as both its critics and supporters attempted to influence public opinion in Britain. Kenya's unique status of a Crown Colony under direct control of the Colonial Office in London was a source of numerous conflicts (Wasserman 1974). This fact, and the constant negotiation between settlers' demands and the Crown's interests it brought about, will reflect in several domains of everyday life in the Kenya Colony. Among them, "Native Affairs" were a pivotal issue.

Settler colonialism was conceived and implemented as "a structure rather than an event" (Wolfe 2006: 390), a political form that combined structural and ideological elements. Life in the colony was thus characterised by "pervasive inequalities, usually codified in law" (Elkins & Pedersen 2005: 8), while the mere fact of European settlers' cohabitation with African populations led to a particular attention to their customs and behaviours. This interest progressively translated into an elaborate system of regulation and control over the Natives' everyday lives. In the quest for information and understanding of "tribal societies and cultures", early colonial administrators and missionaries with ethnographical ambition (Hobley 1903, 1922; Cagnolo 1933), who thoughtlessly reflected European racial prejudices, were succeeded by detached scientific observers (Lindblom 1920; Wagner 1949), who "rarely questioned their 'laboratory condition'" (Lewis 1973: 582).

In these early writings on cultures of Kenya Colony, references to musical and dance practices were both scarce and racially biased. Some examples include the following: "There is little to say regarding Turkana dances as they consist almost entirely of a large number of men walking about, stamping their feet." (Baker Beall 1932);[3] "Music amongst civilized nations represents the soul of a people but with the Akikuyu it expresses merely their present feelings" (Cagnolo 1933: 161), and so on.

When they did not openly pass judgment, the short descriptions of music and dance within small or big monographic volumes on a specific tribe, considered them, without exception, as irrelevant entertainment, which does not seem to carry out any significant role (Leakey 1930).

In this historical and political context, local dances were not spared from interference. On the contrary, they were, since the 1910s, strongly criticised by the colonial administration. Their suppression, prohibition and regulation are "an index of the significance of dance as a site of considerable political and moral anxiety" (Reed 1998: 506).

Added to the specific nature of settler colonialism, one of the key reasons of such an interest in local populations' dances lies in the very nature of dance events. Festive gatherings, ceremonies or rituals, which were also opportunities for dance and song sessions, were often judged by the colonial authorities as dangerous and conducive for riots. They involved more risks than just the gathering of otherwise fragmented and dispersed tribal units, the consumption of alcohol and other celebratory practices. In general, dance reinforces the sensorimotor experience of the ritual event and promotes emotional involvement of the participants (Houseman 2006). While shared, extraordinary bodily experience is lived, emotions and spirits rise high and opportunity for expressing latent or repressed feelings of discontent and anger may be taken. The colonial observer(s) appraised this phenomenon which was particularly threatening in situations where dance was a site of male collective performance (Hanna 1977; Reed 1998).

Additionally, many of the musical and dance practices in East Africa were historically linked to traditional forms of power and integrated into the age-set systems of societies (Peatrik 1995). Once the colonial pacification process abated the need for war dances as physical and psychological preparation for combat, their benefit and functionality for the local populations transmuted into a form of assertion of traditional independence and of symbolic resistance. Thus, to the colonial administration, the control and regulation of these polymorphic practices presented itself as a requisite for successful government.

From Prohibition to Orchestration: The Progressive Development of British Native Dance Policies

As in many other colonial arenas, in Kenya Colony "dance tended to generate multiple and contradictory policies and attitudes" (Reed 1998: 506). This fact is partly explained by the complex nature of the indirect rule system set in place. On the ground, officially protective of "the authority of 'custom'" (Elkins & Pedersen 2005: 24), the British administration in Kenya transferred "the native question" to separate institutions – the Native Councils, established in different tribal "reserves". These were to enforce their own customary law in matters of everyday life issues, "provided it is not repugnant to humanity, or in opposition to any ordinance" (Lugard 1922: 206). Yet, the British administration seemed to have difficulty deciding whether musical and dance practices fall under the jurisdiction of these councils. Resolutions and other legal documents concerning dances could be issued by both the central colonial authority and by native councils, while traces of consultation and discussion between the two on the topic of dancing are surprisingly recurrent.

The most radical approach to control during colonial era in Kenya would be the legal prohibition of specific musical and dance practices. Traces of these extreme measures can be found in the form of lists of prohibited dances in a specific locality, area or district at a given time. The cited reasons for prohibition of certain dances are essentially of two types: moral and political.

When it comes to questions of morality, the most common phrases used to describe "dangerous" dances, those considered for prohibition or already prohibited, are such as "of an indecent or immoral character" and/or "likely to lead to immorality or a breach of peace." The definition of levels of immorality, and consequently controversy, of a dance form stems evidently from the Christian Western European viewpoint and evokes the strong influence of missionary stations in the region.

Several authors have commented on the usage of dance scenes in early missionaries' and explorers' works for the purpose of supporting the assertion that Africans possessed an immoral nature, which was evident in their dance vocabulary and their relationship to individual and mutual bodies. The tradition of depicting Africa as a place with "human sacrifice, highly sexual religious ceremonies, wicked excess of polygamy, and lascivious dances with a childlike ignorance" (Curtin 1964: 327) fuelled missionaries' desire to convert the native populations. Yet, such encounters and their oral or written descriptions reveal a bizarre mixture of disgust and judgement on the one hand, and dance as a site of sexual desire on the other (Thompson 2012). As Father Cagnolo wrote, in 1933, on Kikuyu songs and dances: "When we began to take interest in their music we discovered that native song is an occasion of great corruption, bringing men down to the level of the beasts and blinding them to things of the spirit. It became therefore logical duty to study the causes of this corruption, in order to find a remedy…" (Cagnolo 1933: 173-174).

The impact of early Christian missions, which entered different regions of the Colony at different historical periods (between 1840s and 1920s) is a topic that would merit a separate chapter. According to testimonies collected in the field, we conclude that missionaries' opinions and practical reactions to music and dance practices of the Natives varied on the basis of two essential factors – the Church denomination involved and the (perception of) native beliefs associated to the concerned dance form.

Examples from Western Kenya, notably from Shinyalu constituency - the home of *isukuti* dance,[4] testify to an interesting discrepancy. Whereas the general impression early Christians – largely Quaker Protestants, left in this region is that of opposition to traditional music, frequently associated with confiscation and destruction of drums, the Catholic mission established in 1906 in Mukumu village in reality favoured the development of *isukuti* dance genre. Father Withlock, who headed the Mukumu mission in its' early days, used to organise the local youth for dance and wrestling sessions on Sundays, after the service. The impact of these dance sessions was so significant that the community elders state "*isukuti* started there."[5]

This case can only partly be explained with a specific priest's personal liking for *isukuti* dance or with the Catholic Church's more inclusive approach to worship[6]. It is our hypothesis that the missions were permissive of *isukuti* mainly because it was considered an entertainment form. Even though the White administration and the clergy were aware of *isukuti* being played at burials, its' connection to the spiritual life of the natives and consequently to their potential spiritual corruption was not judged central. Thus, when in March 1934 Mrs Ingels, a British lady living within the native reserve in the region of Kakamega, approaches the authorities concerning an incident in which a large number of natives following a funeral *ngoma*[7] sought shelter from the rain under her veranda, the District Commissioner does not take action but rather expresses the opinion that prohibiting native *ngomas* "will merely intensify the idea that the Reserve is theirs no longer" (North Kavirondo DC 1934).[8]

Contrary to *isukuti* which is nowadays, in a somewhat lighter form, integrated into Christian worship, the *gonda* dance of Giriama Mijikenda populations, who inhabit the coastal and the interior coast regions of Kenya, has never been accepted by the Christian Churches. We argue that the reasons for prosecution of traditional music and dance practices of the Mijikenda is essentially their manifest connection to traditional worship of ancestor spirits, regularly interpreted as or associated with witchcraft (Brantley 1979). Even in the 21st century, one excludes the other – "Either you are a Christian or you do *gonda*."[9]

The alliance between the Christian missions and the colonial government in controlling dance events is justified by more than just morality concerns. A frequently raised issue, which reappears in several districts of the Colony, is equally a health one. Overnight dances, originally related to communal ceremonies, but later recast for the sole purpose of entertainment, are reported on for being "harmful for the health of the people" (Vicar Apostolic of Kisumu 1942).[10] The consumption of alcohol by youth (especially girls), sexual orgies, spread of venereal diseases and subsequently infertility are mentioned as principal risks of such occasions.

The discussions of the connection between dance occasions and libertine behaviour among native youth are even more frequent in the 1940s with the appearance of couple dances. These are designated as "European types of dances" and their proliferation in different corners of the colony is investigated with fervour, concluding that these dances "not infrequently results in murder, seduction, adultery and assault, and it is considered essential in the interests of law and order to prohibit their use. The African is hot blooded, jealous and sensual, and close bodily contact with one of the opposite sex in the case of Africans is almost incapable of being confined to decent dancing" (Hunter 1940).[11]

The political reasons for prohibition of certain songs and dances relate mostly to songs with lyrics that incite or question the existing colonial order and legislation. A historically famous example is that of *Mūthīrīgū* song and dance in Kikuyu reserves in Central Kenya. In 1930, in a document entitled "Political Situation in the Province", the Fort Hall District Commissioner reports to the Provincial Commissioner on "forbidding it", as well as on twenty or thirty offenders which had received sentences of imprisonment. The *Mūthīrīgū* had emerged as a popular protest song after the colonial government, in concert with missionaries and Churches established within the areas inhabited by the Kikuyu, declared war on the custom of female circumcision. However, the lyrics of these controversial songs reveal a much larger spectrum of concerns and "clearly show how a defence of sexual order became entangled with a revolt of younger Kikuyus against the British and their African collaborators and with a political protest against the loss of Kikuyu land." (Pedersen 1991: 563)

However, we argue that prohibition was, in fact, a mere fraction of the regulative system set in place by British colonial authorities towards "native dances" in Kenya. Regardless of its undoubtedly detrimental effect on certain practices, it was not necessarily the most significant effect of this historical era. When we confront legislative papers with testimonies of living informants, it is revealed that prohibition neither led to the extinction of targeted practices, nor is remembered as a primary trauma. We believe that other forms of regulation were even more influential in the process of heritagisation of dances – their progressive transformation into "cultural dances of Kenya".

The British colonial administration controlled native dances by reducing their duration and their attendance, as well as by dictating the calendar of their performance. One of the responses to reports on an increase in dances in native reserves is the idea that "…some of these dances can be shortened and circumcision ceremonies permitted only during a fixed period of the year, say two months" (District Commissioner of Kiambu 1926).[12]

This type of ordering of music and dance events progressively led to a very elaborate section in the native control regulations. In 1926, the Chief Native Commissioner G.V. Maxwell proclaims:

> "...I hereby declare that any headman may from time to time issue orders to be obeyed by the natives residing within the local limits of his jurisdiction prohibiting or restricting excessive dancing by natives or the public performance of any native dance of indecent or immoral character or of such nature that it is likely to lead to immorality or a breach of the peace and determining the hours within which, the place or places at which, and the conditions under which any native dance may be publicly performed" (Maxwell 1926).[13]

These interventions into traditional performance of music and dances made them not only easier to survey and control, but also corresponded to some of the requirements for their "staging" - for performance in front of an audience. The reconfiguration of time, space and number of participants originally conceived for reasons other than performance itself is an important part of what we fetchingly refer to as *colonial choreography*, a process that progressively modified not only dance forms and events, but also their perception in the minds of local population.

One of the paradoxes of Kenya's colonial history was the fact that "the increasing scope and intensity of state intervention against the African population, in order to establish the viability of the settler sector, coincided with a rising level of conflict between the settlers and officials who were determined to defend African interests." (Lonsdale & Berman 1979: 494) Agreement on native affairs policies was, thus, difficult to attain and in a state of continuous negotiation. In relation to native dances, some administrators did not agree with proposed or implemented repressive measures, but rather defended the opinion that "native customs which are not objectionable will not ordinarily be interfered with" (Montgomery 1934).[14] Some recognised music and dance practices as central to local populations' social universe(s), as "the chief amusement" which "affords exercise and contentment" and therefore does not have "any more evil effect on them than dancing has among Europeans" (DC of Embu 1926).[15] Those are the opinions that progressively gained momentum, once negotiation gave place to a common policy in regards to native dances, a historical and political decision that can be explained by both internal and external factors.

The 1950s were a period of profound restructuring of the British colonial policy. Although Britain and the Empire had emerged victorious from the Second World War, the effects of the conflict were profound, both in Europe and in the colonies. Anti-colonial movements, supported by the two new axes of world power, the United States and the Soviet Union, who both opposed European colonialism were becoming stronger and Britain progressively adopted a policy of disengagement. Simultaneously, the colonial administration expanded its efforts "to knit their African settler colonies more tightly into the metropolitan economy" (Elkins & Pedersen 2005: 2).

These significant changes reflected, among other things, in an alteration of attitudes towards the native populations and towards their cultural expressions. The British were now seeking to ensure that the increasingly urbanised and modernised native populations maintained their "tribal identities" through traditional music and dance performances.

Interestingly, the cited politically induced changes coincided with international developments in the field of folklore. In 1947. International Folk Music Council was founded and "preserving the performed cultures of African tribes" (Bushidi 2015: 13) was consistent with their declared objectives. In the same period, Hugh Tracey, famous ethnomusicologist and founder of the International Library of African Music (1954), toured Kenya Colony recording traditional music. In this research and documentation task Tracey was logistically assisted by British administration officials.

Accordingly, proofs of early "professional" associations of music and dance in the colony can be noted in archival documents from the early 1950s. These groups are mentioned in documents referring to their movements around the territory of the Colony (and even outside it), where they perform on stages of festivals and agricultural or commercial fairs. Such native performances are still closely regulated and directed. Firstly, they are limited to a certain type of venues – the so-called Native Stadiums, existing in large urban centres. From this fact the term *stadium dancing* is derived. Secondly, performances of this kind are subject to permission by the District Commissioner's office of the group's respective location. Thirdly, if the permission is granted, native musicians and dancers are to be transported to and from location of performance, fed and, in the case of festivals and events longer than a day, accommodated by the organising body (in most cases Nairobi District, the Colony's Agricultural Cabinet, etc.). Native musicians and dancers could be rewarded with an ox or a similar form of compensation (sugar, firewood), yet never paid. Any payment, if negotiated, was to be credited to locational funds and to the so-called African District Councils of their region of origin.

A rare footage from this era shows stadium dancing by native groups at its best. In 1952, at the occasion of her historically famous visit to Kenya Colony, Princess Elisabeth is entertained with a showcase of tribal dances. Several teams of dancers are present, notably we can identify the Wakamba - who exhibit the acrobatic movements inherent to their traditional dances, and the Masaai - whose plain appearance and a run through the stadium stage seem to constitute sufficient attraction.

The early initiatives of staging native dances generated several transformations. Among them, possibly the most important one is that of both spatial and mental separation of active participants – musicians and dancers themselves from passive observers - their audience. As Barber (1997) argued, these changes in ways of being an audience reflect much wider transformations in institutionalisation and economics of entertainment. They are equally related to "the degree to which performances are 'embedded' in other social forms" (Barber 1997: 347).

This consideration reminds us of another social practice the colonial administration commenced in the same historical period, a practice that would become crucial for the creation of dance heritage in the region. Building on the competitive nature inherent to a large number of musical and choreographic practices in East Africa (Ranger 1975; Gunderson & Barz 2000), the British proceeded to what we call *the institutionalisation of competiveness* (Kiiru 2017). "African Tribal Dance competitions" proliferated in most districts of the colony in the mid-1950s, while the earliest found record of efforts to organize an "All Kenya" competition that would bring together teams of dancers from different communities dates from 1960. The African Cabinet of Business and Entertainment hopes that it might "…add to the standard of Kenya economics through such social activities whilst trying to make some of our people refrain from politics, worries, use of violence, etc." (Githuku 1960).[16]

An important role in the progressive establishment of colony-wide, and later nation-wide, competitive festivals, which live up to today, was played by the British musicologist and music educator Graham Hyslop. In 1957, in view of the administration's new enthusiasm for music and performance arts, Hyslop was designated the *Colony Music and Drama Officer* whose duties included: "(1) Organisation of Music Courses…; (2) Choice of music for festivals; (3) Adjudication at festivals; [and] (4) Development and recording of African Music…;" etc. (Buttery 1957). His efforts in the promotion of what he considered African folk sensibilities, as well as his idea of the benefits a syncretism between those and European sensibilities, have left an undeniable trace on traditional music performance in Kenya. He prescribed the first reconfigurations of African folk songs and dances performed on competitive festival stages, and some of them are still retained in the contemporary system of national annual festivals (Kidula 1996; Omolo Ongati 2015).

As processes of staging traditional dances of Kenyan communities in the late colonial period resume, their presence can be noted in more and more diverse contexts. Soon groups of dancers are being hired for private parties by the settlers and recruited on occasions of tourists' safari visits to the Colony. Like so, in 1957 a safari tour company that specialises in "big game hunting and photographic expeditions" writes to the District Commissioner of Kitui with a requests for permission to bring to one of the locations under his jurisdiction a party of three British citizens, stating that they "are mainly interested in taking photographs of a Wakamba dance" (Stephens 1957).[17]

In the following years, administrators discuss frequent requests for tribal dance displays closer to Nairobi, in order to satisfy the demand of both tourists and urban populations. Such displays are occasionally organised at the Kaloleni Native Stadium, while a project of forming a permanent dance troupe in Ngong area of Nairobi is in the pipelines. Minute number 31/58 from the District Commissioners' meeting reports the following on the topic of tribal dance displays:

> "Mr. Mackley[18] explained that it was the policy of his Ministry that Africans should receive a greater share of growing profits of the tourist industry and that the way to achieve this was to commercialise all the more colourful aspects of tribal life, in particular tribal dancing. The difficulty at present was that such dancing as there was in the reserves took place too far away from Nairobi to be of any use to overnight visitors and it was hoped to establish regular dancing displays nearer to the City. An attempt to hold a dancing contest for urban Africans in the Nairobi stadium on the Johannesburg lines had been unsuccessful as it had ended in pitched battle; but it was suggested that a permanent dancing team might be set up in the Ngong area which was ideal setting."[19]

However, the putting in place of rudiments of cultural tourism during the colonial era did not circumvent the controversy of commercialisation, associated to folklore ventures worldwide. Certain administrators were concerned with the effects ongoing processes would have on native populations and considered commercialising native dances "distasteful". Yet, the progressive process of *folklorisation*, defined as the processes of selecting the most visible cultural particularities of a community (tribe) for its "promotion", was under way and could not be stopped or slowed down. On the contrary, it exemplifies the characteristic continuity of a great number of institutions and usages imported from the colonial Empire into the new Independent State, which became in 1963 Kenya.

Cultural Dances of Kenya, their Perceptions, Imageries and Vocabularies

Aside from reshaping dance forms and events, what are the long-lasting effects colonial prohibition, regulation and orchestration had on the dance practice and on the perception of dance heritage in Kenya? Based on observations made in the contemporary research context, we shall now explore some of the more complex and latent effects of the described historical developments.

The first invention of the colonial dance heritage tentative is not in its essence specifically Kenyan, but common to heritage ventures on the continent (Andrieu 2010; Castaldi 2006; Djebbari 2011, etc.) and, in a somewhat different form, around the world (Shay 2002; Trebinjac 2008, etc.). In discourse, as well as in folklore practices of the late colonial period, diversity appears as an ideal and an important motivator for all ventures. Thus, where the colonial administration openly expresses the wish to "keep alive the Traditional dances of all tribes" (Githuku 1960),[20] we discern the germs of orchestrated cultural diversity. Simultaneously, the aspiration to present, preserve and promote all music and all dances of all tribes of the colony reveals an intriguing paradox. In order to paint the picture of diversity, one must start by identifying the differences. This process of identity construction, also referred to as ethnic essentialization, is characteristic of colonial rule all over Africa, and is echoed in most folkloristic projects. The "will to distinguish sets of homogeneous populations that are characterized by a specific type of musical and choreographic culture" (Djebbari 2011: 198) was inherited and further pursued by most newly independent states in the 1960s. Kenya was no exception to this rule.

Our previous research on the Kenyan equivalent of a national troupe – *Bomas Harambee Dancers* (Kiiru 2014) has now revealed its rooting in pre-independence developments. Although the troupe's official date of establishment (1973) defines it as a late nation-building project, when compared to similar projects by other African states, we had previously identified the seed of the idea of "formation of a national troupe" in archival documents as early as 1966 (Martin 1966).[21] With the analysis of pre-Independence folklorisation processes, we can now state that it was indeed a project long time in the making. If we remember the late 1950s discussions of "tribal dance displays" closer to Nairobi and the suggestion of its location in Ngong area, and addition that fact of orchestration of cultural diversity, we can extend the argument to stating Bomas of Kenya was in fact an idea of the colonial government. Nevertheless, the idea was subsequently reshaped to correspond to the national agenda with a characteristic use of music and dance as preferred media for identity creation.

The second residue of colonial cultural policies we wish to discuss is the unequal representation of different tribes, which were after Independence renamed as different "ethnic communities". The process of commercialisation of native dances commenced by the colonial administration included an important judgement of value. This judgement was based on Eurocentric definitions of what "entertaining", "exciting", "authentic", "unique" or "original" is. For example, in 1948. The Kitui District Commissioner writes: "As you may know, Akamba dancing is first class entertainment – it is the only good tribal dancing in Kenya (except perhaps the Turkana)" (Kelly 1948).[22]

This and similar judgements of value translated into favouritism for certain traditions and their prominence in the colonial cultural tourism endeavours. Thus, the most popular dance performances were that of the Akamba, with their spectacular acrobatic elements; the Luyia *isukuti* dancers, notably a famous group led by Chief Shivachi from Iguhu location in Ikolomani area; and, of course, the Maasai, whose warrior jumping dances had already become internationally known symbols of East Africa.

Our research[23] revealed that some of these preferences and prejudice remained imprinted into the national consciousness even after Independence and partake in the stereotypes Kenyan have of the musical and choreographic traditions of their country up to date. As such they are reflected on various levels of representation: the presence, frequency, quality and type of representation of specific traditions in the national repertoire; their valorisation, which can lead to specific preservation and promotion initiatives; their track record in cultural dance competitions; their acceptance and knowledge in everyday life of contemporary Kenyans; etc.

Lastly, the topic of representation guides us to another reminder of the colonial era in the context of Kenyan dance heritage creation processes. We wish to tackle the sensitive issue of self-representation, often associated to tourist destined performances. Essentially, the colonial narrative and the performance scenario inspired by it staged images and sounds of "old Africa". "Tribal" or "native" dance performances were conceived and presented so as to be as authentic as possible, and in this context, authenticity translated into timeless, ahistorical images of natural and primitive Africans whose practices are unpolluted by modernity. These representations extended into the era of tourist realism which gave "tribalism and colonialism a second life by bringing them back as representations of themselves and circulating them within an economy of performance" (Brüner & Kirshenblatt-Gimblett 1994: 435) Thus, what is interesting to observe here are elements of tourist realism in a contemporary performance context, as, since the second half of the 20th century, "we have replaced the stage (for the African Other), but left the format of the imagery intact" (Wels 2002: 64).

At the present day and age, the old image of a native "undergoing" in a way his own "tourismification" without possibility to resist it, is a matter of the past. Local people are no longer theorized as passive objects of the tourist gaze, but as active subjects who consciously build representations of their culture for tourists (Cousin 2008). Or, as Brüner had put it: "Identities are not given, they are performed by people with agency who have choices." (Brüner 2001: 895) At the same time, the representations they build are based both on their own system of references and on their interpretation of tourists' expectations.

In the Kenyan, and more widely African context, these circumstances of creation often leads to auto-exotisation. Music and dance performers frequently paint images of their own culture from the perspective of a past, no longer existing state. Their self-representation echoes some of those same stereotypes and colonial images of African "tribal" dance. In the 21st century Kenya, this fact can be easily traceable in the wide-spread scenes of enactment of different aspects of tribal life as well as in the discourse that accompanies cultural dance performances. When in September 2016, we attend a cultural dance show on the terrace of one of Malindi's largest hotel resort, we are struck as much by the representations of "the Giriama tribe", as by the discourse that accompanies dance pieces. As the master of ceremony announces a piece with an explanation of how the Giriama "always have a lot of kids because they love *ugali*[24] and somebody needs to dig the soil for the maize to grow", or how "here, at our place we don't just fall in love, *questo es cultura europeana*[25]...", the "ancient" layers of representation are revived.

The group's artistic direction relies on their own interpretation of the audience's expectation up to the point of preferring spectacular misinformation to historical or cultural accuracy. Following such reasoning, another angle of staging emerges and the "exotic" nature of gestural, choreographic and musical traits becomes crucial. And so, within their "Giriama show", the members of the group in question introduce elements from Tanzania, Congo and build extensively on the Western conception of "African dance"[26] (Wierre-Gore 2001).

Liberated from repressive politics of the colonial government, Kenyan creative dance responses are not entirely relieved of the effects colonial staging and orchestration of native dances had on the forms themselves or on their mental perceptions.

Conclusions

We believe that dance, as a social and political practice, serves as an excellent media to further the academic investigation of "the full meaning for Africans of the incorporation of their societies into the colonial state" (Lonsdale & Berman 1979: 493), since it cuts across two crucial domains of native populations' lives – their leisure and their ceremonial practices.

A general consideration of the impact British colonial administration's regulations and policies had on music and dance practices in Kenya Colony reveals complex and continuous negotiations between several actors. Extreme repressive politics, such as the prohibition of certain practices, were just a part of a much more elaborate system of regulation that had more than just an adverse effect. Some of the regulatory laws and procedures put in place during those times favoured the creation of dance heritage. By limiting and controlling attendance, forms of participation, duration and timeline, as well as by conditioning dance events to previous permission, the British unconsciously and unintentionally facilitated the staging of local dances. They advanced the idea of performance for an audience and in front of an audience and all the dance material transformations that accompany such ideas. This is a particular use of *spectacularization* and *folklorization*, in which choreography is a tool of partial censorship.

In the 1940s and 1950s, the same administration championed cultural tourism by adding to the safari big game hunting experience of the Colony the offer of "spectacular native dances". And, as in many of their endeavours, the British made use of the pre-colonial practices and uses, notably the competitive character of many musical practices in the region, and staged competitions all over the Colony. By the time Kenya was gaining Independence, a solid colony-wide system of stages/stadiums for performance, festivals and competitions was already in place. The new nation-state took it over with major agenda adjustments, but did not go far in challenging some of the existing formats.

These interventions, referred to as "colonial choreography", progressively modified not only dance forms themselves, but also their perceptions, imagery and vocabulary. It is relevant to observe traces of these transformations in contemporary Kenyan "cultural dance" repertoires, as the polysemy and the intertextuality of staged dance products makes them particularly fertile reading ground. The study of these transformations has the ability to teach us about representations of self and of others we maintain and perpetuate for different reasons in a much larger global context.

Endnotes

1. Administratively the term "Colony of Kenya" referred to the interior lands, whereas the "Protectorate of Kenya" designated the 16 km coastal strip together with several islands which remained under the sovereignty of the Sultan of Zanzibar.

2. By 1928 the number of European settlers in Kenya Colony was estimated to 12 000 (Buell 1928) and in the 1960s there were some 61,000 Europeans, which still made up for less than one per cent of the Kenyan population (Wasserman 1974).

3. Baker Beall, 1932, District Commissioner of Southern Turkana, Notes on Native Tribes and Their Customs, Kenya National Archives and Documentation Service, Nairobi (GF 572 KEN)

4. *Isukuti* is a traditional dance of Isukha and Idakho Luhya communities of Western Kenya characterised by vigorous dancing to a set of percussion and its processional nature (Kiiru 2014).

5. Personal interview conducted with Elder Joseph Lubulela (born 1928) conducted on December 16th 2015 at his brother's home in Shibuye village (Shinyalu, Kakamega County).

6 On the topic of incorporating traditional music of different Kenyan populations into contemporary worship see Katuli (1998), Miya (2004), Kidula (2010) and others.

7 Recurrent in the East African region, *ngoma* is a term which can have different meanings. We can assume that the initial meaning was the designation of a particular percussive instrument, then, by extension, it evolved to designate a musical/dance event, and even music and dance in a broad sense of the word. Yet the linguistic path might have followed the opposite direction, from generality to particular instrument designation.

8 District Commissioner of North Kavirondo (signature illegible), 1934, a letter to the Provincial Commissioner of Nyanza, Kenya National Archives and Documentation Service, Nairobi (PC NZA 2 1 68)

9 Personal interview conducted with Chengo Emmanuel Munyaya, Chairman of the Malindi Cultural Association, conducted on April 8th 2016 at Mekatilili wa Menza Centre (Malindi town, Kilifi County)

10 Vicar Apostolic of Kisumu, 1942, a letter to the Provincial Commissioner of Nyanza, Kenya National Archives and Documentation Service, Nairobi (PC NZA 2 1 68)

11 Hunter, 1940, District Commissioner's Recommendation, Minute 17/40 of a Meeting of the Central Kavirondo Local Native Council held on 5th & 6th February 1940, Kenya National Archives and Documentation Service, Nairobi (PC/NZA/2/1/68)

12 District Commissioner of Kyambu (signature illegible), 1926, Re: Native Dances, report to Senior Commissioner, Kenya National Archives and Documentation Service, Nairobi (PC/CP /6/4/5)

13 Maxwell, Chief Native Commissioner, 1926, Attorney General's Office, 1926 Native Authority Ordinance, Kenya National Archives and Documentation Service, Nairobi (AG/25/18)

14 Montgomery, Provincial Commissioner of Nyanza Province, 1934, a letter to the District Commissioner of North Kavirondo, Kenya National Archives and Documentation Service, Nairobi (PC/NZA /2/1/68)

15 District Commissioner of Embu, 1926, a report to Chief Native Commissioner on Dances in Native Reserves, Kenya National Archives and Documentation Service, Nairobi (PC/CP/6/4/5)

16 Githuku R., for African Cabinet of Business and Entertainment, 1960, African Tribal Dancing, a letter to District Commissioner of Kakamega, Kenya National Archives and Documentation Service, Nairobi (DC/KMG/2/1/130)

17 Stephens, Manager at Ker & Downey Safaris Ltd., 1957, a letter to the District Commissioner of Kitui, Kenya National Archives and Documentation Service, Nairobi (DC/KTI/3/1/48)

18 Mackley was the Assistant Secretary at the Ministry of Tourism and Common Services at the time.

19 Minute 31/58 , 1958, Tribal Dancing Displays, Kenya National Archives and Documentation Service, Nairobi (DC/KTI/3/1/48)

20 Githuku, 1960, op.cit.. (DC/KMG/2/1/130)

21 Martin, 1966, District Commissioner Nairobi Area, Formation of National Troupe, a letter to the Permanenrt Secretary, Kenya National Archives and Documentation Service (KNADS), Nairobi (PC/EST/2/21/2)

22 Kelly, District Commissioner of Kitui, 1948, Kitui Dancers - Kanziko Location, Kenya National Archives and Documentation Service, (DC/KTI/3/1/48)

23 This chapter presents some of the findings of an extensive research conducted on both national policies evolution and on national cultural dance performance events since Kenya's Independence, as well as on the presence, history and current forms of existence of dance practices in different communities of the country.

24 *Ugali* is a dish made of maize flour. It's considered a national dish in Kenya.

25 The historical presence of Italians in Malindi town and surrounding areas of the Kenyan coast progressively made Italian language a sort of a lingua franca which a large majority of Kenyans employed in the tourism industry speak and attempt interacting with any European visitor in.

26 The use of singular is here intentional to refer to the idea of a certain homogeneity in characteristics of all dances of the African continent, built on the premise of a common aesthetic, settled in popular consciousness and strengthened by research and scientific theories from the 1960s and 1970s (ex. Farris-Thompson 1974).

Bibliography

Andrieu, S. 2010. *Le spectacle des traditions, Analyse anthropologique du processus de spectacularisation des danses au Burkina Faso*. Marseille, University Aix-Marseille, unpublished PhD diss.

Barber, K. 1997. Preliminary Notes on Audiences in Africa. *Africa* 67 (3): 347-362.

Buell, R.L. 1928. The Destiny of East Africa. *Foreign Affairs* 6 (3): 408-426.

Bushidi, C.F. 2015. Reflections on the fabrication of musical folklore in Kenya from the early 1920s to the late 1970s. *Les Cahiers d'Afrique de l'Est*, 50: 8-21.

Brantley, C. 1979. A Historical Perspective of the Giriama and Witchcraft Control. *Africa* 49 (2): 112-133.

Brüner, E.M. 2001. The Maasai and the Lion King: Authenticity, Nationalism, and Globalization in African Tourism. *American Ethnologist* 28 (4): 881-908.

Brüner, E.M. & Kirshenblatt-Gimblett B. 1994. Maasai on the Lawn: Tourist Realism in East Africa. *Cultural Anthropology* 9 (4): 435-470.

Cagnolo, C. 1933. *The Akikuyu, Their Customs, Traditions and Folklore*. Nyeri, Mission Press.

Castaldi, F. 2006. *Choreographies of African Identities, Négritude, Dance and the National Ballet of Senegal*. Riversdale, University of California Press.

Clark, C.M. 1989. Louis Leakey as Ethnographer: On the Southern Kikuyu before 1903. *Canadian Journal of African Studies* 23 (3): 380-398.

Cousin, S. 2008. L'Unesco et la doctrine du tourisme culturel, *Civilisations*, 57, p.41-56.

Curtin, P.D. 1964. *The Image of Africa: British Ideas and Action, 1780–1850*. Madison, University of Wisconsin Press.

Dagan, E.A. (ed) 1997. *The Spirit's Dance in Africa, Evolution, Transformation and Continuity in Sub-Sahara*. Montréal, Galerie Amrad African Arts Publications.

Djebbari, E. 2011. Musiques, patrimoine, identité : Le Ballet National du Mali, in Desroches, M.; Pichette, C. & Smith, G. (eds) *Territoires musicaux mis en scène*. Montréal, PUM: 195-208.

Duder, C.J.D. 1991. Love and the Lions: The Image of White Settlement in Kenya in Popular Fiction, 1919-1939. *African Affairs* 90 (360): 427-438. Oxford University Press.

Elkins, C. & Pedersen, S. 2005. *Settler Colonialism in the Twentieth Century: Projects, Practices, Legacies*. New York, Routledge Taylor & Francis.

Evans-Pritchard, E.E. 1928. The Dance. *Africa: The Journal of the International African Institute* 1 (4): 446–62.

Farris-Thompson, R. 1974. *African Art in Motion: Icon and Act*, Berkley and Los Angeles: University of California Press.

Gearhart, R. 1998. *Ngoma Memories: A History of Competitive Music and Dance Performance on the Kenya Coast*. Gainsville, University of Florida, unpublished PhD diss.

Gunderson, F. & Barz, G. (ed.) 2000. *Mashindano!: Competitive Music Performance in East Africa*. Dar es Salaam, Mkuki na Nyota Publishers.

Hanna, J.L. 1968. Field Research in African Dance: Opportunities and Utilities. *Ethnomusicology* 12 (1): 101-106. University of Illinois Press.

Hanna, J.L. 1977. African Dance and the Warrior Tradition, in Mazrui A. A. (ed) *The Warrior Tradition in Modern Africa*. Leiden, E.J. Brill: 111-133.

Hobley, C.W. 1903. British East Africa: Anthropological Studies in Kavirondo and Nandi. *The Journal of the Anthropological Institute of Great Britain and Ireland* 33: 325-359.

Hobley, C.W. 1922. *Bantu Beliefs and Magic*. London, H.F. & G. Witherby.

Houseman, M. 2006. Relationality, in Kreinath, J.; Snoek, J. & Stausberg, M. (eds) *Theorizing Rituals. Issues, Topics, Approaches, Concepts*. Leiden, Brill: 413 – 428.

Huntingford, G.B.W. 1944. *The Eastern Tribes of the Bantu Kavirondo*. Nairobi, Ndia Kuu Press.

Huntingford, G.B.W. 1953. *Nandi of Kenya: Tribal Control in a Pastoral Society*. London, Routledge & Kegan Paul Ltd.

Hyslop, G. 1958. Kenya's Colony Music and Drama Officer. *African Music Society Journal* 2 (1): 37-39.

Katuli, J.K. 1998. *Ethnic Music in Christian Worship: A study of specific aspects of Akamba traditional music in the liturgy of the Catholic Church in Mwingi Deanery*. Nairobi, Kenyatta University, unpublished master's diss.

Kidula, J.N. 1996. Cultural Dynamism in Process: The Kenya Music Festival. *Ufahamu: A Journal of African Studies* 24(2-3): 63-81.

Kidula, J.N. 2010. "There is Power": Contemporizing Old Music Traditions for New Gospel Audiences in Kenya. *Yearbook for Traditional Music* 42: 62-80.

Kidula, J.N. 2015. The Kenya Music Festival: A Retrospective History, in Akuno E.A. (ed) *Talanta – Yearbook of the Kenya Music Festival*. Nairobi, Kenya Music Festival Foundation: 1-4.

Kiiru, K. 2014. Bomas of Kenya: local dances put to the test of the national stage. *Mambo! Research Chapters on East Africa* 12 (1).

Kiiru, K. 2017. National competitive festivals: formatting dance products and forging identities in Kenya. *Cultural Analysis* 5 (2): 1-28.

Kirshenblatt-Gimblett, B. 1995. Theorizing Heritage. *Ethnomusicology* 39 (3): 367-380.

Leakey, L.S.B. 1930. Some Notes on the Masai of Kenya Colony. *The Journal of the Royal Anthropological Institute of Great Britain and Ireland* 60: 185-209

Leakey, L.S.B. 1977. *The Southern Kikuyu before 1903*. London, Academic Press.

Lewis, D. 1973. Anthropology and Colonialism. *Current Anthropology* 14 (5): 581-602.

Lindblom, G. 1920. *The Akamba in British East Africa, an Ethnological Monograph*. Uppsala, Appelbergs Boktryckeri Aktiebolag.

Lonsdale, J. & Berman, B. 1979. Coping with the Contradictions: The Development of the Colonial State in Kenya, 1895-1914. *The Journal of African History* 20 (4): 487-505.

Lugard, F.D. 1922. *The Dual Mandate in British Tropical Africa*. Edinburgh & London, William Blackwood and Sons.

Miya, F.N. 2004. *Educational content in the performing arts: tradition and Christianity in Kenya.* Cape Town, University of Cape Town, unpublished PhD diss.

Ochieng, W.R. 1985. Moralism and Expropriation in a British Colony: The Search for a White Dominion in Kenya 1895-1923. *Présence Africaine* 133/134: 214-232.

Omolo-Ongati, R.A. 2015. Performance of Traditional Folksongs and Dances at the Kenya Music Festival with Reference to Style, Instrumentation, Movements, Authenticity, Costume and Choreography, in Akuno ,E.A. (ed) *Talanta – Yearbook of the Kenya Music Festival.* Nairobi, Kenya Music Festival Foundation: 62-74.

Peatrik, A.M. 1995. La règle et le nombre: les systèmes d'âge et de génération d'Afrique orientale. *L'Homme* 35 (134): 13-49.

Pedersen, S. 1991. National Bodies, Unspeakable Acts: The Sexual Politics of Colonial Policy-making. *Journal of Modern History* 63: 647-680.

Ranger, T.O. 1975. *Dance and Society in Eastern Africa, 1890-1970: The Beni Ngoma.* Berkley, University of California Press.

Schechner, R. 1990. Wayang Kulit in the colonial margin. *TDR* 34 (2): 25-61.

Shay, A. 2002. *Choreographic Politics: State Folk Dance Companies, Representation, and Power.* Middletown, Wesleyan University Press.

Sutton, J.E.G. 2006. Denying History in Colonial Kenya: The Anthropology and Archaeology of G. W. B. Huntingford and L. S. B. Leakey. *History in Africa* 33: 287-320.

Thompson, K.D. 2012. "Some were wild, some were soft, some were tame, and some were fiery": Female Dancers, Male Explorers, and the Sexualization of Blackness, 1600-1900. *Black Women, Gender & Families* 6 (2): 1-28.

Trebinjac, S. 2008. *Le pouvoir en chantant. L'art de fabriquer une musique chinoise.* Paris: Société d'Ethnologie.

Wagner, G. 1949. *The Bantu of North Kavirondo,* Volume 1. London, Oxford University Press.

Wasserman, G. 1974. European Settlers and Kenya Colony: Thoughts on a Conflicted Affairs. *African Studies Review* 17 (2): 425-434.

Wels, H. 2002. A critical reflection on cultural tourism in Africa: the power of European imagery, in Akama, J.S. & Sterry, P. (eds) *Cultural Tourism in Africa: Strategies for the New Millennium.* Arnhem: Association for Tourism and Leisure Education: 55-66.

Wierre-Gore, G. 2001. Present Texts, Past Voices: The Formation of Contemporary Representations of West African Dances.*Yearbook of Traditional Music* 33: 29-36.

Wolfe, P. 2006. Settler Colonialism and the Elimination of the Native. *Journal of Genocide Research* 8 (4): 387-409.

"Dancing is Part and Parcel of Someone who is Cultured": Ballroom Dancing and the Spaces of Urban Identity in 1950s Nairobi

Bettina Ng'weno[1]

If you read any city guides about Nairobi in the 1950s you will be struck by the listings of places to dance where live music is played. It was obviously a large part of the social life of the city. What is less obvious at first sight is that these reference dancing available to European audiences only. Was everyone else dancing? Africans resident in Nairobi indeed were dancing. They were dancing to similar and different music, getting their styles both from traditional music and dances of Kenya and across the world through films and through travel. As the end of the decade approached along with the prospect of an independent Kenya, musicians transformed music from outside to develop a particular urban Nairobi sound. This sound made it to the radio and stage changing the sound to which people moved. This chapter looks at ballroom dancing and the music that sustained it in Nairobi, in the spaces of African residential estates and the social halls that hosted the dances in the late 1950s, to understand the spatial layout of dance activities in Nairobi and the urban identities these activities created.

Introduction

I am seated in Loresho, a leafy neighborhood of Nairobi, in a house on the edge of town interviewing a lady who lived in Makongeni (African Railway housing) at the end of the 1950s. As she recalls the dances, her 80-year-old face lights up. She smiles and with a twinkle in her eye she tells me: "The slow waltz. The slow waltz was *my* dance" (ML 2013). She stands up and starts to sing, swaying her body to the music. I imagine this elegant woman dancing, full of fire and grace, to a slow waltz. I see her in the umbrella ball gowns she told me she had worn and which she had made for others, copied from dresses ordered by catalogue from Britain. Her skirt twirls around her, lifting up into an almost horizontal line as she turns. A pearl necklace at her neck.

Today I imagine that she is dancing with someone she probably never knew. I interviewed him in Karen, an upmarket suburb of Nairobi. I see him dressed in the white tuxedo jacket he told me he got a tailor to make the first time he traveled to England. Black trousers and patent leather shoes. The soles of the shoes leather-smooth. Socks matching his trousers exactly. He glides across the floor, improvising as the music changes, attuned to every detail of the song. Hair parted at the side. A bow tie at his neck.

They would be surrounded by similarly dressed dancers. Men in double-breasted suits, in either black or white. Women in calf-length skirts in floral patterns that billow out toward the horizontal as they turn. Some women would have a shawl around their shoulders. Elegant and dignified. They dance as couples on the polished wooden floors in a dance hall, which has tall windows lining both sides like a church. There would be a band playing on stage and drinks served at the end of the hall. Chairs would line the hall in a single row for dancers to return to once tired. They would be dancing in a social hall in one of Nairobi's African residential housing estates. They would be dancing ballroom dances, Continental and Latin American. Their dance would be inflected with movements and gestures revealing their ancestry in different parts of Kenya as they danced to a unique Nairobi sound.

If you read any Nairobi brochures or city guides about Nairobi in the 1950s and 1960s you will be struck by the listings of places to dance where live music is played. They list *"dancing nightly except on Sunday"* at the Equator Club, Queens Hotel, City Hall Gardens, Flamingo Club, Mogambo Club, Ambassador Club, Boomerang Club, the Planter Punch, La Mazot, Sans Cinque Tavern, the Swiss Grill and the Stanley Grill (Nairobi City Council 1957; Nairobi City Council 1962). In addition, there were *"night clubs which are open till the early hours of the morning for dancing and good eating although in these cases membership is necessary"* (Nairobi City Council 1962: 21). One was able to dance to live music almost any day of the week. Photographs show bands with full grand pianos, trumpets, cellos, guitars, saxophones, maracas and drum sets. The dancing couples are finely dressed and look well off. Dance was obviously a large part of the social life of the city.

What is less obvious at first sight is that these venues were segregated and reference dancing available to European audiences only. Right from the beginning, parts of Nairobi were reserved for European settlement. Nairobi is often, even today, referred to as a European city. The colonial government tried to curtail the presence and permanence of Africans in the city (Achola 2002). Not only was housing scarce, insecure and substandard but the colonial government made every effort to limit the amount of time Africans spent in the city and the attractions of the city to Africans. Nevertheless, Europeans were never the majority population of Nairobi. In 1931 the city of Nairobi had an 11% European population – the largest percentage reached (Omenya 2011). Considering the information on dance places in Nairobi makes references European clubs, were other people going out to dance? If so, where? And to what were they dancing?

This chapter examines ballroom dancing in Nairobi in the spaces of African residential estates and the community halls that hosted the dances in the late 1950s to understand the spatial layout of leisure activities in Nairobi and the urban identities these activities created. To do so, it looks at the social, economic, political and architectural context of the spaces of music and dance in colonial Nairobi of the late 1950s. Through the African residential social halls' role as leisure and entertainment centers, the social halls helped form a certain modern, urban, African, Nairobi identity. This chapter looks at how these social halls provided a space in which this modern urban identity was best expressed, in the form of ballroom dancing; the music developed that supported the dancing and gave voice to the identity; the art and styles of being it enabled; the advertising and industries that recognized its power becoming instrumental in its promotion; and the people who made it their own, retooling the dance, music, and social halls for local and national political purposes.

Housing Labor in Nairobi

Burton (2003) argues that urban colonial policies that promoted social halls grew out of British government experience of 1930s Britain and the rise of fascism. He states that, *"community centers were first established in the UK in the 1930s, particularly associated with fostering 'community life' on new housing estates arising out of slum clearance schemes"* to occupy the idle urban dweller (Burton 2003: 348). In Eastern and Southern Africa this fear of the idle urban resident took on particular colonial form and concerns. In settler colonies like Kenya or Rhodesia (now Zimbabwe), control in urban spaces was based on ideas of racial difference and segregation and this included the control of recreation and recreational spaces. Similar to Rhodesia, in Kenya, the *"building of African recreational facilities in the cities was therefore a matter of pragmatic 'native' management. The facilities were designed as infrastructures of control"* (Chikowero 2015: 114).

Frederiksen argues that, *"work in the form it was needed by Europeans, wage labour, presupposes a certain way of computing time, of dividing a day in one's own and somebody else's time. And a certain view of space, accepting one place for work, and another for reproduction and free time"* (1994: 9). Creation of recreational architecture like social halls enhanced these notions of time and space. Institutions such as the Railways, with the schedule of the trains, excelled in the control of time and space, not just in the timing of the trains and workers' shifts, but the architecture of workers' environments and the relationship between work and home. As such, colonial authorities and institutions invested in recreational and educational services provided through housing estates.

Spaces of Leisure in a Working City

In Nairobi, a standard feature of African residential housing estates was the estate social hall. At first the community center provided a venue through which to resettle returning soldiers, whom the colonial government wanted reintegrated into local life (Frederiksen 1994). From the 1930s through the 1960s, almost every housing estate built for Africans had social halls. This was not only a desire of the colonial governments; African workers also came to want and control recreational spaces. The majority of these estates are located in what is now known as Eastlands, a short distance from the Railways.

One of the first and most important social halls to be built was Memorial Hall in Pumwani built by the Municipality of Nairobi Council in 1924 (Muchugu 2016). The name of the area, Pumwani, means *"resting place"* (White, 1990) *"derived from 'pumua' (breathe, relax)"* (Muchungu 2016: 1). Pumwani as a planned Native Location was built in reaction to the *"1921 rise of the East African Association of Harry Thuku, Kenya's first real 'urban protest movement'"* (Myers 2003: 39). The Railways' Muthurwa or Landhies Social Hall became and has remained an important feature of the area as well. These halls were followed by the social halls at Shauri Moyo (1938), Tobacco Village and Bahati.

Later, as Nairobi approached city status under the new 1948 Nairobi Master Plan, Ziwani, Starehe, Kaloleni and Makongeni halls were built. Kaloleni, the new upscale government housing for Africans, was the largest and most magnificent. Kaloleni housing estate was built between 1945 and 1948 and *"borrows heavily from the Neighborhood Unit Concept (NUC) proposed in the 1948 Nairobi Master Plan"* (Macharia 2012: 171). First used in 1947, *"Kaloleni Social Hall was the largest of all the community halls opened in Nairobi"* (Frederiksen 2002: 229). The Railways expanded their housing accommodations for workers in Nairobi by building Makongeni estate to house 5,000 workers in the late 1940s. Anderson describes the new walled estate of Makongeni as having communal kitchens but it *"could boast welfare clinics, a club, a library and reading room, a dance hall and tea room, football ground and even tennis courts"* (Anderson 2002: 147).

The late 1940s and early 1950s saw a huge expansion of the Railways and of the civil service that brought Africans, especially educated Africans, in larger and larger numbers into Nairobi. During the decade of the 1950s, "*Nairobi's population almost tripled*" (Burton 2002: 21). The expansion of Nairobi's population accompanied a changing wage structure, increased industrialization, private entrepreneurship, development of trade unions and the creation of class-differentiated family housing (Atieno Odhiambo 2002). Because of the timing of this expansion – that coincided partly with the State of Emergency between 1952-1958 which limited the movement of people from certain areas of Kenya – many immigrants to the city came from three regions of Kenya: Nyanza, Western and Ukambani. These three regions were thus to have the most direct influence on the music and dance of Nairobi as immigrants brought with them their traditions, sounds and rhythms.

Out Dancing in Nairobi's Social Halls

The social halls in African residential estates held performances in traditional dances, but when people spoke of going dancing, they referred to partner dances in ballroom styles danced to live music. To raise money, ethnic organizations, other businesses and the halls themselves hosted the dances (Owens 2016). While there were dances held in all the social halls, Pumwani, Muthurwa, and Kaloleni were the most famous. Because of the segregated form of the city, these three social halls are in close proximity to each other (as well as to the halls in Shauri Moyo and Tobacco Village). One resident who moved from Muthurwa to Kaloleni in 1945 when it was "*brand new*" remembers the destruction of the three football fields between Makongeni and Muthurwa to build Kaloleni (HJO 2016). Often, people went to the nearest dance hall to dance, but they also crossed the city for dances, although "*Railway people mainly stayed within the vicinity of the Railways*" (MOO 2014).

Residents describe Pumwani of the 1950s as having "*hotels which were open, all night ... with music going on*" and they remember "*attending ballroom dances, cinema going, and listening to bands hired by the municipal authority*" as well as "*orderly dances in the Pumwani Memorial Hall, supervised by teachers and social workers*" (Frederiksen 2002: 229). In addition, in 1958 "*Kenya's first jukebox was installed in Memorial Hall*" in Pumwani (Frederiksen 2002: 229). People from all over Nairobi came to Pumwani to dance. One Nairobi resident recalled sitting in her aunt's house watching her prepare for the dance at Pumwani although her own father would not let her go there (GW 2015). To give an idea of the scale of leisure activities at social halls, "*in 1956/7 five hundred films were shown in the Pumwani Memorial Hall, and in 1957 alone one hundred and ten dances and three hundred meetings were held there*" (Frederiksen 2002: 229).

The music and dance created in the social halls of the new housing estates and older African residential housing came from two sources: outside international influences from especially radio, film and travel; and internal vernacular influences from the different regions of Kenya that workers in Nairobi brought with them. Both the external and internal influences were circumscribed by the politics of British colonialism. Outside influences were limited to music that was considered safe in the politics of 1950s Kenya and the internal influences were limited by the mobility of different people due to, first, the historic regional pull of the Railways; second, to the location of educational facilities across Kenya; and finally to the restrictions of the State of Emergency.

The Nairobi Sound

Stapleton and May argue that, "*the real beginnings of modern Kenyan pop date from the end of the Second World War, when Kenyan soldiers, returning from the front, brought back disposable cash, guitars and accordions*" (1987: 226). Until that moment local music that was not hymns or marching bands was stigmatized as wrong and evil. Stapleton and May state that, "*After the war gramophones became popular, and so did GV records, which had a strong influence on East African musicians. The chief promoters of the new music were the army and police bands, the best-known being that of the King's African Rifles, all of whom included rumbas and cha cha chas in their dance repertoires*" (1987: 226). These army and police bands played in venues such as City Park to a diverse urban audience (ML 2013; HBN 2014; Nairobi City Council 1957). Musicians such as Fundi Konde, who was sent to Burma, and groups such as the Sudanese Brass Band came out of these military backgrounds. "*After the war, musicians who had been trained in brass band instruments went increasingly into dance-music groups*" (Gerhard 1981: 92). In addition, one resident of Nairobi in the 1940s remembers Italian prisoners of war in bands that entertained in the Muthurwa Social Hall (AO 2014).

In the same way, soldiers coming back from the World Wars brought with them ideas of dance that were influential throughout the 1950s. One signature style that came from the military influence was the manner in which you asked someone to dance. A man would bow when asking a woman to dance and offer his hand (SMO 2015). Many Nairobi residents describe the formality of asking a woman to dance and the crushing feeling if rejected. "*You would cross the big empty hallway to where the woman is seated. Once you get there you bow and extend your right hand saying, 'May I have this dance.' But if she is to say no, you turn around and have to face this endlessly big room to cross back alone*" (DA 2013; Cpt O 2015).

In the 1950s finger picking styles of guitar playing became popular across East Africa (Low 1982). The guitarists were often accompanied by the rasp and ring of a rhythm section made up of a Fanta bottle. This first generation of guitar and bottle musicians drew heavily on Luhya rhythms and progressions associated with the *sukuti* percussion music. They included John Mwale, Jim Lasco, David Amunga, and George Mukabi (Stapleton & May 1987). Luhya guitarists also borrowed for the guitar the *sukuma* and *umotibo* dance rhythms (Low 1982: 21). While guitar music was popular across Africa at the time, Low argues that these Kenyan finger-stylists "*developed their own distinctive styles, easily recognizable from those of other countries*" (1982: 19). Later urban bands combined rhumba rhythms and two-part harmonies (Stapleton & May 1987). In addition, musicians such as Olima Anditi "*pushed Luo dance rhythms into the acoustic guitar*" forming the beginnings of what would eventually become the Nairobi music style *benga* (Stapleton & May 1987: 231).

Kenyan musicians were also influenced by southern Africa picking up *kwela*, twist, *sinjonjo* and township jive (Low 1982). In addition, few escaped the influence of Congolese guitarists Jean-Bosco Mwenda and Eduard Masengo, who were promoted and recorded in Kenya, and who sold all over East and Central Africa. As a result, Kenyan guitarists came to copy the Katanga style from records (Low 1982). And in the early 1950s, in "*Kenya, music from Cuba and other Latin American countries was available on the 'GV' label: rhumbas, cha-cha-chas, sambas and other dances, became enormously popular with African people*" (Low 1982: 23). Throughout the 1950s there was sustained interest in Latin and Congolese rhythms and by the 1960s the influence of twist, based on South African *kwela*, was noticeable in most of the Nairobi music (Stapleton & May 1987). People danced to Congolese, southern African and

Tanzanian musicians who were resident in Nairobi such as Mwenda and Masengo (Congo), Peter Tsotsi (Zimbabwe) and Frankie and Sisters (Tanzania) (HJO 2016; Low 1982; Atieno Odhiambo 2002; Stapleton & May 1987). In the 1960s came Calypso and the influence of Harry Belafonte. Finally there was the influence of western music generally.

The Art and Style of Dancing in Nairobi

Importantly the music produced in Nairobi was always music to dance to and was performed at dances by live bands. In this manner dance drove the production of music and vice versa. To the cosmopolitan mixture of music people danced Kenyanized ballroom styles including waltz, quickstep, foxtrot, merengue, chachacha, samba, rhumba, and tango, in addition to rock and roll, twist, and calypso as social dances (HJO 2016). Some also danced these styles in competitions held in the social halls. Different residential estates would organize teams to compete in ballroom dances for prizes. Some of the competitors would represent their estate and Nairobi in competitions elsewhere in the country. People could even make a living teaching ballroom dancing (Owens 2016). One Nairobi resident remembers coaching a dance group from the residential estate of Ziwani in the late 1950s. The group won a competition in Kaloleni in 1956. The next year he won a competition in Nakuru and in 1961 he won a ram at 1:00 am at a competition at Ofafa Memorial in Kisumu opened by Jomo Kenyatta (HJO 2016).

Although the music and the style of dance, ballroom, were derived from abroad, innovation was an important factor of style and allowed for the mixture of genres and the creation of personal style and identity in dance. Improvisation allowed dancers to combine their heritage with this new form of dance. Frederiksen quotes Dedan Githegi, Assistant African Affairs Officer in the 1940s discussing why Africans did not enthusiastically take up colonial recreation activities at first, *"in the old days Africans used to spend their leisure time in Dances which include: a) Ability to show skill in the way they danced, b) Ability to decorate oneself, which is an inherited instinct, c) Attraction of young girls"* (1994: 16).

However, the distinction between the new and the old dancing was perhaps one needing explanation to colonial officials and not necessarily in dancers' minds. The ballroom coach in Ziwani, explained that he never learned how to dance, rather, he said, *"dancing is part and parcel of someone who is cultured"* (HJO 2016). He went on to emphasize that his mother was an amazing dancer and so was his elder sister. His mother was a leader in traditional dances and he got his ability from her. Then, when still in school, he joined his cousin as part of a dance troupe in the countryside for two years. His cousin was a great *orutu* (one string violin) musician and wandering entertainer and performed with an entourage of dancers made up of his younger relatives. As an elderly man recalling ballroom dancing in social halls this ballroom dance coach made no distinction between these forms of dance. Dance was an ability to respond to music as art. When I asked him if he danced the twist he replied *"The twist? There was no art to it. No art at all"* (HJO 2016). He went on to explain that in order for a dancer to demonstrate skill in improvisation, movement and rhythm – as art – the dance, whether traditional or modern, needed to be complex.

Urban Africans in Nairobi were also able to translate the elements of dance that Githegi references (competition, style and sexuality) to their weekly ballroom dances through improvisation. To create new steps that impressed others was part of the fun and competition of dancing. One Nairobi resident recalls being asked by his friend,-who would later become one of Kenya's attorney generals- about one of his signature steps. He replied, *"Just watch. One day I will teach you. One day"* (SMO 2015). Part of the skill of the dancer was to move with the music, especially if it changed (HJO 2016). Therefore, the dancer had to both listen and have a repertoire of steps to deploy when needed. To do this they drew upon traditional steps as well as improvising new steps to add to learned ballroom steps. In dance competitions this is what made or broke the competitor. In line with African dance traditions Nairobi ballroom dancers incorporated improvisational steps, drawing on local tradition styled in a ballroom context.

And dancing was not an inexpensive past time. People who came to dance in the social halls dressed up. Women had special dresses for dancing; either long ball gowns, or shorter less formal dance dresses depending on the occasion. One Nairobi resident remembers that the skirts had gathers so that it would rise to the sides when you turned, like an umbrella, and which they called "umbrella skirts." For competitive dancing, dress was as important as the steps. Thus, even the color of your socks mattered. In addition, how you dressed was a sign of class. Many people stressed their attention to the details of style, of grace and fashion as a statement about who you were. As Nairobi's population accumulated more and more educated Africans working in the Civil Service during the 1950s, class distinctions became more and more important. Some residents who grew up in Railway housing said that the Railway manual workers with some money – people like train engineers or firemen – received complaints from women because they would come to the social halls to drink apparently with soot or grease from the train engines and did not conform to the ideals of style.

The social halls did not only host dances; they hosted movies as well. Similarly, films were part of what defined urban life and modernity in Nairobi (HBN 2013). Due to the ubiquity of films, people in Nairobi were receiving the latest dance and dress styles from abroad. Musicals and Westerns were some of the limited commercial films authorized to be shown to local audiences by the colonial government and were consumed eagerly in Nairobi (HBN 2013). Although by the late 1950s dancing to live music in other parts of the world such as in the US had started a decline, (Craig 2014) it was kept alive in musicals through the likes of Gene Kelly and Fred Astaire. So with films, and the growing economic autonomy of city people and access to *"international circuits of style and wealth"* (Callaci 2011: 367), came ballroom dancing on the grand scale.

In Tanganyika, social halls were also used to host ballroom dances. Burton points out that *"by the early 1940s, the African Dancing clubs (and others) were pre-empting later colonial initiatives by organizing 'European type' dances (dansi) at the Alexandra Hall [in Dar es Salaam]"* (Burton 2003: 337). In fact, in Tanganyika *"to the consternation of many of the Europeans involved, however, dancing – 'of the European sort, but to African bands' – was the most popular activity at the centers as well as being their principal source of revenue"* (Burton 2003: 351). These dances were originally organized by African dance clubs that, *"invited fellow dance lovers in the town, with cards, where the guest couples were designated the kind of Western clothing they should wear. They rented halls and hired dance bands, i.e. African 'jazz bands,' whose main repertoire was Latin-influenced guitar-based dance music, rumba, usually sung in Kiswahili"* (Tsuruta 2003: 201). Callaci argues that through the medium of *dansi* urban Tanzanians expressed concerns about racial uplift in the context of racism but also *"struggles over pressing matters such as social inequality, the boundaries of urban belonging, female virtue, and male access to intimacy with women"* (2011: 367).

Musicians and dancers in Nairobi worked through similar issues through ballroom dancing. They sang about the difficulty of being urban – a theme that was to last after independence. They sang about the lack of jobs, prostitution, violence, overcrowding, poverty, marital problems, housing, love, having to hustle in the city, and the "*changes that town life brings*" (Low 1982: 24; Atieno Odhiambo 2002). These urban musicians sang in Swahili and in some cases partly in English. Unlike rural musicians, who sang mainly in vernacular, the urban musicians used Swahili to reach the expanding cosmopolitan and multilingual working class audiences of the city.

All the halls charged for entering dances, about the same amount as going to the cinema, so they drew from a salaried audience. Usually, if a couple went to the dance hall, the man would buy the tickets. While the men were in line for the tickets, they would first buy the ladies sodas, so they would not just be waiting with nothing. However, there were many more men than women because of the restrictions on women in Nairobi and the colonial expectation that workers were bachelors or, being temporary in the city, had left their wives at home in the countryside. So for men who were not married they would dance alone (SW 2014). Often single men would come and ask the waiting woman to dance while the husband was in line. Although the situation was recalled in terms of respectability where all men respected the woman's response, the gender imbalance of the city of four men to every woman, caused tensions among men expressed both in song lyrics and dance and sometimes in fights. Pumwani social hall was famous for fights, which broke out often (White 1991). One Nairobi resident remembers that her husband, who was a boxer, loved going there because of the possibility of a fight, while she avoided it for the same reason (MOO 2014).

Muthurwa, being one of the oldest halls, was very popular for music and for boxing. It was also the hall closest to downtown and the European and Asian areas of town. The social halls at the Railways were situated in very clearly bounded spaces, which meant that they were more easily policed. One resident mentions how he was able to buy *chang'a* (moonshine) in Kaloleni, although more upscale, but not in Makongeni because of its surrounding wall (NM 2013). Muthurwa represented the Railways and recorded radio shows such as *Happy Hour* and *Railway Showboat* that drew large crowds. It also hosted many political as well as union meetings, and of course films. Along with the ballroom dancing the social halls hosted traditional dances (especially for weddings and funerals) and allowed people to set up their own concerts and comedy theatre shows (MOO 2014).

Kaloleni, home to mainly Nairobi City Council workers, was thought of as an upscale area whose social hall was distinguished by class and size. It was here that some of the most important dance competitions were held, although participants came from housing estates across the city. In this manner, housing estates and their social halls structured competitive engagement across class and occupation.

Tapping African Modernity through Music and Dance

The dance halls were also spaces that helped create a unique sound. Low argues that from a "*melting-pot of influences gradually emerged distinctively Kenyan styles*" (1982: 24). In agreement, Stapleton and May state that "*despite its outside influences, Kenyan music in the 1950s and early 1960s had a feeling of its own*" (1987: 229). Not only was it distinctive but it was also popular, for "*during the heyday of finger-styles, which lasted roughly from 1958 to 1962*" elite urban guitarists earned good money in concerts, bars, hotels, dances and advertising as well as on the radio (Low 1982: 30). One reason for this distinct sound I would argue was that it was also the first moment of popular music played on the radio targeting a nationally conceived audience – whether through advertising, record studios or railway propaganda. It was a moment, driven by the demands for independence and making the most of a rising consumer class, of using the radio to create a certain kind of national audience.

As guitarists moved from acoustic to electric guitars, "*Kenyan musicians were consciously struggling to develop a truly national music and at their best produced dynamic, original and very exciting dance tunes*" (Low 1982: 30). In order to have a national name, to participate in the new economy and to talk to an international audience, musicians produced new sounds that targeted a national audience. One of the best examples is *Western Shilo* by Daudi Kabaka that manages to be regional and national at the same time. Low goes on to add that, "*quite a lot of the credit for the successes of the '60s was attributed to Equator Records and to its producer Charles Worrod in particular, who was felt had given a strong lead to local musicians*" (1982: 30).

Charles Worrod came to music through advertising, building a new sound for Nairobi through a growing industry. The growing Nairobi populations of the 1950s and their developing classes and consumer society allowed Africans to be seen as consumers for the first time. Atieno Odhiambo points out that along with other cosmopolitan items, "*HMV and Columbia gramophones were popular acquisitions*" (2002: 255) and that these "*affluent urban residents were in a position to kula raha – to consume leisure*" (2002: 257).

The adman Peter Colmore and his team of Charles Worrod as producer and Ally Sykes as his partner from Tanganyika, saw an opportunity to mobilize entertainment – both music and comedy – to sell products. Sykes notes that, "*Peter Colmore built some products into household names around East Africa. The best musicians East Africa had ever known were used to promote these products*" (Sykes 2004: 1). Ally Sykes was the perfect partner for Colmore. He was "*not only a political activist, being one of the 17 founders of TANU [Tanganyika African National Union], but also ... a musician in his own band, the Merry Blackbirds*" in Tanganyika (Tsuruta 2003: 212).

In the 1940s, Sykes' father, Kleist Sykes, had started the controversial Tanganyika Islamic Jazz Club that was part of the complicated system of ballroom dance clubs known as *dansi*. Kleist Sykes had to change the name of the club, but in starting the club "*through dansi, Sykes sought both to create a kind of social status based on pan-urban cosmopolitan culture, and to link Muslim identity with emerging forms of prestige*" (Callaci 2011: 373). In Tanganyika, much like in Nairobi, "*dancehalls were spaces of conspicuous self-display where young urban men and women deployed fashion, dance moves, and an elaborate slang vocabulary based largely on foreign loan words from cinema and imported music as a way of claiming a new urban identity based on consumption, romantic courtship, and privileged access to cosmopolitan cultural knowledge*" (Callaci 2011: 375). Not only did this provide willing consumers but "*by the late 1950s, businesses attempted to capitalize on dansi's modern connotations by using images of dancing couples to market elite consumer items*" (Callaci 2011: 375). Considering the structure of *dansi* in Tanganyika, Ally Sykes was well aware of the power of *dansi* and music to both sell products, proclaim a modern identity and to form an audience and community.

With Sykes, Colmore became a very successful media and entertainment businessman and in 1961 founded his own recording company, High Fidelity Productions Ltd., which promoted bands from across East Africa (Sykes 2004). In 1961 Charles Worrod bought up the assets of East African Records (Jambo Records) and launched Equator Sound Studios Ltd., which was to record some of the best-known Kenyan music of the time with the intention of providing "*East African Music for East Africans*" (Odidi 2013: 1).

The Sound of the Railways

The audience for both the advertisements and the music was boosted by a growing radio culture. Kenya had its first regular radio broadcasts starting in 1927 that broadcast to European settlers (Wilkinson 1972). By the 1950s there were many more radios in Kenya, heavily promoted by the colonial government. Africans in Nairobi frequently bought radio sets for community centers, cafes, and bars. Radios were also *"given free of charge to individual Africans thought to be influential, or might be hired at a reasonable price"* (Frederiksen 1994: 28). However, during the State of Emergency broadcasting served the interests of counter-insurgency policy (Amour 1984).

In 1959 the Kenya Broadcasting Service came into being, with broadcasts in English on one service, Hindi and Gujarati on another and Swahili on a third, with regional vernacular services from Nairobi (Kamba and Kikuyu), Kisumu (Luo and Luhya) and Mombasa (Swahili and Arabic) (Amour 1984; Soja 1968). With the setting up of commercial radio in the form of the Kenya Broadcasting Service, recording studios were able to make money promoting sponsored programs and advertisements (Harvey 2003). As such, the radio also became the platform to promote musicians and entertainers. The radio and recording studios began to influence both rural and urban guitarists.

Civil unrest also influenced what was played on the radio. In the later part of 1959 labor relations deteriorated in the ports and harbors as well as across the East African Railways, reducing rail passenger journeys by about 87,000 journeys (a 1.4% reduction) (East African Railways & Harbours 1960). By late 1959, the East African Railways and Harbours were faced with a massive strike that was East Africa-wide. In 1960 there were continued strikes and work stoppages, contributing to an additional loss of 779,000 passenger journeys (a drop of 12.7%) (East African Railways & Harbours 1960). The loss of passenger journeys took place predominantly in third class, that is to say, among African travelers.

So soon after the end of the Emergency, any civil unrest greatly concerned the colonial government who feared it would restart violence. Keenly aware of this, the Railways tried to counter any popular support for the striking African railway workers through entertainment propaganda. *"Railway strikes necessitated intensive day by day coverage and information was disseminated to the public through the media of the press and radio"* (East African Railways & Harbours 1960: 29). As part of this public relations campaign, the Railways started the radio show *Railway Showboat*. The 1959 Annual Report describes the *Railway Showboat* as follows:

> "Railway Showboat" – a weekly feature broadcast of interest to both staff and public – was first produced in October on the Kenya Broadcasting Service. A measure of the success achieved by this initial attempt at African radio entertainment was demonstrated by the allocation of the peak listening time to this program (East African Railways & Harbours 1960: 29)

This program was not just recorded in a studio. Photos in the Railway Museum archives show some of the newly famous African artists, such as Fadhili Williams and his sister Esther, performing to a live audience on stage at Muthurwa Social Hall. Fadhili and Esther sing in front of a full Latin band set up with congas, bongos, triple base, a brass section and drum set. The *Railway Showboat* logo and title is displayed behind them on the wall.

By this time radio was already used ubiquitously in the Railways. The radio was continuously broadcast on loudspeakers at every railway station all day long. This was a signature feature of railway travel. In addition, every residence in Muthurwa, while not having internal electric lights, had wired radios in each one-room house (HBN 2013). Thus, radio news, entertainment and music were readily available to every Railway worker and traveler. The *Railway Showboat* was not a first attempt in broadcasting either; rather, the radio program *Happy Hour* was already broadcast once a week from Muthurwa. It featured Railway worker-musicians who had formed an orchestra and it drew about 500 people to the recording sessions (Frederiksen 1994).

The *Railway Showboat* featured local popular music, mainly in Swahili but with a few songs in English, and it played nationally. Its aim was to appeal to a national audience; the music could therefore not be reduced to a narrow ethnic sound and it was by local artists. Because of its association with the Railways, Swahili was a natural choice both for artists and those producing the show. The Railways were not local by any means – they were East African in scope and reach, and through this program helped spread the music of artists like Fadhili Williams and his sister Esther, John Mwale, Daudi Kabaka, George Mukabi, Gabriel Omolo, Fundi Konde and others across East Africa. These artists would later to be synonymous with what became known as "*zilizopendwa*" (golden oldies).

Owens reports that, "*as urban laborers returned to the countryside, they brought with them new tastes and influences from the city*" (2016: 168). Reaching beyond a vernacular audience, the combination of urban themes, movement on the railways and the use of Swahili meant that in the 1950s music heard, and danced to, all over Kenya was disproportionally about Nairobi. Even rural guitarists sang about Nairobi, its money, women, education and love, the very themes expressed in music and dance in social halls (Low 1982). In 1993, doing fieldwork in coastal Kenya, I remember that people in the village where I lived sang songs of Nairobi to their children by moonlight – songs made famous in dances in the 1950s and passed down from generation to generation by their grandparents.

Dancing is Part and Parcel of Someone who is Cultured

In 1959, in fear of civil unrest in Nairobi and a return to violence, the British colonial government did a sweeping dragnet raid on a number of political activities in the city of Nairobi. They raided offices of the Nairobi People's Convention Party (NPCP), which were also the offices of the Kenyan Federation of Labor, and of the newspaper *Uhuru*. Thirty-four Members of the NPCP were detained and some exiled to Lamu at the Coast for sedition, others rusticated to their supposed "home" in the countryside. The man connected to all three entities (party, union and newspaper), Tom Mboya, was held at home in Ziwani, along with visiting Julius Nyerere, who later became founding president of Tanzania. Finally, all political rallies were banned by the government (Goldsworthy 1982).

Mboya was a Nairobi politician who represented the "*non-customary, urban developments*" expressed by the dances in the social halls (Parkin 1978: 239). At the time Mboya was the Secretary General of the Kenya Federation of Labor, founder and President of NPCP, which produced the newspaper *Uhuru*, a member of the Legislative Council (LegCo) representing Nairobi (one of 8 African members), and Secretary of the African Elected Members Organization (AEMO) of LegCo. He was 29 years old. In response, "*just two days after the raid he coolly circumvented the current ban on African political meetings by calling an 'African song and dance meeting' in the Kaloleni community hall*" (Goldsworthy 1982: 113). Frederiksen describes Kaloleni as "*perhaps the most important meeting place of nationalist activists in the* late 1940s and the 1950s, becoming colloquially known as the House of Parliament. What had been planned as an institution aimed at the betterment of urban Africans became a center not only for the nationalist elite's plotting, but also for political meetings of Nairobi's African masses" (2002: 229). Mboya turned this song and dance meeting into a political rally, where people sang about Kenyatta and freedom, and where Mboya started every remark with "'*as you know, I am not allowed to make a political speech*'" (Goldsworthy 1982: 113).

A song and dance meeting, however, was not something unexpected for Tom Mboya. Rather, Mboya is described by those who remember him from the social halls as a "*lifer,*" that is to say, someone who lived life to the fullest in all aspects. Mboya is remembered by most people as "*musical*" and an "*amazing dancer,*" their voices softening and their heads nodding in recollection. He is also recalled as a sharp dresser, "*always well turned out,*" "*smart from his head to his shoes,*" a man of style "*in a class of his own*". A very young politician representing Nairobi in the late 1950s and a powerful trade union leader, Mboya appears in the few photographs of Kaloleni (as dancer, musician and politician) and Muthurwa social halls (holding a union meeting) that still exist. There are pictures of him playing maracas with a band in a recording studio and stories of his guitar stolen from him in Kaloleni. At Mboya's mausoleum on Rusinga Island where he is buried, there is a museum in his memory. On a shelf of the museum is a silver trophy cup for a dance competition in Nairobi bearing witness to his ability as a dancer. Mboya most completely embodied all the aspects of social halls in the late 1950s, their dance and youth culture, their class and gender dynamics and divisions, salaried workers, their style of music, their cosmopolitan and international outlook, and of course their urban politics that became national.

Conclusion

At the time the social halls in African residential estates were built, many recreational facilities in the city, including private and public clubs, bars and movie theatres, were segregated spaces. Chikowero argues that British colonial policies on music and dance in urban areas of settler colonies sought to control Africans in the city and to produce a certain kind of urban African. But that African urbanity was hard to control. Owen argues that, "*the social halls, municipal football leagues, and weekend dances became spaces where Africans explored new expressions of socialization, leisure and identity within Kenya's urban centers*" (2016: 171). Africans transformed these spaces from what they were intended to be – spaces for the domestication and control of African labor – to spaces of protest, innovation and creation.

Callaci (2011) emphasizes that dance halls can't be seen simplistically as spaces that transcend difference and create shared national identity. Rather, she argues, they are multiple embodiments and claims about community boundaries. Social halls in Nairobi, I would argue, were also a claim of urbanity and a claim to the city denied to the majority of its inhabitants, that, along with the Nairobi sound defined Nairobi and partly defined Nairobi's dominant position to articulate Kenyan modernity and imaginary.

While Nairobi is often still imagined as European, the idea belies the ideology that tried to make it exactly that, and the people, dancers included, that resisted and transformed the urban spaces to make them their own. In much writing on East Africa inland of the coast, the urban African is someone ill-fitting and maladapted to a city that is somehow not African. There is little attention to long-term residents and what they made of the city. The architectural layout of colonialism in 1950s Nairobi established social halls in African residential estates for leisure activities segregated by race. While meant to placate and domesticate an African labor force, due to the Mau Mau, the demands for labor of the Railways and colonial fear of urban civil unrest, social halls, I would argue, became a site for urban identity formation that bypassed and transgressed colonial imaginations. Rather, the dancers and other users of these spaces made them their own, creating sounds and steps that were uniquely Nairobi.

Endnotes

1 I would like to thank Garnette Oluoch Olunya, Njane Mugambi, Joyce Nyairo, Julia Kunguru, Makau Nzioka, Bill Odidi and Fleur Ng'weno for their help and support and also especially all the people who so generously answered my questions about their life in 1950s Nairobi (including ML, DA, GW, HBN and HJO in Nairobi, NM in Mbitini, SW, AO, MOO and GW in Funyula, and SMO and Cpt. O in Kisumu quoted in this chapter) who for confidentiality reasons are not named here.

Bibliography

Amour, C. 1984. The BBC and the Development of Broadcasting in British Colonial Africa 1946-1956. *African Affairs* 83(332): 359-402.

Anderson, D.M. 2002. Corruption at City Hall: African Housing and Urban Development in Colonial Nairobi, in Burton, A. (ed.) *The Urban Experience in East Africa c.1750-2000*. Azania Special Volume XXXVI-XXXVII. Nairobi, The British Institute in Eastern Africa: 138-154.

Atieno Odhiambo, E S. 2002. Kula Raha: Gendered Discourses and the Contours of Leisure in Nairobi, 1946-63, in Burton, A. (ed.) *The Urban Experience in East Africa c.1750-2000*. Azania Special Volume XXXVI-XXXVII. Nairobi, The British Institute in Eastern Africa: 254-264.

Burton, A. 2002. Introduction: Urbanisation in Eastern Africa: An Historical Overview, c.1750-2000 in Burton, A. (ed.) *The Urban Experience in East Africa c.1750-2000*. Azania Special Volume XXXVI-XXXVII. Nairobi, The British Institute in Eastern Africa: 1-28.

Burton, A. 2003. Townsmen in the Making: Social Engineering and Citizenship in Dar es Salaam, c. 1945-1960. *The International Journal of African Historical Studies* 36 (2): 331-365.

Callaci, E. 2011. Dancehall Politics: Mobility, Sexuality and Spectacles of Racial Respectability in Late Colonial Tanganyika, 1930-1961. *Journal of African History* 52: 365-384.

Chikowero, M. 2015. *African Music, Power, and Being in Colonial Zimbabwe*. Bloomington, Indian University Press.

Craig, M. 2014. *Sorry I don't Dance: Why Men Refuse to Move*. Oxford, Oxford University Press.

East African Railways and Harbours, 1960. *Annual Report for East African Railways and Harbours 1959*. Nairobi, East African Railways and Harbours.

Frederiksen, B F. 1994. Making Popular Culture From Above: Leisure in Nairobi 1940-60. Occasional Paper 145, Centre for Studies in Social Sciences, Calcutta.

Frederiksen, B F. 2002. African Women and Their Colonisation of Nairobi: Representations and Realities, in Burton, A. (ed.) *The Urban Experience in East Africa c.1750-2000*. Azania Special Volume XXXVI-XXXVII. Nairobi, The British Institute in Eastern Africa: 223-234.

Gerhard, K. 1981. Neo-Traditional Popular Music in East Africa Since 1945. *Popular Music* 1: 83-104.

Goldsworth, D. 1982. *Tom Mboya: The Man Kenya Wanted to Forget*. London, Heinemann.

Harvery, F. 2003. Jambo (East Africa), in Shepherd, J., Horn, D., Laing, D., Oliver P. and Wicke, P. (eds.) *Continuum Encyclopedia of Popular Music of the World: Performance and Production Vol. I. Media, Industry and Society*. London, Continuum

Low, J. 1982. A History of Kenyan Guitar Music: 1945-1980. *African Music* 6(2): 17-36.

Macharia, P A. 2013. Design Strategy and Informal Transformations in Urban Housing: A Study of the Contribution of Design Strategy to Dweller-Initiated transformations using Comparative Case Study Analysis of Buru-Buru and Kaloleni Housing Estates in Nairobi, Kenya. *Journal of Housing and the Built Environment* 28(1): 167- 186

Muchugu, F. 2016. Pumwani Social Hall Gets New Lease of Life. *The Star 7 March 2016*. http://www.the-star.co.ke/news/2016/03/07/pumwani-social-hall-gets-new-lease-of-life_c1306888 (Retrieved August 27, 2016).

Myers, G A. 2003. *Verandahs of Power: Colonialism and Space in Urban Africa*. Syracuse, Syracuse University Press.

Nairobi City Council. 1957. *Nairobi: City in the Sun 1955/57*. Nairobi, Nairobi City Council.

Nairobi City Council. 1962. *Nairobi: City in the Sun 1961/62*. Nairobi, Nairobi City Council.

Odidi, B. 2013. The Golden Years of Kenya's Music. *The Daily Nation online Monday August 12th 2013*. http://www.nation.co.ke/lifestyle/DN2/The-golden-years-of-Kenyas-music/957860-1944042-ulh7amz/index.html (Retrieved December 23, 2017).

Omenya, A. 2011. The History of Nairobi 1900-1950s: Colonial Capital in *Nairobi: An Exploration of the City by Photographers and Writers*. Nairobi, Kwani?: 2-3.

Owen, C. E. 2016. *Lands of Leisure: Recreation, Space, and the Struggle for Urban Kenya: 1900-2000*. East Lansing, Michigan State University, unpublished PhD diss.

Parkin, D. 1978. *The Cultural Definition of Political Response: Lineal Destiny Among the Luo*. London, Academic Press.

Soja, E W. 1968. *The Geography of Modernization in Kenya: A spatial Analysis of Social, Economic and Political Change*. Syracuse, Syracuse University Press.

Stapleton, C & May, C. 1987. *African All-Stars: the Pop Music of a Continent*. London, Quartet Books Ltd.

Tsuruta, T. 2003. Popular Music, Sports, and Politics: A Development of Urban Cultural Movements in Dar es Salaam, 1930s-1960s *African Study Monographs* 24(3): 195-222.

White, L. 1990. *The Comforts of Home: Prostitution in Colonial Nairobi*. Chicago, University of Chicago Press.

Part II:

The Performance of Local Politics and National Identities

Pan-Somalist Discourse and New Modes of Nationalist Expression in the Somali Horn: From Somali Poetic Resistance to Djibouti's *Gacan Macaan*

Kenedid A. Hassan

This chapter explores the evolution of nationalist discourses in the Somali Horn through the expression of Somali musicians, poets and a Djiboutian band, Gacan Macaan ("Sweet Hand"). After first exploring how the development of musical expression tracked with the rise of Pan-Somalism in the late colonial period, I look at the way that Somali poets in the 1960s and 1970s began to deconstruct the notion of Pan-Somalism – a universalist, clan-transcending political ideology central to the anti-colonial independence project. I then explore the impact this critique had on Gacan Macaan who, by the 1970s used their artistic productions to articulate a different type of anti-colonial, nationalist agenda in Djibouti. I draw on Gilroy's Black Atlantic and Amselle's Branchements to make sense of the ways post-nationalist cultural productions may be used for nationalist ends, and argue that greater attention be paid to the interplay of local historical developments and transnational cultural flows.

Introduction

During the 1960s and 1970s, the Somali-speaking territories underwent profound social and political changes. In 1960 the Somali Republic was born – a union of the newly independent British and Italian Somalilands – and Pan-Somalism, a clan-transcending universalist nationalist discourse was touted as the way forward. While it found initial purchase in Djibouti, a city-state with a significant Somali-speaking community country then a colony of France, by the time of Djiboutian independence in 1977, a different type of anti-colonial nationalist discourse had taken hold. This chapter explores how this transformation was reflected in, and precipitated by, poetry and music in the Somali-speaking territories of the Horn of Africa, and particularly the influence that developments in one area (Somali) had on another (Djibouti). From the 1960s, Somali artists and musicians explored the tension between the past and the present in unprecedented ways, beginning to unpack Somalis' infatuation with the ideology of Pan-Somalism and their unwillingness to renounce irredentist views of the region. I will argue that these poetic interventions altered the balance of discursive power in the region, obliging Djibouti's vibrant and creative artistic community to rethink its position to capture this mutation. *Gacan Macaan,* Djibouti's most popular band of the 1970s and 1980s, serves as a case study of how these shifts became manifest.

The first section of this chapter sets the theoretical stage by outlining certain features of Gilroy's *Black Atlantic* and Amselle's *Branchements* relevant to the analysis of Somalis' artistic productions. I suggest that Gilroy provides helpful insight into the transnational flow of ideas and artistic expression, though the Somali-Djibouti experience complicates his Atlantic focus and "post-nationalist" perspective. Amselle provides a remedy to Gilroy's tendency to "essentialize" culture, as well as a longer view of the history of transnational flows. Following this, I provide an overview of the emergence of Pan-Somalism as a political ideology, and trace how this was reflected in the developing musical scene of the time. Next, I discuss how the post-1969 regime incorporated the arts into its governing agenda, before exploring in more detail how poetry was eventually used to de-construct Pan-Somalism. I then turn to an exploration of the impact these developments had on the emerging Djibouti music scene, paying particular attention to *Gacan Macaan*. I show how cultural producers, fusing different musical and poetic genre, re-articulated their artistic and political agenda – by this time a nationalist agenda that rejected pan-Somalism in favour of a distinctively Djiboutian agenda. I conclude by discussing the implications of this case for our theoretical understanding of the intersections of artistic expression, the transnational flow or cultural ideas, and nationalist discourses.

Theorizing Cultural Expressions

The work of Paul Gilroy constitutes one of the most innovative contributions to *black studies* forms of *diaspora* analysis. Adapting some of the perspectives and expressions of historical black studies debates, Gilroy's *Black Atlantic* (1993) attempts to fill certain gaps by conceptualizing black studies as a zone of interactivity between various spaces and continents, namely Africa, America and Europe. This analysis suggests that black studies representations of black experiences may be much more complex than cultural studies (Gilroy's own discipline of origin, which sees culture as the central unit of social analysis) characteristically assumes. Within a postmodern perspective, the author argues that *black studies* should move away from ideas of nationalism and "ethnic absolutism" to focus on "intercultural" and "transnational" dimensions – although the book's argument draws partly on W. E. B. DuBois' notion of "double consciousness", which elucidates how Blacks in America struggle with America's mainstream identity model. To Gilroy, cultural studies, in general, is fixated with what he calls "cultural insiderism". Gilroy suggests:

> Regardless of their affiliation to the right, left, or centre, groups have fallen back on the idea of cultural nationalism, on the overintegrated conceptions of culture which present immutable, ethnic differences as an absolute break in the histories and experiences of "black" and "white" people (1993: 2).

Against this "ethnic absolutism" point of view, he proposes "the theorisation of creolisation, metissage, mestizaje, and hybridity" (Gilroy 1993: 2). One way of transcending "cultural insiderism" and the nation state is to avoid focusing either on Africa or the Americas. More than anything else, *Black Atlantic* seeks to grasp black lives, which are the product of incessant reinventions of complex historical dynamics, through the circulations of ideas and "the image of ships in motion across the spaces between Europe, America, Africa, and the Caribbean as a central organising symbol" (Gilroy 1993: 4).

While recognizing Gilroy's undeniable contributions to our understanding of black transatlantic exchanges,[1] I wish to point out quickly two drawbacks of the *Black Atlantic* model that concern this chapter. First, Gilroy does not pay any attention to Africa-Asia cultural productions or exchanges; *Black Atlantic* exclusively builds its theoretical apparatus/ framework on the black English, Afro-American and Afro-Caribbean experiences. Africa is in the whole treated as the silent imaginary interlocutor, except for a few passages on Sierra Leone and Liberia – two nations founded for the resettlement of the freed Afro-Americans.[2] The idea that black experiences can be only framed within the Atlantic space is problematic.

Second, Gilroy's anti-nationalism overlooks how African musicians, for example, while reappropriating Afro-American artistic expressions and styles, incorporate nationalist projects into their artistic productions. As the *Gacan Macaan* case will illustrate, cultural productions that draw inspiration from beyond their own borders can also be used to support nationalist projects.

Writing roughly on the same subject as Gilroy, Jean-Loup Amselle, an Africanist, also examines cultural processes in his seminal work *Branchements: Anthropologie de l'universalité des cultures* (2001). Amselle's *Branchements* represents both an extension and a modification of the many arguments developed in previous books. Like Gilroy, Amselle challenges the theory of "cultural essentialism", but, unlike Gilroy, he criticizes the postmodern discourse of "creolization" and "hybridization" for reproducing the very "biological-culture" it sets out to deconstruct. In opposition to the illusion of "original purity", Amselle elaborates the metaphorical theme of "connection"; he suggests we see "cultures" as constantly interconnected by "a network of planetary signifiers" "already there" (Amselle 2001: 7). Amselle sees these constant interconnections of cultures as the result of all historical globalizations that predate those of Islam, of European colonization or of the current "globalization". To avoid the idea of biologisation of globalization or the racialization of societies, Amselle prefers the term "connection" to that of "mestizo society" to show the openness of all cultures. This thesis is illustrated by an "African" example: the creation in 1949 of a real "cultural multinational" (in Conakry, Cairo, Bamako), the N'Ko movement, founded by the Mandingo thinker, Souleymane Kanté. While our subject of study embodies some features of Gilroy's transnational black expressive cultures, Amselle's *Branchements* would certainly guard us against the essentialism inherent in *Black Atlantic*. In the remaining sections of this chapter, we will see how well these models play out in practice.

Pan-Somalism and Popular Music Before the Union

In the Fall of 1946, just over a year after the end of the WWII, Mr. Ernest Bevin, then the British Foreign Secretary of the post-war Labour Government, delivered a speech at the UN. In a strategy designed to give Britain more political clout in world politics, he proposed that all the Somali territories be administered by British colonial power under UN trusteeship. Following the fall of the fascist regime in the Somalilands in March 1941, all Somali territories, except for Djibouti, had been administered by a British military general. Mr. Bevin suggested "that British Somaliland, Italian Somaliland, and the adjacent part of Ethiopia, if Ethiopia agreed, should be lumped together as trust territory, so that the nomads should lead their frugal existence with the least possible hindrance and there might be a real chance of a decent economic life, as understood in that territory" (cited in Touval 1963: 79). Britain's good intentions, however, raised suspicions among the other superpowers, who proposed to send a fact-finding commission to investigate the political sentiments of Somalis.

Long before the so-called Bevin Plan, sentiments of uniting Somali territories, including the British and Italian Somalilands, eastern Ethiopia, northeastern Kenya and Djibouti, were advocated by various Somali political figures. Politicians such as Ali Bahdon Buh, a charismatic leader from Djibouti, and others had been fighting for some forms of Pan-Somalism in the 1930s. His party, Al Khairya, one of the few parties in place at the time, had a reasonably coherent Pan-Somali platform. But it was only in the late 1940s that Somalis were able to channel their political aspirations into formal and legal organizations, when they were granted permission to form political parties by the British. Parties competed across the political spectrum to re-evaluate Somalis' place and role in the region and the world. Most emerging parties were either regionally or clan-based, with the exception of the Somali Youth League (SYL), Somaliland National League (SNL) and the National Front United (NFU), whose Pan-Somalism dominated the political landscape for almost two decades. The object of pro-Pan-Somalism was to abolish the customary law - *Xeer* – which many viewed as a source of inter-clan violence, real or imagined, and as a hindrance to progress. Pan-Somalism served as a critical ideology in the late-colonial period, guiding efforts to unify Somalis in one, independent state. While Pan-Somalism did have its detractors – particularly the likes of Sheikh Abdullahi Sheikh Mohamed "Bogodi" and the *Hisbi Digile Mirifle* (HDM) party (see Touval 1963) – Pan-Somalism was indisputably the political ideology *du jour* up until the independent Somali Republic unified the north and south in 1960.

With no competing ideology in play, Pan-Somalism featured strongly in the popular music that was developing at the time. In the colonial Somalilands, *qaraami* – a popular music genre that originated in British Somaliland, closely associated with urbanization and influenced by the *balwo* genre invented by Abdi Deqsi Sinimo[3] – dominated public spaces in the 1950s and the first part of the 1960s. The first and only band for almost a decade – *Walaalaha Hargeysa* (Hargeysa Brothers) – typified the rich and expressive *qaraami*. The creation of Radio Hargeysa[4] in Hargeysa, the largest city and the seat of the colonial administration,[5] contributed to the spread of this genre and the success of the group. While *qaraami* musicians embraced new sounds, they also remained attached to the older forms of artistic sensibilities. Musicians appropriated and imitated Sudanese and Arabic sounds, but they also connected with the Somali Sufi style. In Somalis' first experimentation with musical instruments – oud and violin were introduced in the mid-1940s and were more easily adaptable to Somali rhythms and melodies – Sudanese sounds served as a major source of inspiration for popular music, because Afro-American and European music were not yet available. Mohamud Mohamed Good "Shinbir" (a composer) and an Indian-Somali Rashid Buulo (a violinist) were sent to a music school in Cairo to contribute to the nascent popular music.

In British Somaliland, *Walaalaha Hargeysa's* rudimentary music studio was the centre of Somali popular music for the most part of the 1950s, buoyed by the musical creativity of Abdillahi Qarshe, the writing and poetic imaginations of Hussein Aw Farah and Sahardid Mohamed Jebiyeh, and the extraordinary performances of Ahmed Ali Dararamleh, Ahmed Mohamed Kulu and Omar Dhuleh Ali. Initially, members came typically from the urban social class, those who had some access to cultural imports. Later, adherents came from various socioeconomic and regional background, including women. In the early development of Somali popular music, women were absent from the musical scene. In part, music was associated with debauchery, just as the *balwo* dance performances was falsely linked with sexual transgressions in the 1940s.[6] A few women succeeded in breaking the social and cultural rule, despite the negative perceptions (though at times with serious repercussions). Early pioneers of Somali popular music, such as Kadija Dharar ("Kadija Balwo"), Shamis Abokor ("Guduudo Arwo") and Faduma Kahin ("Maandeeq") not only contributed to the acceptance of women in the artistic field, but also they played a major part in the development of arts in the Somali context. Suffice to say that Somali popular music took a monumental leap forward with the creation of *Walaalaha Hargeysa*.

Politically, *Walaalaha Hargeysa* were well in tune with the political climate of the times. Members of the band were disenchanted with the colonial administration and the way it ceded portions of the Somali territory to Ethiopia in 1955.[7] They adopted the anti-colonial narrative for the return of their land, and, buoyed by the unity platforms of the nascent political parties of the day, invited Somalis to espouse the politics of unity. Abdillahi Qarshe, who never disguised his pro-independence and pro-Pan-Somalism, openly criticized the colonial power in "*Dhulkayaga*" ("Our Country/Our Land"), a song that advocated independence by any means necessary, including shedding blood through liberation struggle:

Dhulkayaga, Dhulkayaga	Our Land, Our Land
Waan uu Dhimanayna,	We will Die, For Our Land
Dhallin iyo Dhallan	The Youth and The Children
Waayeelka Dhurugsagay	The Unyielding Elders
Dhiig Inaan ku Shubo	We Will Shed Blood for our Land
Aan Dhagar ku Galo	We Will Kill for Our Land

Throughout his career, Qarshe stressed shared ideology and regional solidarity among Somalis in Ethiopia, Djibouti, Kenya, British Somaliland and Italian Somaliland. His unity message was not anathema to the Somali territories' political elites, who presented Pan-Somalism to the world as panacea for Somalis' political and socioeconomic problems. In essence, musicians and poets of *Walaalaha Hargeysa*, at least in the 1950s, had identified the colonial administrations in the Somalilands with political and economic exploitation of Somalis by foreign powers, and espoused Pan-Somalism as the way forward. The band's first play *"Cantar iyo Ceebla"* ("The Foolish and Perfect Woman"), which on the surface was a love story, had powerful anti-colonial and Pan-Somalism undertones.

In the early decades of Somalis' experimentation with musical instruments and new forms of musical expression – which incorporated Sudanese sounds but remained rooted in indigenous Sufi styles – musicians for the most part reflected the popular political attitudes of the day; anti-colonial discourse, a Pan-Somalist agenda and the nationalist fervor of the pre-independence years was clearly reflected in artistic work. This continued, to a degree, in the early years of independence. After the Union, *Walaalaha Hargeysa's* creativity, popularity and pro-Pan-Somalism attracted the attention of the civil government (1960-1969), but members continued to enjoy a degree of independence. The place of artists in the nationalist project, however, was to take a sharp turn after the revolution of 1969, when they became incorporated into the regime's strategy of government, but at the same time started to use their work to question the pan-Somalist agenda.

The Revolution of 1969: Music in the New Regime

Right after the military junta led by General Siyaad Barre assumed power in October 1969, multiparty politics was banned and replaced by the Supreme Revolutionary Council (SRC), putting an end both to the political pluralism introduced by the British Colonial Administration and artistic diversity[8], as music was becoming one of the most important cultural forms of expression for Somalis. Although music was highly popular historically, it was not lucrative economically for artists. A year after the coup d'état, music, poetry and drama were marshaled to carve out a national class consciousness against the perceived threats of a nomadic mentality. The SRC established an artistic committee scout called *Heesahaga Hirgalay* ("New Talent"), led by Abdillahi Qarshe,[9] who was tasked with searching for new talents to bolster the artistic potential of musical bands such as *Horseed* and *Waaberi*" (Dawn) national music band symbolized an era of progress after a long period of uncertainty and ignorance. Music was no longer considered a mere entertainment art craft, but a tool to harness for the purposes of *"cilmiga hantiwadaga"* (scientific socialism). Clearly, this was an attempt by the political power to commandeer musicians' artistic capital in order to gain greater legitimacy. This did not however stop artists from producing anti-government lyrics, as we shall see in the following sections.

As the period of political uncertainty became more profound in the 1970s, musicians were called upon more and more to perform in the "revolutionary" Party's orientation centres in Mogadishu and Hargeysa, and at spectacular socialist-style gatherings to promote the ideals of the revolution. This strategy of presenting music as a powerful propaganda tool of the Revolution impacted negativly on poets' artistic creativities. While there were sincere desires on the part of musicians to support the government's so-called revolutionary programs, the regime's framework of the artistic community's role and place were haunted from its inception by its own contradictions. As Bourdieu (2013 : 229) highlights, such strategies represent an attempt to define who is an artist and what constitutes artistic production. The regime's policy of co-opting the artistic community continued throughout the 1980s during the national tragedy of the civil war. Singers, lyricists and poets were forced to compose songs in honour of the General-President.[10] Some leading musicians did willingly put their artistic capital at the service of the regime. For example, Abdi Muhumed Amin, a celebrated musician and lyricist, composed *Caynaanka Hay* ("Hold the Reins of Power Eternally"):

Caqli Toosanoo, Cafimad Qaba	Righteous and Healthy Mind
Nagu Caymisee	You Saved Us
Cududdo Midoo iyo	United Force and
Caanahah Wadaag	Sharing of Milk
Waa Caaddilnimee	Bring Equality
Caynanka Hay	Hold the Reins of Power
Waliga Hay	Forever
Hay, Hay	Hold, Hold

This song praised Barre's so-called divine leadership qualities, which was often used as a signature tune on national radio. The song was later unmasked by various artists and pilloried mercilessly by the people.

During this era, musicians and poets were frequently used to advance Barre's agenda, and the reputation of artists reached new heights during this era, in part as their voices were given greater prominence on state radio and venues. However, artists also used their craft to heap scorn on the pervasive rhetoric of nation-building of the regime. Popular poets such as Mohamed Ibrahim Warsame "Hadraawi" and Mohamed Hashi "Gaariye'" who had initially welcomed the Revolution, eventually turned their words against the regime (often resorting to elaborate metaphors to do so). With Said Salah Ahmed and Muse Abdi Ilmi "Muse Gadleh", Hadraawi and Gaariye founded the Lafoole[11] Group, who wrote in 1972 *Aqoon iyo Afgarad* (Knowledge and Understanding), a pro-revolutionary play.[12] The group was briefly very influential in the intellectual space, especially during the first part of 1970s. As we shall see below, this early pro-revolutionary stance was not the case for Abdi Aden Haad "Qays", who rejected the Military Junta's unlawful removal of the democratically-elected government of Mohamed Haji Ibrahim Egal in October 1969 from the very beginning. In the next section, I explore in more detail how poetic expression, which until this point had generally kept time with the political ideology of the day, began to depart from the status quo and espouse a different kind of political vision – a vision which, in turn, altered the course of musical expression across the Somali-speaking territories.

Poetic Critiques of Pan-Somalism

Much of the Somalis' intellectual tradition occurs outside academia. Poetry, not political treatises or novels, is Somalis' preferred means of intellectual expression. Far more Somalis listen to Abdillahi Suldan Timaadde's poems, Mohamed Omar Huriyo's rhapsodies and storytelling in the politically charged "*Dalmar iyo Daabbad*" ("The Traveler and The Horse") or Mohamed Mooge Liban's revolutionary melodies than are able to read any contemporary writer. Poetry traditions are rooted in Somali life and grounded in Somali social imaginaries, able to articulate the themes and challenges of any given period of time. In the words of Lewis and Andrzejewski, "[p]oetry occupies a large and important place in Somali culture, interest in it is universal, and skill in it something which everyone covets, and many possess. The poetic heritage is a living force intimately connected with the vicissitudes of everyday life" (1964: 3). Moreover, the poetry field has its own accepted rules of procedures and criteria for judgment,[13] and sets up a rigorous intellectual framework to deconstruct various cultural and political categories. Naturally, it is only the poet who can set out to prove many of the institutions society holds dear are illegitimate. In the past, there simply have been no literate "intellectuals"[14] who interpreted Somalis' rich imaginaries as intelligently as Salaan Arrabay, Ali Dhuh, Qamaan Bulhan, Abdi Qays, Hadraawi, Abdi Idaan, Gaariye, Ibraahim Sheikh Saleban Gadhleh, Aden Farah, Hassan Ilmi or Ali Suguleh, just to name a few.[15]

In response to the social and political upheaval of the era, from the late 1960s modern critical poetry took unconventional paths, aiming its bile at Pan-Somalism, an ideology essentially based on anti-clan universalism fossilized by various Somali regimes, on which the entire post-colonial projected relied for meaning. Somalis were uneasy about how best to approach the idea of Pan-Somalism. The idea was presented to them as de-clanized and de-territorialized citizenship. Proponents of Pan-Somalism viewed clan solidarities as inheritances of the old order, totally out of step with modern times. The new citizenship idea had been accorded sacrosanct status in the first Somali constitution. The citizenship law states: "Any person living beyond the boundaries of the Somali Republic but belonging by origin, language, or tradition to the Somali Nation may acquire Somali citizenship by simply establishing his residence in the territory of the Republic" (Muhammad 1972: 302). This law has been broadly welcomed, albeit grudgingly, by most Somalis.

From today's vantage point, the end of 1960s seems to be the era of disillusionment with the idea of Pan-Somalism. Accordingly, in the 1960s, many Somali poets examined, with unparalleled sophistications, the conceptual foundation of Somalism used by nationalists in their effort to invent the Somali people as a political and ethnic identity. With their panoply of Somali metaphors,[16] these poets were not simply contesting the all-encompassing current in the poetry field: they were also investigating the way in which Pan-Somalism, an inherently protean notion, was imposing a one-dimensional nationalism. For these remarkable poets, the post-independence meta-narrative simply lost its performative power, in the Austian sense. The fantasy of unity, they argue, ought to be consigned to the scrap heap of history. They understood, with prescience, that "nationalism is not the self-awakening of nations to self-consciousness: it invents nations where they do not exist" (Gellner 1964: 169). Curiously,

Abdillahi Suldan Timaade, who was perhaps the best-known expounder of Pan-Somalism, appears in hindsight as one of the pioneers of the anti-Pan-Somalism mood. On his first visit in Mogadishu in 1961, he confessed his astonishment when, at the height of Pan-Somalism, he shrewdly observed the tribal politics of the South in the following verse:

Goortaan horoo loo durkiyo, darejo eegaayay	Promise of progress and Enlightenment
Hadduun baa sidii buul-duqeed, daaha loo rogay	Turned into obscurity
Immikaa la doon-doonayaa, Dir iyo Daroode	In Search of Kinship politics between Dir and Darood[17]
	(Ducaale 2006: 126, *translation mine*)

Heralded by the 1961 insightful homespun anti-constitution philosophy of Cali Sugule and others, the new critical poetry, unusually attuned to peoples' postcolonial sensibilities, started challenging Pan-Somalism by putting the political rhetoric of the nationalist in its local context, away from the "isms" in vogue. Disillusioned by the nationalist parades, Qays, one of the most renowned and revered cultural critics, articulated the first significant blow during his early philosophical broodings in the 1960s. He went against the grain of sanguine observations of unsavory poets who had bonds to the status quo and who spent their time ruminating endlessly on the haughty Pan-Somalism that typified post-independence Somali life. Qays' distinctive turn of phrase pithily captures the turning point in his *Aakhiro* ("After Life") song. In this song, Qays' addresses the afterlife – here a metaphor for the illusive "Pan-Somalist" ideal – using the vocative, then proceeds to question his subject as to her elusive whereabouts:

Aakhirooy	Oh Afterlife!
Halkeed baad naga xigtaa,	Where Could we Find You?
Xiddigaha ciirka sare	Stars Way up the Sky?
Inaad xubin ka mid tahay	Star among the Stars?

From a political perspective, Qays' keenly evocative tune unveils the elusiveness of Pan-Somalism in Somali representations and challenges mainstream poetry giddy with self-satisfaction, utterly bereft of reason and political groundings. By invoking examples from his own political life to symbolize new meanings, Qays unwaveringly questions the prevailing notion of Pan-Somalism and urges Somali "intellectuals" to stop being unmindful of dominant "regimes of truth". *Aakhiro* clearly highlighted Pan-Somalism's main flaws, which resided in the fact that it confused political imaginations with objective characteristics (i.e. language, culture, religion and geography). Most importantly, *Aakhiro* reflects a time of mourning and lamentation about Somalis' postcolonial predicament where the "nation" suddenly becomes unsure of itself and unsettled about its future. Eventually, Qays was excommunicated, hounded, and forced into exile by the regime for criticizing Pan-Somalism.

Predictably, Somalis' political conditions took a sharp turn for the worse in 1969 when the so-called revolutionaries suspended the controversial 1961 constitution and their leader assumed dictatorial powers. Evidently, the new cohort in power reduced Pan-Somalism to its simplest expression and did not shun from populist contrivances. The rest of the story has been solidly documented in bloodshed, as the country slid slowly into a lawless abyss. As history evidences, the postcolonial project based on Pan-Somalism has dismally failed, and recent attempts at reviving it by radical Islamists or self-proclaimed Republicans are destined for failure. Qays, an affable poet and playwright feted everywhere in the Somali-speaking territories, voiced a poetic critique to mirror the real spirit of post-independence cultural and political anxiety, later expressed in the form of political action by various post-liberation movements. The new anti-Pan-Somalism political mood that he articulated had significant impact on the regional politics of the Somali territories, particularly Djibouti, a country where some segments of the population had strong affinities with their kin in Somalia. In the final sections of this chapter, I consider how Qays' critique of Pan-Somalism helped to turn the tides towards a new form of nationalist discourse in the nearly-independent French colony.

Djibouti's Artistic Scene in the 1970S[18]

Qays' critique of Pan-Somalism reached Djibouti's artistic elite at a time when the very basis of popular music was being transformed by non-Somali cultural traditions. In contrast to the Sudanese and Arabic influence in the early periods of Hargeysa musical sound, the development of popular arts and music in Djibouti is closely associated with French artistic production and Afro-American music. Although the country's Somalis had access to the Somali Republic's artistic expressions with their Pan-Somalism political undertones, Djibouti's urban elites were more concerned with cultural contradictions.[19] Hassan Abdi, one of the first Djiboutian playwrights, translated Pierre Corneille's tragicomedy *Le Cid* around 1965-1966.[20] Abdi's *Laba Dab Dheexdood* ("Between Two Fires") re-imagined Corneille's play in a new way by evoking a particular mood in the Somali-Djiboutian experience of honour and love, with their dilemmas and contradictions. The artistic experience of Djibouti's first-generation cultural producers did not emerge solely out of Somali tradition: it began as a connection, in the Amsellian sense, with the French cultural tradition. Abdi played a pivotal role in Djibouti's cultural scene and his approach would inspire the next generation of dramatists, who would appropriate and imitate major French playwrights, both classical and contemporary. His influence flourished among artists and people who were brought up in Djibouti's multi-clan and multicultural experience.

Amsellian connections were also visible in the development of Djibouti's musical scene. In the late 1960s, Afro-American music rapidly becomes one the most relevant forms of musical expression in Djibouti, the largest city in the country and the seat of the colonial regime, with the arrival of recordings of R&B and Blues singers such as James Brown, Marvin Gaye, BB King, and Ray Charles, just to name a few. By the early 1970s, youth from the emerging middle class formed R&B and Blues groups, as Afro-American music and the movement of Black and Proud sounds had increasingly become the mediums for youth to express their artistic demands and exasperations with dominant Somali, Afar and Arabic genres.[21] While Afro-American music had been present in Djibouti since the early 1960s, it gained prominence and popularity following the spread of the black movement identity politics in the United States and Pan-Africanism. As an imported genre, Afro-American music provided a transcontinental appeal for youth and an opportunity for them to articulate their own experiences of Djibouti as actors in search of an alternative community. Although Djiboutian musicians appropriated Afro-American music, one of my interlocutors observed that it reflected the specificities of Djiboutian artistic expressions and experiences. In his words, "we were experimenting with new Afro-American sounds, but always using local material."[22]

The Djiboutian soul scene consisted mostly of Westernized men, who embraced Afro-American popular music and laid the artistic groundwork for the emergence of the genre. In contrast with local genres composed mainly of male musicians from modest families, the soul scene consisted of youth from more affluent families. In the context of the 1970s Djibouti scene, the conspicuous absence of female musicians in soul music reflected the male dominated space of popular music in both private and public performances.[23] With the French presence in Djibouti, youth had relatively better access to Western cultural sounds and materials – musical instruments, recordings – than their peers in Hargeysa (Somali Republic) and Diredawa[24] (Ethiopia). In addition, as imported Afro-American pirated tapes flooded the market via Djiboutians who visited France, Djibouti developed into a major centre of the cassette duplication industry, making the city a leading musical hub to the growth in popularity for Afro-American music in the region This aspect heavily influenced the distinctive sound of Djiboutian popular music. With their bellbottoms, Afro hairstyles and platforms shoes, youth soul bands such as *Filsan* (Somali), *Iglumao*[25] (Afar), and *Harlem Soul*[26] (diverse), among others, emerged in the native ghetto quarters of the colonial city. Formed in the 1970s, *Filsan* (which included lead guitarist Almis Haid, rhythmic guitarist Jama Haid, and drummer Omar Gerdon) exemplified the musical mood of this era. Although *Filsan* was mostly playing soul music, the band was able to appropriate Afro-American music to produce a distinct mix of Djiboutian music genres and Afro-American soul.[27] While these youths had little chance of transforming their artistic capital into a profitable career, the emergence of soul music was symbolically representative of a relative shift in sensibilities. Although most musicians never left the country, Djiboutian soul artistic producers Afro-Americanized the country's popular music through their exposure to programs such as *Soul Train*, and to Kenyan soul through Somali-Kenyan Slim Ali, who performed with *Filsan* band in Djibouti's famous venues, *Les Salines* and *Cinéma Le Paris*.

A mix of soul and Somali influence guided the artistic experience of the talented and the most soulful of all Djiboutian singers, Abdo Hamargod. According to Gerdon, Abdo, who was one of the few musicians who succeeded in crossover musical experiences, combining elements of style and thematic content from both musical traditions, Afro-American and Djiboutian. Hamargod was not, however, the only singer who took advantage of Afro-American music's malleability. With the introduction of electrical guitar in 1960's, Abdi Bowbow and Mohamed Ali Furshed, two giants of Djibouti's musical experience, were also able to re-invent blues and soul to fit local musical sensibilities and situations. Bowbow, an excellent guitar player, re-invented Said Hamargod's *Guux*[28] (murmur or groan), a blend of Afro-American shuffle and the Somali wailing genre *Calaacal*. Other youth appropriated and imitated Hassan Abdi's style in *"Laba Dab Dheexdood"* ("Between Two Fires"). In 1972, *L'Union de la Jeunesse*, a youth club led by Ali Abdi Farah, translated *Adunyadu Wa Sidee*, ("World Complexities") a play by Abdi Qays. In addition to covering philosophical and existential themes, the play – with its a myriad of poems, songs and storytelling – also deconstructed the negative perceptions surrounding the artistic community, viewed as an immoral milieu. But the focus on social and cultural issues changed into a new political independence discourse as the anti-colonial nationalist movement started to take shape.

Gacan Macaan's New Direction

As the anti-colonial struggle intensified in the early 1970s (especially, in the backdrop of the anti-Charles de Gaulle unrest in August 1966 that ended with the violent colonial army crackdown) in contrast to the less political overtones of the mid-1960s, Djibouti's popular music more explicitly expressed Djiboutians' political demands. Into this era of social and political upheaval *Gacan Macaan,* the most influential art and music band in Djibouti, was born. From its establishment in 1972 through to the early 1980s, *Gacan Macaan* used music to provide political commentaries, describe the country's living conditions and articulate anti-colonial and Pan-Somali discourses. Through fusing various musical styles, and in response to the poetic critique of pan-Somalism taking hold at the time, *Gacan Macaan* proposed an alternative way to conceptualize and categorize the colonial power. In this last section, I trace how the group's nationalist, anti-colonial vision was re-articulated, drawing on Gilroy and Amselle to make sense of their artistic and political project.

Before *Gacan Macaan's* founding, the band's main figureheads – Ibrahim Sheikh Saleban Gadhleh, Hassan Ilmi, and Aden Farah had identified with Somalia's poets' pro-Somalism. In 1965, Ibrahim Gadhleh wrote *Guubaabo* (Awareness) in which he is expressing his desire to unite the Five Somali Territories:

| *Shanta kala go'doomaan lahaa* | My Aim for the Five[29] |
| *Meel isugu geeye* | Is Unification |

At the time, Somali music bands in Djibouti were also all pro Pan-Somalism, even though the artistic scene was clearly divided along clan lines: *Caareey* (led by Aden Farah) was predominantly Isa, *Bonne Espérance* (led by Hassan Ilmi) was mostly Gadabursi and, finally, *Union de la Jeunesse* (led by Ibrahim Gadhleh) was mainly Isaaq[30]. On a night in 1972 at a house on Rue de Zaila, the leaders of these bands came together to create something new.[31] Significantly, the new band's founders decided to tone down their Pan-Somalism messages. The role of the artist was about identifying important political problems caused by the French colonial power that required artistic imagination to be creatively addressed. After the demise of Pan-Somalism, precipitated in part by Qay's poetic interventions, they all became broadly preoccupied with what the colonial administration did or did not do. These changes in focus can be ascribed to a fundamental shift in *Gacan Macaan*'s political perspective. French colonialism became the only target. There was virtually nothing about the Northern Frontier District (NFD, i.e. the Somali-inhabited region of northern Kenya), nor about the Haud and Reserve Area. In addition, the band's political outlook was further shaped by other events that spelled the demise of Pan-Somalism in Djibouti. While a significant proportion of Djibouti's population was Somali, 80% of the territory was inhabited by Afars, who had their own culture and language. In the 1950s and 1960s, the French colonial power, with the support of the Afars and some segments of the Somali community, reconfigured Djibouti's local political dynamics culminating to the 1967 official change of *Côte français des Somalis* (French Somaliland) to *Territoire des Afars et des Issas*[32] (French Territory of Afars and Issas). This move served to turn aspirations of independence away from a Pan-Somalist ideal towards a distinctly Djiboutian state. The story of *Gacan Macaan*'s creation seems to support this turn.

Gacan Macaan's new direction was also reflected in the style and tone of their music, which fused traditional genres and referents with Afro-American, Arabic and Indian styles. On the one hand, many songs and poems used by the band in its attempt to deconstruct the colonial discourse evoked traditional Sufi musical genres. In an effort to reconnect with the country's pre-colonial Islamic period, the band's main figures had spent most of their time collecting every Sufi piece they could find. This approach resonates with Amselle's *Branchement* framework, connecting with one tradition in order to mount resistance against another by mixing artistic creativity with political and social commentaries. Yet the band also drew influence from Afro-American music, particularly in their performance of *Guux*. Some of the metaphors, analogies and poetic and musical styles in their music can also be traced to Asian roots (Islamic, Arabic and Indian). While *Gacan Macaan*'s nationalism is a clear departure from Gilroy's post-national model, and his focus on the Atlantic obscures important Asian/Middle Eastern conjectures, these musical fusions could be read within Gilroy's analytical approach as post-national cultural constructs.

Sensing the new collective political and artistic project of *Gacan Macaan*, *La ligue populaire africaine pour l'indépendance* (LPAI), the main political movement, commissioned the group to create a pro-independence play to move away from the long years that were rife with ambiguities. In a way, the band co-opted LPAI's nationalist rhetoric and took a populist turn[33]. Still, *Gacan Macaan*'s willingness to articulate an oppositional political and social discourse through a reinvention of black expressive cultures could be viewed as a counter-culture production of modernity, to use Gilroy's terms. Hassan Ilmi produced the first play of the band: "*Ilmo Geeska Afrika*" ("Children of the Horn of Africa") one of the most memorable pro-independence plays, which reconstructed the arrival of the French colonial enterprise. Ilmi's play attempted to demonstrate how the French colonial drive constituted the "natives" as static clan groups rather than historical peoples. According to him, erasing the Djiboutian history, after all, was fundamental to full colonial rule. In some ways, Ilmi's vision of a new national narrative was a vision of what official history should become. History was to draw from all the sources: notably Sufi musical traditions, Afro-American and Pan-African genres, and Arabic musical resistance. *Ilmo Geeska Afrika* laid out the goal and purposes of *Gacan Macaan*.

As Ilmi did in *Ilmo Geeska Afrika*, others members in the band started composing music and poems about the French occupation. In their view, colonialism discourse presented Djiboutians "in the imagery of static, almost ideal types, and neither as creatures with a potential in the process of being realized nor as history being made" (Said 1979: 321). But it was Gadhleh who openly declared the specificity of Djiboutian political experience in a 1973 poem, which was part of the *Siinley*[34] debate:

Aniguna sidaydaba	Personally,
Kama helo sawaxankoo	Noise does not confuse me
Waan ka meel samaystee	I control my destiny

Departing from his previous political stand, Gadhleh depicts Pan-Somalism as Somalia's own problem, and implicitly advises Djiboutians against adopting the trans-clan ideology noise advocated by some segments of Somalia's political elite. Such outright critiques of Pan-Somalism, combined with *Gacan Macaan*'s use of multiple artistic references provided audiences with an alternative nationalist discourse – one based on local specificities, and against the all-pervasive Pan-Somalism. Out of this confluence of Qays' critique of Pan-Somalism and *Gacan Macaan*'s methods of appropriating multiple music experiences, there emerged a particular Somali-Djiboutian form of popular music that came to define the 1970 Djiboutian way of artistic – and nationalist - expression.

Conclusion

This chapter has explored the evolution of nationalist discourses in the Somali Horn through the expression of Somali poets and a Djiboutian band. I have suggested that while at times Somali poets and musicians lent their creative talents to supporting the idea of Pan-Somalism, they were also responsible for its deconstruction. By the early 1970s, this critique of Pan-Somalism re-shaped *Gacan Macaan's* political and artistic productions, when they began to articulate a different kind of nationalist discourse, now divorced from the ideal of Pan-Somalism. I have suggested that certain aspects of Gilroy's model help to explain *Gacan Macaan's* new directions: in particular, their musical fusions, particularly *Guux,* represent a form of post-national cultural productions. But against Gilroy's predictions of the demise of nationalism, *Gacan Macaan* used these productions for nationalist ends, re-articulating anti-colonial agenda in the process. In *Gacan Macaan's* work we also see a longer and broader network of cultural exchanges that reach beyond the Atlantic, as Amselle's notion of '*branchement*' suggests. In sum, this chapter has highlighted the way that artistic modes of expression sometimes tack with, and sometimes against, prevailing political discourse, at times being shaped by them and at other times – drawing on myriad musical inspirations – playing a critical role in defining the terms of debate. *Gacan Macaan's* artistic productions, as in the work of the Somali poets' who influenced their work, also highlight the need to pay attention to the interplay of local historical developments and transnational cultural flows, while being wary of framing nationalist and post-national discourses in dichotomous terms.

Endnotes

1 Many authors have been critical of *Black Atlantic*, but they have not ignored it or dismissed it.

2 Also, Latin-America is absent from Gilroy's conceptualization of black experiences

3 Interview with Abdillahi Qarshe, London, 1997.

4 Radio *Goodir* (Kudu), later known as Radio Hargeysa, was created in 1942-43. Abdirahman Abby, a Somali-British whose mother was white, was one of the first Heads of the station.

5 In March 1941, the British Colonial Office moved to Hargeysa from the coastal city of Berbera as part of its hinterland policy.

6 Interview with Abdillahi Qarshe. The *balwo* dance company was founded by Abdi Deqsi 'Sinimo' and a few artists, including Kadija Balwo, close to him.

7 The Haud and Reserve Area.

8 Even though the British colonial office allowed musical and artistic expressions, the imprisonment of anti-colonial artist was common throughout the 1950's. Abdillahi Qarshe and Mohamed Ahmed Kuluc were jailed for composing subversive songs or speaking out against colonial rule.

9 Qarshe was a prominent musician and an original member of *Walaalaha Hargeysa* band, whose Pan-Somalism position attracted wide popularity thanks to his patriotic songs. Hussein Aw Farah, a brilliant poet and an original member of *Walaalaha Hargeysa*, was also one of the members of *Heesahaga Hirgalay* committee.

10 Interview with Ibrahim Meygag Samatar, Ottawa, Canada, 1998.

11 Lafoole was the teachers' training college created by the military regime in 1972.

12 The play's messages included the importance of local intellectuals over foreign-trained elite, women's rights and work ethics. But in reality, the Lafoole Group was legitimising the military regime's pseudo-nationalist stand.

13 Poets are evaluated on their knowledge of law (customary law, religious law, and previous legal cases), their ability to

remember previous and current arguments, and persuasiveness.

14 Perhaps, with the exception of I.M. Lewis and B.W. Andrzejewski, thanks to their reasonable command of Somali and longtime close proximity with Somalis' ups and downs.

15 Here, we are not arguing that poets have better understanding of Somalis' cultural, political and social realities.

16 For example, Somalis conceive of the he-camel as the driving force of pastoral life and the she-camel as the mother of all humankind, and related pastoral metaphors infuse Somali poetry. *Maandeeq*, a popular name of the she-camel, symbolises the nation. Although poets in the 1960s and 1970s were mostly city-dwellers, the pastoral mode of production was still the main source of inspiration when composing poetry.

17 Dir and Darood are two major Somali clan families.

18 This section does not cover the equally significant sounds and expressions of the Afaar and Arab artistic communities. The works of such towering figures like Ali Oudun, Taha Nahari, Mohamed Houmed Moussa "Petit Fanaan" ("Petit Artist") and the multi-genre and versatile musician Kamal Haji Ali, just to name a few, shaped Djibouti's multicultural music sounds. It is worth noting that Djibouti's three main communities -Afar, Arab and Somali – shared at the bigining one music studio group, whose members were all Arabs, because Afar and Somali artists were around this period just starting to incorporate new musical intruments - oud, violin, flute, piano- into local traditional sounds (finger snapping, feet stamping, hand clapping, etc.)

19 Djibouti was home to two famous Somali studios, which copied and distributed massive volumes of cassettes: in Quartier 5, Abdi Sinimo Studio (named after Abdi Deqsi "Sinimo", the inventor of the balwo genre); and in Quartier 4, Boodhari Studio, (named after Ilmi Bodari, the father of Somali love and owned by Ibrahim Gadhleh, one of the founders of *Gacaan Macaan*).

20 Interview with Ali Abdi Farah, former Djiboutian Minister of Communication and Culture and former president, in the 1970s, of l'Union de la jeunesse (Djibouti, 2016).

21 Interview with Omar Gerdon (Gabiley, Somaliland, 2017).

22 Ibid.

23 Hawa Geelqad (first Djiboutian woman to join a musical ensemble), Amina Abdillahi, Faduma Ahmed and Nimo Jama were the few only female singers in the late 1960's and early 1970's.

24 Dirdawa, a city in the Somali region of Ethiopia, never produced any Somali musicians and never had a significant musical scene to my knowledge. Often, many musicians from this town discovered their artistic calling either in Djibouti or the Somali Republic.

25 *Iglumao* was led by the talented Abdulaziz Ali.

26 Harlem Soul, led by Geudi as lead guitarist and vocalist, used to perform at the historical and symbolic *Les Salines* venue throughout the early 1980s.

27 Interview with Hussein Abdi Aidarus. (Djibouti, 2016 and 2017). Aidarus is a famous Djiboutian musicologist, composer and singer.

28 *Guux* is the sound that camel makes when approaching the water. Said Hamargod (Abdo's older brother) first introduced *Guux* by reworking *Guux* sounds from the Somali Republic. This genre's tradition continues with the Guux Brothers Band, a musical group that reincarnates the sounds and expressions of popular music from the 1970's and 1980's.

29 The poet is referring here to *Shanta Somaliyeed* (the five Somali territories): British Somaliland, French Somaliland, Italian Somaliland, the Northern Frontier District (NFD) in Kenya and the Somali Region in Ethiopia.

30 It goes without saying that Farah, Gadhleh and Ilmi were not the only leaders of these artistc collectives.

31 Interview with Abdi Nur Allale (London, England, 2004). Allale is an original member of *Gacan Macaan* and one of the most gifted performers produced by the Djiboutian musical experience.

32 By associating the territory with only one Somali clan, the Issas, the Colonial Office's intention was to label other Somali clans as foreigners, an exogenous population. The assumption here was that Issas constituted a distinct group and were less concerned with Pan-Somalism, even though historical Issa figures such as Ali Bahdon Buh and Mohamud Harbi wanted to bring all Somalis under one nation-state.

33 Aware of arts' subversive potential, the colonial administration had established a censorship committee to check Djiboutian plays beforehand. During the performance, about 10-20 censors were dispatched to observe if playwrights added new anti-colonial messages, hidden or otherwise. Interviews with Ali Abdi, Abdi Nur Alaale and Mohamed Jama Abdi Gahnug.

34 *Siinley* was a poetic debate started in 1972 by Abdi Qays, where close to 35 poets discussed the state of Pan-Somalism and the military regime of Siyaad Barre. Somali poetry uses the method of alliteration: in the Gadhleh's poem, *Siinley* **S** is the alliterating letter. So, *Siinley* simply means the poem that has **S** as the alliterating letter.

Bibliography

Adam, H. 2008. *From Tyranny to Anarchy. The Somali Experience.* Trenton, NJ, Africa World Press & Red Sea Press.

Amselle, J-L. 2001. *Branchements: Anthropologie de l'universalité des cultures.* Paris, Flammarion.

Austin, J.L. 1970. *Quand dire, c'est faire.* Paris, Éditions du Seuil.

Andrzejewski, B.W., Lewis, I.M. 1964. *Somali Poetry: An Introduction.* Oxford: Oxford University Press.

Bourdieu, P. 2013. *Manet. Une révolution symbolique.* Cours au Collège de France (1998-2000) Suivi d'un manuscrit inachevé. Éditions du Seuil/Raisons d'agir. Cours et travaux.

Ducaale, B.Y. 2006. *Diiwaanka Maansada: Cabdillahi Suldan Maxamed (Timacadde)*, Daabacaadi 2aad. Addis Ababa: Flamingo Printing Press.

Gellner, E. 1964. *Thought and Change.* Chicago, The University of Chicago Press.

Gilroy, P. 1993. *The Black Atlantic: Modernity and Double Consciousness.* London and New York, Verso Press.

Muhammad, N. 1972. *The Legal System of the Somali Democratic Republic.* Charlottesville, VA: Michie Company.

Said, E. 1979. *Orientalism.* New York, Vintage Books.

Samatar, I.M. 1997. Light at the End of the Tunnel: Some Reflections on the Struggle

of The Somali National Movement, in Adam H & Ford R (ed.) *Mending Rips in the Sky: Options for Somali Communities in the 21st Century.* Larenceville, The Red Sea Press: 21-48.

Touval, S. 1963. *Somali Nationalism.* Cambridge: Harvard University Press.

The Symbolism of *Gada* in Local Political Campaign Songs among the Boran of Marsabit County in Northern Kenya

Hassan H. Kochore

This chapter looks at how the Boran of northern Kenya use their traditional institution of gada[1] to make dialogue with and make sense of the Kenyan political system. Despite its historical ubiquity and importance in the socio-political life of the Boran of Marsabit, the system has however been on the decline in recent decades; however, here I argue that gada has come to be memorialized in popular culture like songs and continues to influence the way in which the Boran navigate new social and political realities. Drawing on earlier ethnographies on the Boran and colonial archives reports, the first part of the chapter discusses the ethnographic background of the Marsabit Boran and locating the historical centrality of gada and its associated rituals and ceremonies in their socio-political life. The second part looks at how this system is remembered in contemporary Boran political campaign songs by analyzing the lyrics of the music and teasing out the imagery of gada contained therein. This part also puts the songs in their longue durée and expounds on their contemporary usefulness for the Boran in making sense of the Kenyan political system. The analysis reveals that despite having 'practically' declined,[2] the Boran socio-political institution of gada and its associated ritual site of ardha gadamojji[3] in Marsabit are symbolically useful resources for imagining and making sense of the Kenyan political system. Finally the chapter argues that despite having been presented as existing on the periphery of the Kenyan nation and at times portrayed as anti-national, – the Boran have in their own ways syncretized the Kenyan experience as can be discerned from their popular culture.

Introduction: Music, Identity and Politics

Music and society, as Martin Stokes (1994) argues, are intricately interwoven in a way that one could arguably study important socio-political aspects of a society through its music. Aidan Russell echoes this proposition by introducing the concept of 'communities in music' (Russell 2011: 303). He contends that "music can provide the framework and expression in which social organisation, beliefs, group identity and historical memory can be formalised or confirmed" (ibid.) In this chapter, I look at the ways in which people use music to constitute and express their identity, especially when they emphasize and reproduce a 'traditional' past in musical performance. In this respect, I explore the role of music in "continuity maintenance", that is, when music is used as a mnemonic tool to recount a past that is deemed useful for a society through emphasizing their tradition as well as adapting to new socio-political conditions.

In Marsabit County of northern Kenya, composition and performance of political songs have become an important part of the periodic election campaigns. The songs contain, among other themes, praise of preferred local candidates (and in some cases national party leaders), mock rivals, and contest communal boundaries with other communities. More generally, they record and comment on the political context since the previous elections. These commentaries on social, political and economic conditions range from the state of education, drought and instances of conflict to any other issues deemed significant for the community. In a way, as Nyairo and Ogude posit, this type of "music documents the people's history" (Nyairo and Ogude 2005: 226) by identifying, recording and memorializing certain social and political events. In Kenya, while the politics of such music has been explored at the national level, for example, through the analysis of artists, Gigigidi *Majimaji*'s song, *unbwogable* by Nyairo and Ogude (2005), more localized political campaign songs have not been given much attention even in the context of a devolved political structure. Basically, this chapter therefore seeks to move the analyses of such music to the county level in a bid to explore the interplay between local and national politics, production of citizenship and belonging.

In the case of Marsabit, the music is laden with strong symbolism of *gada* - a traditional socio-political system whose practice and influence has hitherto been eroded by the coming of nation-states, namely, Kenya and Ethiopia. Gunther Schlee, writing in a context in which he argues that *gada* has lost its historical potency, asserts that in some places, '*gada*' has become part of folklore or historical romanticism' (Schlee 1998:145). Following up on Schlee's statement, I would like to explore, through the example of Marsabit Boran, the first part of this statement where *gada* is argued to have been relegated to 'folklore'. At this level therefore this chapter seeks to understand the contemporary relevance of the almost structurally defunct Boran *gada* system among the Boran of Marsabit. It especially focuses on how *gada* is appropriated as a language in music to syncretize the hitherto 'external' ideas and experiences of the post-colonial Kenyan nation-state. More specifically, it explores how a marginal group constitutes and expresses its identity by invoking a revered traditional system in popular discourse in the context of socio-political change. Drawing on Kelly Askew (2002)'s insight into Tanzanian *taarab* music and nation building, I demonstrate and argue that in (northern) Kenya music is a particularly salient form of social and political discourse that provides an important window into understanding ethnic, regional and national identity politics which are actualized through *'performing the nation'*. Askew essentially argues that musical performance is fundamental to understanding nation-building. He demonstrates how the genre of *ngoma* (traditional dance), *dansi* (urban jazz), and *taarab* (sung Swahili poetry) influenced the official presentations of "Tanzanian National Culture" over the years. Following this line of inquiry, in this chapter, I look at how the Boran articulate their own ideas and conception of Kenyan political culture through 'local-national' lens as manifested their political campaign songs that draw on traditional ideas of political representation.

The chapter is structured as follows: Firstly, I start by giving a short ethnographic background of the Marsabit Boran and their historical relationship to the *gada* system. I then delve into the composition and lyrics of the songs which I discuss. The final part then explores the symbolic meaning and resonance that *gada* has for the Marsabit Boran as can be gathered from political campaign songs.

Marsabit Boran: The Ethnographic Setting

The Marsabit Boran are a branch of the larger Oromo - the majority ethnic group in Ethiopia. They however have largely been disconnected from their kin in Southern Ethiopia due to not only geographic barriers but also the colonial and post-colonial process of state building where the Boran were divided into 'Kenyan Boran' and 'Ethiopian Boran'. The Kenyan Boran are further divided into Marsabit Boran who reside in Marsabit County and Waso Boran who live in Isiolo.

Due to the 'Somalisation' of the Waso Boran (Aguilar 1998) - mainly conversion to Islam and becoming (like) Somalis –, the Marsabit Boran may be considered the cultural core of Kenyan Boran. The Marsabit Boran were formerly pastoralists who moved long distances (as far as southern Ethiopia) with their herd in search of water and pasture; but in the last few decades they have mainly settled on Marsabit mountain and engage in farming alongside keeping livestock (mainly cattle). Despite having been disconnected from their homeland and ritual and pilgrimage sites in southern Ethiopia, they have, to a certain degree, maintained most of their rituals and reproduced the associated ritual sites in Marsabit. Indeed, the slopes of Marsabit mountain aredotted with ritual sites such as Kubi Dibayyu, Qilta Korma, Sagante wells, *gadamojji* and so on.

Despite some of these rituals disappearing and sites following into disuse, I argue that these physical sites and the (memory of the) rituals held at the sites have a powerful symbolism for the Boran in the contemporary times. To illustrate this argument, I will use the example of how *gada* and its associated ritual of *gadamojji* is appropriated in music to construct a strong narrative of Boran identity in the context of electoral politics.

There is no space here to get into the detail of the structure and inner workings of the *gada* system (for this refer to Asmarom Legesse 1973). Suffice it to say, it is, according to Megerssa & Kassam (2004: 53), "a complex system of temporal differentiation through which all the male members of a society undergo a series of initiations and are socialized into the social, legal and religious roles that they will fulfill in the course of the life cycle."

The Boran pride themselves as the 'people of *rabba-gada*'- as a demonstration to their strong commitment to their customs and institutions- and participation in the generation-set ceremony associated with the *gada* system which is held every eight years to cement a common identity and entrench beliefs about how to ensure the continuity and the proper leadership for the community.

The *gadamojji* ceremony was always held in Southern Ethiopia- considered as the homeland and ritual headquarters. However, after settling on Marsabit Mountain, and due to colonial restriction of their movement between Marsabit and Southern Ethiopia, the Marsabit Boran founded a *gadamojji* site on the slopes of the mountain where the ceremony was held.

In 1939, a famous colonial administrator in Marsabit, Gerald Reece noted that:

> "The holding of these ceremonies is all too good since it encourages the cohesion of the local Boran and strengthens tribal authority."

Gada was so salient and central to the lives of Marsabit Boran that another colonial administrator concluded in 1951 that:

> "The whole social framework of the people appears to depend on the eight years cycle associated with the name of gadamojji."

Despite such usefulness and ubiquity in the lives of Boran, the *gada* system has been on the decline not only in northern Kenya but even in its 'home' in southern Ethiopia. The weakening of the system in Ethiopia has inevitably been felt in Marsabit as people there draw inspiration from the *gada* rituals and leadership in Ethiopia. For example, Paul Baxter notes that:

> "In 1951, it was assured by elders in northern Kenya that the times, even then, were so out of joint that it was unlikely that the gada would ever be performed again in Kenya, and that, even in traditional homelands of the Kallu in Ethiopia, it was likely they would soon be given up."

Despite this pessimism, *gadamojji* continued to be held in Marsabit until late 90s as Baxter himself quoting a letter from a 'friend' in Marsabit notes:

> "The Borana Gadamoji [i.e those elders about to assume ritual responsibility for the Boran people] are getting ready for buffat [i.e to perform the essential rituals]…Marsabit Boran are participating too…maybe for the last time!"

Indeed in the last about 60 years, the decline of the traditional gada system has been accompanied by conversion to either Christianity or Islam. A decline in the practice of *gada* and the conversion to a world religion might be considered as a weakening of ethnic identity or cultural loss as often cited in the example of Waso Boran (Aguilar). However, as various researches have shown, Marsabit ethnic identities and particularly the 'brand Boran' continue to flourish despite the rapid socio-political changes. Elisabeth Watson (2010), for example, notes that there has been 'a hardening of lines' where competition over resources and boundaries have led to intense ethno-nationalist sentiments and, in some cases, violent conflict. Gunther Schlee explains this as a process of 'territorialising ethnicity' (2013). Drawing on Watson (2010) and Schlee (2013), Carrier and Kochore (2014) also advance a similar argument where they observe that electoral politics have led to a consolidation of various ethnic identities in Marsabit. Drawing on and extending my research on 'ethnicity and electoral politics,' in this chapter I look at how the Boran identity is forged, articulated and emphasized through skilful appropriation of the hitherto 'disappeared' *gada* system in music. For this I draw inspiration from Andrea Nicolas (2007) who, in the case of the Oromo in Ethiopia, argues that nostalgia for *gada* has been productive for the (re-)invention of social institutions, namely clan assembly, in Hiddi, Eastern Shewa Ethiopia. I argue that the nostalgia and at times the 'romanticism of *gada*' as it manifests itself in popular culture can provide a useful window into understanding socio-political change among the Boran.

Composition, Dissemination and Provenance of the Music

The music I discuss here is recorded and produced locally in Marsabit at a low cost. Essentially it takes a basic guitar and drum performance of about 5-10 people with the composer being the lead singer. An audio recording of the performance was previously done with a radio cassette player and more recently, a digital voice recorder. The music is then disseminated on cassettes (previously) but recently on flash drives at the local music 'studios' and cyber cafes. The music is then played at rallies from Land Rover stereos amplified through public address system fitted on the back on the vehicles. It is also played on *bodabodas* (motorbike taxis) to the preference of the operator. The whole town is abuzz with these sounds for about two to three months during the Kenyan election campaign period. After that the music is usually relegated to individual households, shops or miraa chewing 'bases'[4] as the owners or operators desire. I collected these songs in two ways. The songs between 1997 and 2002 elections was obtained from 'Gen electronics', operated by Genno Jarra, since closed down but Genno has been generous enough to allow me to access his 'studio' at home even many years after he closed his shop. Originally recorded on cassettes, Genno has digitized the songs from 1997 and 2002 election campaigns and sold them on CDs as part of his business. Due to the original tape recording or due to the conversion (or both), the quality is not good but is still audible. The 2013 songs were obtained from a local cyber café on a CD and the recording is fairly good.

The songs I analyse here are composed and recorded by a local artist Aga Galgallo during election campaigns. I especially concentrate on the songs composed and sang for Abdi Tari

Sasura, a candidate for the position of MP in the 1997, 2002; but I also occasionally draw on his songs for other candidates in 2007 and 2013 general elections. Mr. Sasura went on to become MP for Saku Constituency of what was then Marsabit district (now Marsabit County) between 1997 and 2005 (when he died in a plane crash in Marsabit while still in office). Sasura (and by extension his supporters) identified as *LATTU*. In normal usage, the name means, 'young shoots', but in this context, it represents Sasura as a new entrant into competitive politics and a 'game-changer' and also has connotations of him breathing new life and bringing fresh ideas to (re) invigorate the politics of Saku constituency which had previously been dominated by MP Jarso Jillo (1988 -1997) who was considered by the *LATTU* supporters as an 'old guard' and non-performer at the time of going to the polls in 1997.

The Elements and Vocabulary of Gada in Election Campaign Songs

Coincidentally, both writing in 1998, Gunther Schlee and Mario Aguilar have shown the significance of *gada* in the politics of identification (in northern Kenyan-Southern borderlands in the case of the former and among the Waso Boran in the case of the latter). Aguilar posits that *gada* is used "by the Boran of Eastern Kenya so as to provide a continuation with their own sense of tradition and genesis, but with the aim of self-generating identity and ethnicity for the following generations to come" (Aguilar 1998: 27). As for Schlee, he observes that, "Beyond their actual workings in age-grading people, living *gada* systems, and even the memory of defunct ones, are important elements of identity discourses, and these discourses become increasingly important with the ethnicization of politics" (Schlee 1998: 145).

Following these two scholars, I explore in this section the importance of *gada* by looking at popular songs during Kenyan election campaigns. I particularly concentrate on outlining the use of the names of positions of leadership in the traditional gada system as applied and used in interpreting and 'localizing' Kenya's current political structure.

In the songs the Kenyan parliamentary term of five years is referred to as '*gada*' and it is named after the Member of Parliament from Saku constituency who was in office during that period. This is in line with the naming of the eight-year periods after the name of its leader in the *gada* system (eight years being equated with two four-year MP mandates). For example, the current *gada* is called 'the *gada* of Kura Jarso' – named such after the office holder, Kura Jarso (2017-2025). Here I will give an example of a song in which the *gada*, or the terms in office, of two former Saku Members of Kenyan Parliament are compared using the idiom of the *gada* terms. This association is usually emphasized in order to show that the preferred candidate's term in office was more peaceful, prosperous and propitious (having *kayo-* the good omen and quality of auspiciousness) for the community. Voters are then urged to vote for the candidate praised in the song as s/he attracted good fortunes.

> "Gada *J.J qabannaa ta Abditin wolt lalanna,*
> We remember the gada J.J's Gada, and compare it with Abdi's
> *Wor Saku chubu laganna tamit gom isan gafanna?*
> The people of Sakhu let's shun sin (by saying the truth), we ask you which one is better?
> *Wolt in d'uf tan it kakanna Kitaballe itqabanna*
> They (the two gadas) can't even come close to each other, we can swear by the book (the Koran)
> *gada Lattu Kayo Tamanafu Abdi jaranna*
> In the gada of Abdi we were more prosperous

Gan kud'an ka Jarso Jillo Jarsi nanno finna d'abe,
Ten years of Jarso Jillo ('s rule), the elders were denied the nanno finna (elders planning meeting)
tisse tisan ule d'abe, some soman uji d'abe
times were hard for the herder, the educated couldn't find jobs
Gan shanaan ka Abdi Tari, Abdin kor d'etha nubasse,
(in) the five years of Abdi Tari, Abdi organized the meeting of *d'etha*
Tisitu Aburun d'aqe, ijolle college it naqe
He took the herders in search of pasture, and took children to colleges."

In another song, a two-term parliamentary MP, Jarso Jillo, is criticized for seeking a third time even though he had already surpassed the maximum eight years of being a leader according to the *gada* system.

"*Gadan abba toko gan sathetin chitte bekhi,*
The gada of one abba gada ends at eight years
Gadan Jarso Jillo gaan lamman thabarte bekhi..
The *gada* of Jarso Jillo has already surpassed that."

Two other key concepts associated with *gada* are ubiquitous in the songs: *kayo* and *nagaa*. At face value nagaa means peace but it has other philosophical underpinning. Mario Aguilar (1996: 63) notes that: There is 'the union and communion of all Boorana through the keeping of the *Nagaa Boorana* (the Peace of the Boorana), an ethno-philosophy that permeates the actions and beliefs of every Boorana'.

Kayo on the other hand describes the quality of propitiousness of a particular time or period. Leus and Salvadori (2006) define kayo as: "*good* fortune: *warri kayo qabu, homaa indhibani:* those who have good fortune nothing troubles them. *Oba arra kaayo dhabe:* the watering of the catlle (today) lacked grace/was unfortunate (i.e. everything went wrong)."

In the case of the songs that I discuss here, a particular *gada* is expressed has having both *nagaa* and *kayo*:

"*gada Lattu Kayo tanafu Abdi jaranna*
In the gada of Lattu—we had *kayo*[6] so we will continue choosing Abdi (as M.P)
Thao nagaa nubulchinna Sasura kura kennani
And make us live in a peaceful shelter, (Marsabit), and give the elections (victory) to Sasura
Nagaa wol afat kalala, d'iro naga manit challa
Look at this peace that has spread all over (the land), people, what surpasses peace? (It is important than everything else)
Kaayo gabo tan nusatha, wor Saku me Abdi jarra
Praise this good fortune (during his gada), the people of Saku build Abdi (vote for him)
Thuri gosan gargar banna nyanyoomne nunchuf wolhanna
In the past we used to separate into tribes, become hostile and fight one another."

The above examples illustrate how the terminologies and concepts of the *gada* system have been deployed to understand the Kenyan parliamentary system. The use of the gada terminology is also meant to appeal to the ethnic sentiments of the Boran by demonstrating how the preferred candidate had supported the Boran cultural system and livelihood during his term in office. The words and adjectives that are associated with describing *gada*, namely *nagaa* and *kayo* which represent the abundance of peace, rain, the growing of grass and livestock udders full of milk and so on and so forth. Here then I show how the different parliamentary terms (which is equated to *gada*) are remembered and memorialized in the same way *gada* is in the Boran folklore.

The *Gadamojji* Site and its Significance

Apart from a general appeal to the *gada* system and its leadership, the *gadamojji* site in Marsabit where the *gada* rituals used to be held also features in the songs. While the site has largely fallen into disuse, it is still passionately preserved in Marsabit. The site is considered a 'physical' link to Southern Ethiopia 'homelands' which host the most important ritual sites. As such even though for most Marsabit Boran *gadamoji* has become an imaginary pilgrimage, the site on the slope of Marsabit mountain is symbolically a strong expression of a link to a wider 'imagined Boran community' in Southern Ethiopia. While *gadamojji* has not been held for about two decades now, the memory of previous ceremonies continues to influence the way the Boran make sense of their contemporary social and political predicaments. Nowhere is this more evident than in the campaign songs I discuss here. In the songs, this status of Marsabit as a ritual site is emphasized and recounted strongly.

For example, a line from a song composed by a local artiste Bonaya Doti goes:

"*Sakhuun ardha jilati d'uguma, gadhamojjin bufaat matuma; korma korbess qalum aadhuma Chama KANU jaran nu kura….*
Sakhu (a Boran name for Marsabit mountain) is indeed as ritual center (where) gadamojji initiates shave their hair and other ritual activities is performed."

While I argue here that these gada symbols and the gadamojji site have a meaning that appeals to a majority of the Boran, I am aware and acknowledge Schlee and Shongolo's (1995) argument that in fact for other non-Boran Oromo, the use of these symbols have been unattractive. However, as I have shown here, for intra-group Boran identity, the past glories of Boran and the symbols associated with the *gada* system have been to an extent useful in expressing a strong Boran ethno-national sentiment. Therefore, while the invocation of gada might be 'unproductive' " in areas/counties populated by populations of diverse origin who are not all Boran"as Schlee and Shongolo argue, it does actually provide a strong narrative on 'boran-ness' as expressed in this particular type of music. Indeed, this attraction to *gada* is not only limited to an abstract appeal; rather blessings and endorsement of the Boran *aba gada* in Ethiopia is key and is actively sought by candidates even in the present times. For example, in 2013 the current Aba gada of Boran, Guyo Gobba was practically involved in the campaigns in Marsabit in which he arbitrated between two Boran candidates and later endorsed one of them (Carrier and Kochore 2014).

In the next section, in order to demonstrate the 'Kenyan side of the story', I show how the *gada* of different candidates are evaluated in terms of the Kenyan values that are deemed Kenyan. I especially focus on education and *maendeleo* (development).

Embracing Kenya(N)?: Education and Development

Since the colonial times, the north has been administratively treated as a thing apart. In the words of Charles Chevenix Trench, "the north was another world," and it was perceived as "the silent north" by Glanday, both administrators during the British Colonial period in northern

Kenya (Chevenix Trench 1993:48, 122 quoted in Aguilar 1998: 261). The Boran and other groups in the north have indeed felt disconnected from a state they are, geographically and administratively, be supposed to be a part of. Colonialism and independence have therefore brought little in the way of development in northern Kenya (Arero 2007; Kochore and Carrier 2014). To date when heading down country, people would say, 'we're heading to Kenya'. Indeed, campaign songs as recent as the 2013 elections in Marsabit county reveal that people still regard Kenya(ns) as 'other'. For example, a line from one of Aga's song goes:

> "*Wor Kenyalle nugafannan inwakatan thaimtu tessan*'
> when we asked the people of Kenya about the whereabouts of our MP, they too didn't have an answer for us."

This is a song in which the incumbent MP was being accused of running away from the people, being inaccessible and 'hiding' in 'Kenya', the land of the other.

While the Boran (and other peoples of northern Kenya) have continued to feel alienated, however, a closer look at these campaign songs reveals that people emphasize the role various politicians have played in integrating them with the Kenyan nation. They particularly cited the support toward *maendeleo (development)* and Kenyan education as tools through which they continue to get integrated and emphasize their quest for a Kenyan identity.

Indeed, "Education (together with the fight against diseases and poverty, was identified, after Kenya's independence, as one of the three instruments for creating a progressive nation" (Arero 2005). The transformation in social and political perception that took place among Boran, and indeed in the whole of Kenya after independence is also significant as to understand processes of identity formation. Formal education became fundamental and the means of accessing the 'national cake' (read resources) and economic opportunities in the post-colonial nation-state. The education system entrenched a sense of nationalism whose ideals was 'new and educated citizens' of the Kenyan nation (Aguilar 1998: 261).

As such Boran children managed, through the involvement in formal schooling, to access the national resources through representation and employment in the national government (Aguilar 1998). Therefore socialization through formal education and subsequent integration into the government system has become, quite literally, a path to national belonging. This fact is well articulated in the songs I discuss as various candidates for political positions are praised for their role in supporting the education of Boran children.

This verse from one of Aga's 2002 campaign songs comparing Abdi Tari's first five-year term with Jarso Jillo's previous ten-year term is illustrative here:

> "Gan shanaan ka Abdi Tari, Abdin kor dheetha nubasse,
> *(in) the five years of Abdi Tari, Abdi organized the meeting of dheetha (to discuss pasture and water issues)*
> Tisitu Aburun d'aqe, ijolle college it naqe
> He took the herders in search of greener pastures, and took children to colleges
> Gan kud'an Jarso Jillo kasom maqa lagatani
> Ten years of Jarso Jillo, he fell out with those who were well educated (because of ideological differences)?
> Ka infen transfer d'awani, kiwanjat nam arabsani

Those whom he didn't like he transferred them to other places (often hardship areas), and insulted others in public
Shanaan gada Abdi Tari, mchango nama changanni
The five years of Abdi Tari's gada, funds were raised (through harambees)[7]
University d'aqani akanan ejat tharatani
And people went to the university."

Various development projects especially those supporting livestock production are also appreciated and applauded. In the Kenyan context, James Howard Smith (2008) has pointed to the ubiquity of the concept of development in official discourse, national politics and in popular discourse. It is a concept that is also deployed and reproduced in the songs at the local level in Marsabit showing how they plug into a Kenyan discourse as they simultaneous draw on their hitherto 'non-Kenyan' Boran identity.

> "*Urji wor Sakut angae, gof chobat eli nubae,*
> It's the star of the people that shone (since Abdi became M.P), we got a well at Gof Chopa (A crater on the Marsabit-Moyale road)
> *Biliqit Haron nubae, dhalach kenat d'ebu bae,*
> We got a pond/ a dam at Biliq (name of a dam), and the thirst of our livestock was quenched
> *Wor Saku Waqat nunae Jaldessi gaf colony bathe*
> The people of Saku, it's God's mercy (that he gave us Abdi for M.P), the Jaldessa borehole become dry during the colonial period
> *Gada issa bisan nubae Abdi wan gutho nubae*
> But it is during his *gada* that water was found there again (through Abdi's efforts to revive the wells)."

But Still not Quite Kenyan

While the above discussion paints a picture of how the Boran, drawing on the *gada* vocabulary and symbolism, have domesticated Kenya's post-colonial political system and its imaginaries, it should not be interpreted to mean that they have fully embraced the Kenyan identity. On the contrary, their ambivalence to national identity indeed persists. Hassan Arero discusses this perception of Boran considering themselves as outsiders in his chapter aptly named, 'coming to Kenya'. This is a sentiment that is expressed in the songs I discuss here as well. As Carrier & Kochore (2014) note:

> Indeed, campaign songs for the 2013 elections in Marsabit county reveal that people still regard Kenya(ns) as 'other'. For example, a line from one song states, 'when we asked the people of Kenya about the whereabouts of our MP, they too didn't have an answer for us'. This is a song in which the incumbent MP was being accused of running away from the people, being inaccessible and 'hiding' in 'Kenya', the land of the other.

Marsabit may be removed from Nairobi and the residents joke that it is not Kenya at all but an analysis of how they have domesticated Kenya's political system by interpreting it through a vernacular lens reveals that they are more 'Kenyan' than they might appreciate. This is despite the continued sense that they were neglected by the Kenyan government, a trend which is slowly being reversed through improvement of infrastructure like roads and appointment of educated community members to top government jobs.

Conclusion

This chapter has argued that despite its influence having generally been on the decline, the nostalgia for and attraction to the *gada* system continues to influence the perception of governance and the state by the Marsabit Boran. *Gada*'s terminology and symbolism comes in handy in imagining and understanding the Kenyan political system. While the Boran do not entirely consider themselves as 'Kenyan', an inquiry into their music reveals the ambiguities of their association with the Kenyan nation and political system.

As Nyairo argues, there are different ways of becoming Kenyan; not just one monolithic identity. Being Kenyan is in fact being able to be versatile and drawing on multiple lines of identities and citizenship.

Lastly, the chapter demonstrates that the often overlooked elements of popular discourse such as music can provide a fertile ground for analyzing some of the socio-political changes happening across Kenya particularly issues surrounding ethnic, regional and national identities.

Endnotes

1. For the definition of the gada system, I find Megersa & Kassam (2004:253) explanation quite apt: "Gada is a complex system of temporal differentiation through which all the male members of a society undergo a series of initiations and are socialized into the social, legal and religious roles that they will fulfill in the course of the life cycle".

2. The eight-year age-grade transition ceremony of *gadamojji* has not taken place in Marsabit since 1995 meaning the

3. The site on the slopes of Marsabit Mountain where the ceremony and rituals associated with the age-grade transitions (*gadamojji*) are conducted.

4. These are tin and timber kiosks where Miraa (a stimulant plant mainly grown in the Nyambene area of Meru and also on a small scale on the slopes of Mt. Marsabit) widely chewed in northern Kenya and other parts of the country.

Bibliography

Aguilar, M.I. 1995. African conversion from a world religion: Religious diversification by the Waso Boorana in Kenya. *Africa*, 65(1:525-544.

Aguilar, M.I. 1998. *The politics of age and gerontocracy in Africa: ethnographies of the past & memories of the present*. Africa World Pr.

Amborn, H. 2006. The contemporary significance of what has been. Three approaches to remembering the past: Lineage, gada, and oral tradition. *History in Africa*, 33: 53-84.

Arero, H. 2005. Pastoralists of northern Kenya: Education as a response to a shifting socioeconomic process. (Unpublished Manuscript)

Askew, K. 2002. *Performing the nation: Swahili music and cultural politics in Tanzania*. University of Chicago Press.

Baxter P.T. 1990. Oromo Blessings and Greetings, in A. Jacobson-Widding and W. Van Beek, (ed.), *The Creative Communion: African Folk Models of Fertility and the Regeneration of Life*. Uppsala, Acta Universitatis Upsalienis: 235-50.

Carrier, N., Kochore, H.H. 2014. Navigating ethnicity and electoral politics in northern Kenya: the case of the 2013 election. *Journal of Eastern African Studies*, 8(1): 135-152.

Legesse, A. 1973. *Gada: Three approaches to the study of African society*. Free Press.

Leus, T., Salvadori, C. 2006. *Aadaa Borana: A dictionary of Borana Culture*. Shama Books

Megerssa, G., Aneesa, K. 2004. The 'Rounds' of Time: Time, History and Society in Borana Oromo in, *The Qualities of Time. Anthropological Approaches*, London, Berg: 251-65.

Nicolas, A. 2007. Founded in Memory of the 'Good Old Times': The Clan Assembly of Hiddii, in Eastern Shewa, Ethiopia. *Journal of Eastern African Studies*, 1(3):484-497.

Nyairo, J., Ogude, J. 2005. Popular music, popular politics: Unbwogable and the idioms of freedom in Kenyan popular music. *African Affairs*, 104 (415): 225-249.

Oba, G. 2013. *Nomads in the shadows of empires: contests, conflicts and legacies on the southern Ethiopian-northern Kenyan frontier*. Brill.

Russell, A. 2011. Home, music and memory for the Congolese in Kampala. *Journal of Eastern African Studies*, 5(2): 294-312.

Stokes, M. 1994. Ethnicity, identity and music. *The musical construction of place*. Oxford, Berg

Schlee, G. 1998. Gada systems on the meta-ethnic level: Gabbra/Boran/Garre interactions in the Kenyan/Ethiopian borderland in, *Conflict, age & power in North East Africa: age systems in transition*). Oxford, James Currey: 121-146

Schlee, G. 2013. Territorializing ethnicity: the imposition of a model of statehood on pastoralists in northern Kenya and southern Ethiopia. *Ethnic and Racial Studies*, 36(5):857-874.

Schlee, G., & Shongolo, A. 1995. Local war and its impact on ethnic and religious identification in Southern Ethiopia. *GeoJournal*, 36(1): 7-17.

Schlee, G. 2013. Territorializing ethnicity: the imposition of a model of statehood on pastoralists in northern Kenya and southern Ethiopia. *Ethnic and Racial Studies*, 36(5): 857-874.

Smith, J.H. 2008. *Bewitching Development: witchcraft and the reinvention of development in neoliberal Kenya*. University of Chicago Press.

Wario Arero, H. 2007. Coming to Kenya: Imagining and perceiving a nation among the Borana of Kenya. *Journal of Eastern African Studies*, 1(2): 292-304.

Watson, E.E. 2010. A "hardening of lines": landscape, religion and identity in northern Kenya. *Journal of Eastern African Studies*, 4(2), 201-220.

Archival Documents

Gerald Reece, Handing Over Report Marsabit District, 1939, Kenya National Archives, PC NFD 2/2/2

G.M. Bebb, Handing Over Report Marsabit District, 1951, Kenya National Archives, PC NFD 2/2/3

Songs

Aga Galgallo, '*Lat ken Waaqi biqilichinna*' 2007

Aga Galgallo, '*Gada Jey Jey qabanna*' 2007

Bonaya Doti, '*Aban Finna Jabaan Waqum*' 2007

Aga Galgallo, '*Kupi Qalloti qabe isan bae Jaldessat*' 2013.

Part III:

Music and the Politics of Love and Gender

Singing Love in(to) Somaliland: Love Songs, "Heritage Preservation", and the Shaping of Post-War Publics

Christina J. Woolner

In August 2014, Hiddo Dhawr *– a cultural restaurant and "tourism village" – opened its doors in Hargeysa, becoming the first live music venue to operate in Somaliland since the war. In this chapter I explore how* Hiddo Dhawr, *and particularly the live performance of old love songs, are implicated in the shaping of post-war publics in contemporary Somaliland. Drawing on ethnographic data, I seek to unravel how* Hiddo Dhawr's *mission of "heritage preservation", twinned with its near exclusive focus on love songs, work to create space for the performance of music in contested terrain, providing audiences with the resources to reflect on the past, imagine different futures, and enact different ways of being in the present. I suggest that in so doing,* Hiddo Dhawr's *audiences constitute a kind of alternative public, one where a "traditional" Somali identity is celebrated while audiences are freed to push the limits of everyday social conventions.*

Introduction

On August 26, 2014 *Hiddo Dhawr* – a cultural restaurant and "tourism village" – opened its doors in Hargeysa. While a host of new restaurants and cafés have opened across the city in recent years, *Hiddo Dhawr* is no ordinary restaurant. Roughly translating as "take care of heritage", the restaurant became the first and only live music venue to operate in Somaliland since the civil war decimated the capital, displaced the artistic community and, according to some Somali commentators (Afrax 1994; Samatar 2010), precipitated the demise of Somalis' artistic soul. Two evenings a week, *Hiddo Dhawr's* house musicians delight audiences diverse in age and gender with love songs popular from the 1950s-80s, now "contextually recomposed" (Johnson 2010: 239) and somewhat nostalgically re-cast as "traditional" or "classic" Somali music. Audience members hum along to popular vocal melodies, accompanied simply by an *cuud*[1] (oud) and drums, while enjoying traditional Somali dishes of camel meat, *suqaar*, (meat stew) *shuuro* (cornmeal porridge) and *laxoox* (pancakes made from sorghum). While not immune to criticism – particularly from conservative religious groups who view music as *haaraan* (Islamically forbidden) – in its early years of operation the venue has gained a reputation as both the "theatre" of Hargeysa and a key centre of "heritage preservation", indelibly shaping the city's contested urban landscape in the process.[2]

Starting from Barber's premise that popular arts both reflect and inform processes of social change – as both "constellations of social, political and economic relationships" and "expressive acts […] through which consciousness is articulated and communicated (1987: 2, 4) – in this chapter I explore how *Hiddo Dhawr*, and particularly the live performance of old love songs, are implicated in the shaping of post-war publics in contemporary Somaliland. I am particularly interested in unraveling how *Hiddo Dhawr's* mission of "heritage preservation", twinned with a commitment to the live performance of pre-war *love* songs both reflect contemporary socio-political-religious dynamics of the city while actively seeking to re-shape Hargeysa's urban landscape. In what follows, I argue that by recourse to "heritage preservation", *Hiddo Dhawr* has opened space for a music venue to operate in contested terrain, and in so doing has provided people with resources to reflect on the past and its potential enduring importance. Yet rather than simply being a space for nostalgic reflection on an irretrievable (and romanticized) past, I suggest that *Hiddo Dhawr's* focus on *love* songs, and the space occasioned by their live performance, provides audiences with resources to imagine different futures and to enact alternative ways of being in the present. In this way, *Hiddo Dhawr's* audiences constitute a kind of alternative public, one where a "traditional" Somali identity is celebrated while audiences are freed to push the limits of everyday social conventions.

This chapter draws on ethnographic research conducted from July 2015 to December 2016 as part of my broader PhD research,[3] which focuses on the social and political lives of love songs in contemporary Somaliland. I proceed in three parts. First, to "set the stage", so to speak, for an understanding of *Hiddo Dhawr's* significance for Hargeysa's contemporary cultural landscape, I provide an overview of the city's pre- and post-war music scene. Second, I turn to an ethnographic consideration of how *Hiddo Dhawr's* founding and commitment to "heritage preservation" have opened space for the performance of love songs, and provide a description of what this space looks like in practice. Third, drawing on insight from musicians and audience members, I attempt to unpack why *Hiddo Dhawr* has emerged as it has, and consider its unfolding impact on post-war public spaces. I conclude with a brief reflection on the possible relationships between audiences, publics and processes of social change. This chapter is both an exploration in the multifaceted and often subtle ways that music "speaks", and an attempt to shed light on the contours and contestations of everyday life in a post-war, unrecognized state.

Hargeysa's Pre- and Post-War Music Scene

Understanding *Hiddo Dhawr's* significance for Hargeysa's cultural landscape requires comprehending something of the socio-political and artistic context into which it was born. While a full accounting of Somalis' musical heritage is beyond the scope of this chapter, it is important to highlight that music has long been both a source of pride and a site of contestation, put to different uses as the socio-political climates of various historical eras demanded.[4] In this section, I provide a basic overview of Hargeysa's pre-war music scene, before considering the impact of the war and various post-war developments on Hargeysa's urban soundscapes.

Fondly known as *Hoyga Suugaanta,* or the "home of literature", Hargeysa has long been a critical site of Somali artistic production.[5] It was in Hargeysa that the first Somali theatre group, *Hargeysawi* emerged in the 1950s, and the first cooperative of musicians, *Walaalaha Hargeysa* ("The Hargeysa Brothers"), was established (Ducaale 2002: 36). Members of this group, including Cabdullahi Qarshe, are widely credited with ushering in a new era in Somali artistic production, fusing traditional nomadic poetic genres with Arabic, Indian, Sufi and Western musical influences to create *qaraami* – love songs performed by and for mixed-gender audiences, accompanied by an *cuud* and drums. Radio Hargeysa, the first Somali-language broadcast service in the region,[6] also played a critical role in mainstreaming music into Somali social and political life, helping to quell the criticism early musicians faced from both religious and colonial authorities (cf. Adam 2001; Johnson 1996). By the time of independence in 1960, Hargeysa had developed into an energetic artistic hub, and music played an important part in fomenting feelings of nationalism and *Soomaalinnimo* (Somaliness) in the early years of independence.

While Mogadishu was the centre of Siyaad Barre's regime and the many state-sponsored artistic troupes it developed, Somalilanders are quick to point out that many of the most famous national artists of this era began their careers in Hargeysa. Throughout the 1970s and 1980s, the large National Theatre regularly hosted plays, concerts, and other cultural events, and many national artists and government-sponsored and associated bands – like *Waaberi Hargeysa, General Da'uud, Horseed* and *Danan Hargeysa* – were based in the city. Hargeysa residents fondly reminisce about roadside merchants who copied cassettes of the most popular singers for eager fans while they waited, public buses competing for bragging rights as to who could play their music the loudest, and attending regular open-air concerts with thousands of other music-lovers at the outdoor *Timo-Cadde* basketball court.

This music-loving hub of Somali artistic production, however, was quite literally decimated in 1988, when aerial bombardments by Barre's regime, by now engaged in a full-blown war with the Somali National Movement (SNM), turned much of the city to rubble. The National Theatre was "deliberately and totally razed to the ground" (Ducaale 2002: 38), the homes of national artists were demolished or pillaged, instruments were stolen and sold, ruined or converted for other purposes, Radio Hargeysa's musical archives were looted, and artists, along with much of the rest of the population, were forced into refugee camps. Significantly, musicians – including some who would later become the core of *Hiddo Dhawr* – did continue to make music, even in refugee camps. Music sung directly for the troops, as well as broadcast over Radio Halgan (*halgan* = "struggle") was used to support the SNM's struggle. After declaring independence from the rest of the former Somali Democratic Republic in 1991, music also featured in the series of reconciliation conferences dedicated to re-building Somaliland in the wake of the civil war. Nevertheless, so great was the violence and its social-psychological effects that were to follow that in the wake of the war at least two Somali scholars have lamented the "loss of [Somalis'] literary soul" (Samatar 2010: 208; see also Afrax 1994).

In the decades since declaring independence, Somaliland has managed to achieve an impressive level of stability, and social-political reconstruction efforts in various sectors have fostered modest development. The artistic community, however, has been much slower to recover. Many of the artists who fled during the war eventually made new homes in the diaspora, and those who did return to Hargeysa found little opportunity to practice their craft. Instruments were nearly impossible to find, the city's primary stage (the National Theatre) had been destroyed, reconstruction efforts were focused in other areas, and the strong financial and organizational government support for the arts provided under Barre disappeared. In 1993, President Cigaal did put in place efforts to organize and support artists, and today over 100 artists are on the payroll of the Ministry of Information, Culture and National Awareness. However, the support they receive is insufficient to launch major productions, and their responsibilities do not extend beyond performing for national holidays; artists are thus "under-employed and have suffered a concomitant decline in morale, creativity and prestige" (Ducaale 2002: 38). While groups in the diaspora continued to produce music, it was not until 2013 that the first locally-based music group, *Xidigaha Geeska* ("The Stars of the Horn"), established itself. While this is certainly a welcome development, younger musicians are frequently lambasted by older artists and music-lovers of all ages for their reliance on the use of the synthesizer instead of more complex instruments, lack of musical knowledge and skill, and lyrics deemed superficial and frivolous compared to earlier times. Concerts by younger artists are few and far between, and usually rely entirely on playback and lip-synching.

Beyond constraints of resource and skill, the changing religious landscape of Hargeysa has had a further impact on the artistic scene. While Islam has deep roots in the Somali regions, public and private forms of religiosity have undergone significant transformations since the war. Although reform Islamic movements took root in the region from the 1950s, they were repressed by Barre's agenda of "scientific socialism"; when the state collapsed, however, such movements gained influence, seeking to reform or displace the Sufi traditions that previously predominated (Adam 2010; Hoehne 2015). While many turned to religion in the 1990s in the wake of war and state collapse, since the early 2000s funding for mosques and schools from Salafist groups in the Gulf – who uniformly and unambiguously teach that music is *haaraan* (forbidden) – has further altered the city's religious landscape. Significantly, conflict between Salafists who oppose music, and those who take a less rigid approach to music's religious permissibility (and other religious issues more generally) is frequently described as a competition for "audiences": if people are enjoying music, or frequenting places where music is played, they are less likely to be praying in the mosque.

While the penetration of reformist, Salafist-inspired Islam is difficult to ascertain, it has certainly had an impact on Hargeysa's urban soundscapes, individuals' private music-listening habits, and the socio-economic status of artists. Although one may hear music from inside a car or bus, or filtering onto the street from teashops and *majlis* (qat^7-chewing house), for the most part music is conspicuously absent from public spaces. Today it is the five-daily *aadaan* (call to prayer) that echo from the city's hundreds of mosques that define Hargeysa's urban soundscapes. While many still enjoy listening to music, and some will challenge the notion that music is always *haaraan,* some of my most avid music-loving friends concede that it "might be *haaraan*" (even if a "minor" sin) and that they "probably shouldn't listen to too much music". Most music is thus enjoyed in private, and for some is accompanied by a sense of shame or guilt. The status of artists has likewise been affected; while they are sometimes treated as cultural or national heroes, most live socially and economically precarious and marginalized lives. Few artists receive adequate compensation for their work, and despite public adoration for singers, music remains a profession that, as one friend put it, "no one would ever want their daughter to pursue". While being a poet remains a respectable pursuit, the decision for youth, particularly young women, to sing is often fraught with familial and personal anxiety. Even the children of musicians and poets are sometimes encouraged against following in their parents' footsteps. The complicated social position occupied by artists is perhaps best summed up by a saying often repeated by artists themselves: *fannaanku waa ubax guddaafad ka dhex baxay* ("artists are flowers growing in the rubbish"): admired for their beauty, yet poorly cared for, tossed aside and forgotten.

The government, it should be noted, has an ambiguous relationship both to these religious groups and to music. State-run Radio Hargeysa continues to broadcast music, the government organizes large nationalist-flavoured outdoor concerts for Somaliland's two independence celebrations (18 May and 26 June), and, as mentioned above, over 100 artists remain on the government payroll. Despite this clear government support for artists, members of the government have periodically spoken out against music. In August 2016, for example, the Minister of Religious Affairs cancelled a concert of a young female singer from Puntland over complaints from religious leaders that that her online music videos suggest she "had a bad culture" and "didn't behave like a Muslim." While alternative explanations for why the concert was cancelled have been suggested,[8] that religion was used as the primary public justification highlights the ways in which the government will at least pay lip-service to the concerns of financially-powerful religious groups when it suits their interests. Whatever the case may be, this incident helps to illustrate that Hargeysa's contemporary cultural (and political) landscape is contested to say the least. While still shaped by the memory of a rich (if sometimes controversial) artistic history, today's urban soundscapes bear the indelible marks of a devastating war, and have been further impacted by broader socio-political and religious changes in Somaliland's precarious, internationally-unrecognized, post-war development. It is into this complex and contested terrain that *Hiddo Dhawr* was born.

Making Space for Love Songs: "Taking Care of Heritage" in Contested Terrain

Given the contested urban environment into which it emerged, it is in many ways a wonder that a live music venue has come to operate at all. How, then, has *Hiddo Dhawr* come into being? What do "taking care of heritage" and the live performance of love songs look like in such a context? In this section I detail how *Hiddo Dhawr*, guided by a mission of "taking care of heritage" came into existence in the first place. I then explore what this "heritage preservation" looks like in practice: first, by considering how "tradition" or "heritage" – including old love songs – are envisaged and presented; and then by detailing a typical performance evening, and the atmosphere occasioned by the live performance of love songs.

Like many new cafés and restaurants in Hargeysa in recent years, *Hiddo Dhawr* opened its doors thanks to the initiative of two diaspora Somalilanders: Ismaaciil Cawl, a Dutch-Somali businessman and development worker; and Sahra Halgan, a singer. During his teenage and early adult years in Holland, Ismaaciil found it "difficult to feel at home". To cope with this sense of displacement, he would listen to Somali music and read everything he could get from his homeland. On returning to Somaliland in 2012, however, Hargeysa was no longer the place he remembered from his childhood. Of this first trip back to his homeland he recalled: "there were new buildings and new cars, and nothing I recognized from when I was young." Inspired in part by travels abroad, where he had enjoyed museums and cultural centres, he endeavoured to return home and open a centre devoted to preserving Somali heritage.

While Ismaaciil's early proposals to build a village of traditional *aqallo* (nomadic huts) and get people to pay to visit were met with laughter, he eventually found a kindred spirit in Sahra Halgan, who would become the public face of *Hiddo Dhawr*. The granddaughter of a folklore dancer and singer, who explains that she has music "in [her] blood", Sahra first rose to fame as a member of the SNM in the late 1980s. During this time she used her music to soothe weary soldiers, and to rally support for their cause, earning the nickname "Halgan" from her association with Radio Halgan. While Sahra performed at the 1994 Burco Conference, soon thereafter she became disillusioned with continued inter-clan conflict, and migrated to France. In France she went on to a successful singing career, and continues to regularly tour and record albums with her band *The Sahra Halgan Trio*. Like Ismaaciil, on trips back to Hargeysa she was saddened by what she found, particularly the state of the artistic sphere, lamenting the failure to rebuild the National Theatre, and the fact that "artists had no place to call home anymore." Like Ismaaciil, in her tours abroad she had been impressed by various venues dedicated to preserving and celebrating the culture and heritage of different locales. Driven by a shared commitment to "showcasing Somaliland's cultural productions", Sahra gathered a number of artists with whom she had collaborated during her SNM years, including the *cuud* player Cabdinaasir Macallin Caydiid, to discuss the idea. While one of the collaborating musicians originally suggested the name *Dhaqan Dhawr* ("take care of culture"), concerns were raised about its similarity to the term "*dhaqan celis*" ("return to culture") – a pejorative term used to describe diaspora kids who come to Hargeysa in the summers, sent by parents afraid they are losing their language and culture, and considered by some locals to be a nuisance. While the alliteration in "*Dhaqan Dhawr*" would have resonated to Somali ears, wanting to avoid any associations with "*dhaqan celis*" eventually they settled on the term "*Hiddo*", which roughly translates as "heritage". And thus *Hiddo Dhawr* was born.

While generally warmly received, the venue has not been without controversy. Early in their operation they were approached by a group of conservative religious leaders, who wished to voice their concerns about the inappropriate activities mixed-gender audiences of music might get up to, and specifically highlighted that they heard the venue was serving alcohol. In response, the manager invited them to visit the venue, to clearly see for themselves that alcohol was not being served. According to Ismaaciil, once they clarified that "heritage preservation" was their principal mission, these leaders agreed to leave them alone. The fact that they do not serve alcohol, that female singers are always covered when on stage, and that they encourage patrons to dress modestly also left their religious objectors with weak grounds for further harassment. Reflecting on this early criticism, Sahra, is more assertive in her response: "I liberated this land with my *cuud*. I have every right to practice my art." Elsewhere in the city, a number of diaspora-owned restaurants disparaged for playing "Western music" and allowing men and women to mix freely face frequent harassment and periodic visits from security forces sent to investigate reports of nefarious mixed-gender activities. One of the most popular of these cafés, which periodically hosted music evenings, shut down less than two years after opening when the imam of a local mosque seemed to make it his personal mission to encourage neighbours to make it difficult for the venue to operate. The fate of a female singer who reportedly "did not behave like a Muslim" was already recounted above. Yet by recourse to "heritage preservation," upholding standards of "good culture", and drawing on Sahra's social and political capital as an SNM veteran, *Hiddo Dhawr* has been largely allowed to carry out its business undisturbed.

Put into practice, Sahra and Ismaaciil's commitment to "taking care of heritage" has resulted in a somewhat eclectic reconstruction and presentation of rural, nomadic life, the showcasing of music of a more recent, urban vintage, and contemporary nationalist symbols. The grounds are populated by traditional nomadic huts (*aqallo*) lined with textiles woven by women, where guests can enjoy meals of "traditional" Somali food, such as camel meat, *suqaar, shuuro* and *laxoox* – alongside more recent additions to Somali cuisine, like pasta, rice and French fries. Other rural implements – wooden milk vessels, camel bells, head rests, and vats for churning camel milk – decorate the grounds, and are artistically represented on the compound walls. Traditional textiles and fabrics, and pictures of nomadic scenes adorn the two music halls. Guests may sit on *kambadh*, four-legged stools fashioned from wood and goat hide – or, in response to complaints of sore backs and buttocks, on black leather couches or upright chairs. The two music halls bear the names of two of Sahra's greatest inspirations: her grandfather, Nimcaan Hilaac Dheere, and Maxamed Mooge, a popular singer-songwriter and SNM fighter who died during the struggle. Visitors also get a good dose of nationalistic pride: a large map and flag of Somaliland greet visitors at the entrance, and inside the larger music hall hangs a banner featuring Somaliland's flag alongside other national flags, presenting Somaliland as a member in the community of nations. Lights shaped like traditional charcoal incense burners, and painted a patriotic red, green, and white, illuminate the stage. And it is from this stage that a core group of about ten artists take turns performing live music, consisting of vocal solos and duets accompanied simply by an *cuud* and drums.

While most of the heritage on display at *Hiddo Dhawr* depicts a rural, nomadic past, the music performed here is of relatively recent, urban origin – even if it regularly draws on rich pastoral imagery. The venue's repertoire includes the simple melodies and *cuud*-accompanied *qaraami* of the 1950s, as well as more recent songs from the "heyday" of Somali music (1960s-80s), now scaled back in instrumentation to include only *cuud* and drums. As elsewhere in Africa,[9] music of this era was connected both to the mood of nationalist excitement of the late colonial and early-independence era, urbanization, and accompanying changes in social attitudes, particularly towards gender relations, love, and companionate marriage. These songs run the gamut from women's songs that give voice to love's suffering and grievances, men's songs that similarly express the pain of love, songs in which men sing women's praises, and duet's that express a couple's satisfaction or frustration with each other. In their time, these songs worked to "reimagine courtship and put at its center romantic love and mutual consent", thus elevating the ideal of companionate marriage (Kapteijns 1999: 140). In a setting where marriage partners were (and remain) defined by clan and socio-economic status, and where individuals' love ambitions are often thwarted by familial and broader social expectations, the intimate aspirations of love and romance expressed in these songs entailed a kind of claim to new types of social relations, even as they strategically used "'tradition' as an oratorical and moral weapon" to sway their audiences and love-addressees (Kapteijns 1999: 140). Described at the time as "modern" Somali songs (Johnson 1996 [1974]), these songs depicted changing social norms, at once reflecting and stretching social conventions. At *Hiddo Dhawr*, however, they have been "contextually recomposed" (Johnson 2010: 239) and "retrospectively redefined" (Waterman 1997) as "heritage" that needs to be preserved, particularly considering what is perceived to be the sorry state of contemporary or "modern" artistic production.

On Thursday and Friday evenings – and summertime Mondays, to accommodate large diaspora holiday crowds – these songs come alive, brought to life by a dedicated group of musicians and the energetic audiences that gather to see them perform. These evenings go something like this: from about 9pm visitors make their way through two security check-points, before lining up to pay for their pre-booked tickets. A broad cross-section of Somalilanders, from young people to retirees, pass through the doors: groups of middle class women celebrating birthdays and weddings (sometimes with children in tow); politicians and businessmen entertaining potential partners; diaspora men and women on holiday for the summer; groups of colleagues from local NGOs, with the occasional foreign guest; young couples of varying means out for a night of entertainment; and groups of friends of more modest means, who have saved for a rare and special night out, or are being treated by more affluent friends. While in daily interactions – in business, politics, education, and on the street – men and women are usually separated, and women increasingly expected to uphold conservative dress codes, at *Hiddo Dhawr* they mingle freely, laughing and joking with each other as they find their seats. Furtive eyes glance around to see who has arrived with whom, and who is wearing what. Colourful silk scarves slip off of carefully-coiffed-though-usually-unseen-hair, to rest on *dirac*[10]-clad shoulders. While there is a hierarchy of sorts to the pre-assigned seating arrangements – the coveted leather seats at the front usually go to politicians, business leaders and special guests – when the music begins these distinctions fade, as heads nod in time to the music. As a friend remarked after finding himself at a table near the President of his university, "people can't help but move to the music together."

Even though most of the repertoire is older than a large portion of the audience, audience members energetically sing along to most of the songs, originally performed by the "giants" of pre-war Somali music. A male vocalist sings *"Balambaallis"* ("butterfly") – first made popular by Xasan Adan Samatar – which compares the (virgin) woman he loves to a beautiful (untouched) pastoral landscape. Another song by Maxamed Saleban Tubeec compares the search for a good and respectable woman to the wait for a camel to give milk after a drought, while *"Gar Eexo"* ("biased verdict"), a song by Cumar Dhuule, discusses the challenges of marriage, and the need for good fortune and God's mercy to make a marriage work. Songs by Axmed Gacayte, Maxamed Mooge and Axmed Cali Cigaal follow. A young female singer takes to the stage to perform Magool's *"Shimbiryahow ma duushaa?"* ("Oh bird, can you fly?"), a song that laments a woman's love for a man refused to her, and pleads with a bird to send a message to her far-away beloved. Eventually Sahra herself takes to the stage to perform a set of *calaacal,* including songs like Sahra Axmed's *"Laqanyada jacaylka"* ("love nausea"), Magool's *"Siday laabtu doonto"* ("as the heart [chest] desires"), and a set of songs by Khadra Daahir, the "mother of love" and queen of *calaacal*. She closes the first half with Khadra Daahir's *"Caashaqu ogeysiis ma leeyahay?"* ("can love be publically announced?"), a song in which a young woman sings of the pain of not being able to announce her love, constrained by expectations of female modesty and bashfulness, comparing her longing to that of a milking she-camel crying after her calf. Women who empathize with the pain in Sahra's re-voicing of Khadra's words join her on stage, showing solidarity by patting her head, dancing alongside her, and showering her with Somaliland shillings.

When the artists break around 11:30, the energy of the audience is channeled into a raucous joke-telling and sing-a-long session. A large orange microphone is passed through the audience, and those who wish (or are cajoled) sing their favourite songs, recite poems or tell stories and jokes. Sahra has described this part of the evening as a large group therapy session – it provides people the opportunity to sing, and to nostalgically reflect on past loves, or to return to the moment in history when they first encountered these songs. Others have told me that this is a particularly good opportunity to get feelings and emotions of love (both joyful and sorrowful) off your chest – feelings you would never have occasion to otherwise express in public, and whose voicing in song in this setting might also serve to impress the girl you are trying to woo. This is, after all, the best place in town to bring a date. Though discreet in their coupling and likely to deny that what they are doing there is "dating", couples can be seen exchanging flirtatious glances, or stepping out for some private conversation time in one of the *aqal*. Inside the main hall, the microphone circulates for the better part of an hour, and audience members relish in the opportunity to sing, tell stories, and to make each other laugh.

Sahra's "therapy" image aptly describes the energy and mood during the performances. There is a palpable energy in the hall not only of excitement, but also of relaxation and relief – an energy that continues to grow as the musicians re-take the stage for the second set. As the only regular entertainment venue in town, *Hiddo Dhawr* is, I'm told, the best place to come to recover from the pressure of the work-week and other stresses of life. As one of the regular musicians put it, *Hiddo Dhawr* is a kind of "frustration hospital", a place to come to clear your head of all that might worry you. Whether one is tired from housework, lonely and worried about a friend who has left on *tahriib*,[11] anxious about one's own love life, or stressed about employment prospects, *Hiddo Dhawr* provides audiences with the opportunity to leave these worries behind, because, as one friend explained, "when everyone is singing, there is a positive energy everywhere, [there is] nowhere to be negative or sad. When you go to *Hiddo Dhawr*, you will be happy, and this happiness carries you through the next week." When the music finally comes to an end in the early hours of the morning, friends continue to chat and joke with each other, reluctant to depart, preferring rather to dwell in the energy and escape the evening has provided. Or, as a friend explained, exhaling deeply when I asked him how he felt at the end of the evening: "I feel repaired. When you listen to the *cuud*, by the time the evening comes to an end, you feel that you yourself are repaired."

Making Sense of Love Songs: Resistance, Nostalgia, Fantasy and Freedom

While it is still early days in *Hiddo Dhawr's* operation and its effect on the shape of Somaliland's post-war landscape is continually unfolding, the narrative above begins to reveal some of the ways that *Hiddo Dhawr's* presence is serving to re-shape Hargeysa's post-war urban landscape. In this section, I provide some provisional analysis of the ways in which the venue's mission of "heritage preservation", twinned with its near exclusive performance of old love songs, are making their mark on Hargeysa's contested urban soundscapes, and providing audiences with the space in which to reflect on the past, imagine the future, and enact different ways of being in the present.

As the first music venue to operate since the civil war, the importance of *Hiddo Dhawr's* simple presence in the city cannot be overstated. Indeed, that a centre dedicated to the performance of live music could emerge in the first place is in many respects a wonder at all. As many of its patrons describe it, it has become the city's main "theatre", filling the large hole in the city's cultural landscape left by the destruction of the National Theatre nearly three decades ago (and so-far unsuccessful efforts to rebuild it) – and, in so doing, providing both a stage for artists long stage-less, and a space for music-loving audiences to convene. In a setting where music itself is contested, *Hiddo Dhawr's* very establishment entails an implicit claim to inclusion, and demand for the respect that artists once enjoyed. Sahra's comment – "I liberated this land with my *cuud*, I have every right to practice my art" – in no uncertain terms suggests *Hiddo Dhawr's* very establishment entails, at least in part, a challenge to the existing political-religious status quo. As Nooshin notes, where music's permissibility is contested, its "very presence can become a signifier of agency" and a "medium for exercising social and political control" (2009: 30, 25). In a setting where both music's opponents and supporters wield "culture" as a rallying cry (Hadeed 2015), it is no coincidence that Somaliland's first post-war music venue has come into being by presenting music as a display of "traditional" culture, alongside displays of Somaliland patriotism, to be preserved and celebrated. As one cultural activist once remarked to me, "you can't call Hadraawi [a popular poet] un-Somali!"; as long as artistic projects are built around celebrated cultural icons and established national heroes, they remain somewhat protected from a certain form of criticism. Artistic projects that fall outside what is deemed "good Somali culture" have not fared so well.

While *Hiddo Dhawr's* mission to "take care of heritage" has contributed to its reputation as a respectable cultural institution, able to operate in contested political-religious terrain, its impact on Somaliland's post-war public spaces goes far beyond its mere presence. "Taking care of heritage" is, after all, not simply a way to justify their presence, but a mission that grows out of a genuine desire to recover and celebrate ways of being disrupted by war, and further re-figured by decades of political instability and socio-economic uncertainty. Similar "returns" to the past, particularly in times of uncertainty, have been noted elsewhere in the region. Writing about the emergence of "ethnic" theme nights in Nairobi's night clubs, Ogude suggests that "desires to fall back on a known tradition in the cityscape" are a kind of "native cosmopolitanism", which is "indicative of local ways of dealing with modern subjectivity and, quite often, an overwhelming global mass culture" (2012: 162). Nyairo, similarly, suggests that such "romanticized returns work as symbolic gestures whose purpose is providing the idioms and metaphors for confronting the past, thus becoming valuable tools in negotiating the political and even the cultural impasse of the present" (in Ogude 2012: 162). In a time of political uncertainty, economic precariousness and rapid social change, it follows that *Hiddo Dhawr* represents one such symbolic gesture, one that simultaneously nods to Somalis' nomadic rural heritage, and a more recent liberal urban culture; this selective and romanticized retrospective provide patrons with a sense of "Somaliness" and historical continuity, as well as the imaginative tools to remember and reflect on the past and its potential enduring importance in the present.

Significantly, what exactly is at work in the "romanticized return" *Hiddo Dhawr* embodies varies by generation and by whether individuals have lived in the diaspora. For those of Sahra's generation and older, there is a very strong element of nostalgia in a return to this music, a desire to, as Sahra puts it, "relive the era where there was a national theatre and people respected artists." As commentators of the emergence of nostalgia elsewhere on the continent have noted, "nostalgic discourses about the past often represent a means of articulating the failures, dilemmas, and challenges of the present" (Omojolo 2009: 249; cf. Bissell 2005). In many respects, *Hiddo Dhawr's* founding itself was prompted by dissatisfaction with the current socio-political, economic and cultural landscape of Hargeysa, and a sense of frustration and alienation particularly pronounced among the city's diaspora returnees – a sense of alienation reflected in Ismaaciil's lament that Hargeysa was full of "new buildings and new cars, and nothing [he] recognized from when [he] was young." As another diaspora returnee engaged in cultural activist work once remarked to me, he and his peers "used to love a different Somaliland" – a Somaliland where music streamed onto the streets from tea-shops, and you could buy cassettes of your favourite artists from roadside vendors. For those who remember pre-war Hargeysa, *Hiddo Dhawr* provides, in Sahra's words, a kind of "therapy", allowing patrons to return to an earlier, happier, easier time. Yet it is also simultaneously a statement of dissatisfaction about the present context, and an attempt to re-assert something of the past into Hargeysa's contemporary urban landscape.

That *Hiddo Dhawr* is about more than nostalgic reflection on an irretrievable past is evidenced most clearly in the experiences of the "post-collapse generation", i.e. those born around or after the time of the war. Part of *Hiddo Dhawr's* vision, after all, is to expose a younger generation to the "cultural productions" of the past in order to restore respect for artistic production, instill a sense of pride in what is here styled as an "authentic" or "traditional" Somali identity, and inspire further rehabilitation of pre-war ways of being. And there are early signs that *Hiddo Dhawr* is succeeding in doing just that. Singing on stage has inspired some younger performers to establish a group dedicated to (re)learning the art of live music. And the experience of listening to music surrounded by "traditional" materials has served as an effective medium to (re)connect "post-collapse" Somalilanders to their past. Two young female friends explained that *Hiddo Dhawr* is "a place that makes you feel alive," that "makes you to feel unique that you have your own Somali culture, your own Somali food". Another young patron puts it this way: "*Hiddo Dhawr* is the backbone of the Somali traditional system. It reminds the people of the old days, the materials, the food, and the *cuud*. My generation, we forgot this system, but *Hiddo Dhawr* is teaching us how things used to be." Songs are critical to this, for it is "in old songs [that] you can get proverbs, and [learn] about how Somali society was arranged, how people got married, and learn your history…you feel how things were… and you compare the situation to these new decades, and you think about where you are going in the future." As another friend explained, this "traditional" music is important, because "if you know your culture, and how your people lived [before], [you] will know [who you] are now." *Hiddo Dhawr's* mission of "heritage preservation" has certainly struck a chord with patrons eager to encounter their own past in ways that help them make sense of current challenges.

Yet, as the above description suggests, *Hiddo Dhawr* is much more than a museum, where "heritage" is passively preserved and presented: it is the city's hottest (and only) entertainment venue. And, I would argue, it is the venue's exclusive focus on love songs, and the space occasioned by their live performance, that makes *Hiddo Dhawr* particularly significant. For love in this context has long been conceived as a clan-transcending, universal condition that is blind to political ambition and socio-economic cleavages, and singers of love songs are revered (even if sometimes socially marginalized) as the a-political, social-norm-defying-and-transcending bearers of otherwise taboo messages. As one Somali proverb attests, *"abwaan qabiil maleh"* ("a poet is without clan"). While she herself has dabbled in (opposition) politics – to the criticism of some patrons, who suggest artists ought to remain a-political – Sahra herself recognizes the power of love songs to act in this way. She explains her decision to exclusively sing love songs thus: "When you see how people become consumed with things like clan and tribalism, it is good to shift and make them think of something different. Love is the only thing that binds people together, with no animosity." She further explains: "We live in one of the most restive, conflict-ridden regions. Killings and divisive political games dominate media coverage. People need a break from it. [At *Hiddo Dhawr*], we give them the chance to hear something different."

Perhaps precisely because love in the real world is often constrained by the very realities it has the possibility to transcend – particularly clan and socio-economic status – "hearing something different" has given audiences fodder to reflect both on their own experiences of love's suffering and joy, and to fantasize and imagine idealist and other-wordly love futures. Even if many of these songs contain stories of thwarted love, or love constrained by social circumstances, they simultaneously represent "an aspiration or a narrative about something shared, a story about both oneself and others that will turn out in a particular way" (Berlant 1998: 281). Love, after all, is a future-oriented emotion: it "project[s] into the future and infuse[s] … subjects with hope that their dreams of fulfillment will come to pass" (Fair 2009: 79). Young friends have explained, for example, that there is nothing quite like sitting in a traditional *aqal* with the person you love, listening to the music, reflecting on your own love story, and imagining what your future love journey might bring; love songs and the emotions and love-images they evoke serve as the fuel for these conversations. As one young female patron mused about what happens when she listens to old love songs: "Sometimes I remember my old days, the love that I had, my best days. And sometimes if it's a sad song, I remember a failed love that happened before and I am sad. But other times […] I imagine the future that is coming. The songs help me to imagine my love future."

Beyond simply providing fodder for fantasizing about one's potential "love futures," perhaps the most immediate impact *Hiddo Dhawr* has for its audiences is the space it provides to enact different ways of being in the present. For a few hours, audience members are able "escape" both the stress and social conventions – particularly regarding gendered expectations – more common in everyday interactions. The space occasioned by the live performance of love songs is one in which audiences are free to "try on" different ways of expressing themselves – in dress, in mannerism, in speech, in the emotions they can convey. I'm told, after all, that at *Hiddo Dhawr* there is "free life, free music, free everything", and you do not need to feel ashamed about enjoying yourself. Because when you come to *Hiddo Dhawr,* you come, as one patron explained, "wearing the shirt of love" – a "shirt" that frees its wearers from judgment and many of the social conventions of daily life. As Ogude finds of ethnic theme nights in Kenya's night clubs, "[t]he recourse to 'traditional' forms of music [serves] to free the audience of those inhibitions of open expression of pleasure" (2012: 157). In this way, *Hiddo Dhawr* functions as a kind of alternative public, one where, by recourse to "tradition", audiences are freed to express otherwise taboo emotions and enact ways of being that stretch social expectations and transcend the socio-economic, clan and political cleavages that define daily life.

Conclusion: Of Audiences and Alternative Publics

To summarize, in this chapter I have suggested that through recourse to "heritage preservation", combined with Sahra's SNM credentials, *Hiddo Dhawr* has established itself as a culturally-acceptable venue and laid claim to a right to exist in Hargeysa's contested urban landscape. While there is certainly a nostalgic dimension to the way "tradition" has been "retrospectively defined" (Waterman 1997) in this space, rather than simply providing space to reminisce on an irretrievable past, *Hiddo Dhawr* is providing audiences with alternative resources with which to reflect on the current context of their lives. I have also suggested that a focus on love songs, and the space occasioned by their live performance, have provided patrons with additional imaginative resources and the space in which to "try on" different ways of being – freed, in part, by recourse to "tradition." Inasmuch as audiences constitute their own kind of "public" (Barber 1997), *Hiddo Dhawr* functions as a kind of alternative public, one where an "authentic" "traditional" Somali identity is celebrated at the same time that audiences are freed to stretch social conventions. Significantly, in part because of its mission of "heritage preservation", *Hiddo Dhawr* does not represent a "counterpublic" in the way that Warner defines the term, i.e. a public, comprised of a subaltern group, which is "constituted through a conflictual relation to the dominant public… [that] maintains an awareness of its subordinate status" (2002: 423-424). Although *Hiddo Dhawr's* audiences comprise their own kind of alternative public, they are also members of Hargeysa's broader "dominant" public. While conflict with certain religious elements of the population features in *Hiddo Dhawr's* existence, the venue does not seek to simply resist or subvert popular narratives of what it means to be a Somalilander; rather, it seeks to *transform* Hargeysa's "dominant public" by, as one friend put it, "making singing together normal again." If "ways of being an audience are made possible only by existing ways of being in society" (Barber 1997: 348), then the alternative public *Hiddo Dhawr* represents serves to remind its patrons that there are indeed other ways of being – ways of being that are simultaneously rooted in history yet stretch contemporary social norms.

I have, of course, but scratched the surface of the ways in which *Hiddo Dhawr* may be potentially implicated in the re-shaping of post-war public space in Somaliland. This is a story still in the writing. As Barber (1987: 4) reminds us, popular arts do not simply "reflect an already-constituted consciousness," but rather may reveal a critique that is not yet fully formed. As popular arts are both constrained and enabled by particular configurations of power (Okome & Newell 2012: 41), the "moments of freedom" (Fabian 1998) they provide may be as fleeting as the term "moment" suggests. Perhaps it would be apt to conclude that, as has always been the case for Somali audiences of the oral arts, *qof walba xaggii gubeysa ayuu ula kacaa* – each person takes it to the place where the pain burns. It is *Hiddo Dhawr's* audiences, and their interaction with the broader public(s) of which they are a part, who will ultimately be responsible for interpreting and re-interpreting, retrospectively re-defining and presently re-imagining how love songs will continue to shape the contested everyday fabric of a nation unfolding.

Endnotes

1 In Somali, the Arabic letter "ayn" is rendered as a "c". For readers unfamiliar with this sound, omit the letter "c" when reading, i.e., read "Cali" as "Ali", or *cuud* as "oud".

2 This chapter develops themes and material that I first presented in the podcast "*Hiddo Dhawr*: Singing Love in(to) Somaliland", for *Camthropod* (see Woolner 2016).

3 Apart from certain public figures and artists, to respect the privacy of my many interlocutors and to honour agreements of confidentiality I have withheld names and identifying details throughout this piece. All quoted interviews occurred in Hargeysa between July 2015 and December 2016.

4 For more on the evolution of Somali music, particularly its links to political developments, see Johnson (1996) or Hassan (this volume). For a gendered analysis of artistic developments, see Kapteijns (1999).

5 In addition to the referenced literature, the information contained in this section was obtained through dozens of interviews with older and younger artists, as well as others knowledgeable about the development of Somali music.

6 Though it was originally called Radio *Goodir* ("Kudu").

7 *Qat* (also known as *chat* or *khat,* and the Kenyan variety known as *miraa*) is a shrub or small tree whose leaves are chewed in a variety of social and religious settings for their stimulating effect. Chewing *qat* could be described as a national past-time for most men in Somaliland.

8 Some other reasons for the show's cancellation that have circulated include local artists feeling threatened by a singer from Puntland, and possible clan tensions (as the singer was from Puntland, she would have had poor clan connections to mobilize on her behalf). The incident has also led to mockery of the Minister, who has been teased/called out for watching online music videos of young women, earning him the nickname "Khaliil Indho" (after the singer's name, Nasteexa Indho). He's also been trolled on Facebook, with critics re-posting a picture of him shaking hands with the First Lady and highlighting his own double standards (strict practicing Muslims will not shake hands with a member of the opposite sex).

9 For a discussion of the urban origins of "popular art", see Barber (1987). Waterman (1997) also provides an account of the intersection of popular art, nationalism, and the re-definition of "tradition" in urban spaces.

10 A *dirac* is a style of dress made of loose-fitting though sometimes rather sheer fabric worn by women at weddings and other celebrations. In this context it is sometimes referred to as a "traditional" form of dress.

11 *Tahriib* refers to illegal migration abroad, usually to Europe via North Africa and the Mediterranean Sea. It is widely considered one of the greatest social problems facing Somaliland's youth.

Bibliography

Adam, H.M. 2010. Political Islam in Somali History, in M. Hoehne and V. Luling (eds.) *Milk and Peace, Drought and War: Somali Culture, Society and Politics*. London, Hurst Publishing: 117-126.

Adam, S.M. 2001. *Gather Round the Speakers: A History of the First Quarter Century of Somali Broadcasting: 1941 - 1966*, 2nd ed. London, HAAN Publishers.

Afrax, M.D. 1994. The Mirror of Culture: Somali Dissolution Seen Through Oral Expression, in A.I. Samatar (ed.) *The Somali Challenge: From Catastrophe to Renewal?* Boulder, Lynne Rienner Publishers.

Barber, K. 1987. Popular Arts in Africa. *African Studies Review*, 30 (3): 1-78.

Barber, K. 1997. Preliminary notes on audiences in Africa. *Africa* 67(3): 347-362.

Barber, K. 2007. *The Anthropology of Texts, Persons and Publics: Oral and written culture in Africa and beyond*. Cambridge, Cambridge University Press.

Berlant, L. 1998. Intimacy: A Special Issue. *Critical Inquiry*, 24: 281-288.

Bissell, W.C. 2005. Engaging Colonial Nostalgia. *Cultural Anthropology*, 20 (20): 215-248.

Ducaale, B.Y. 2002. *The Role of the Media in Political Reconstruction*. Hargeysa, Academy for Peace and Development.

Fabian, J. 1998. *Moments of Freedom: Anthropology and Popular Culture*. Charlottesville, University Press of Virginia.

Fair, L. 2009. Making Love in the Indian Ocean: Hindi Films, Zanzibari Audiences, and the Construction of Romance in the 1950s and 1960s, in J. Cole and L. Thomas (eds) *Love in Africa*. Chicago, University of Chicago Press: 58-82.

Hadeed, A. 2015 (Feb. 27). Who decides what's good for Somali music: Goth or Good? *Sahan Journal*. Available at: http://sahanjournal.com/abdi-good-bashir-goth/#.V77by0uGP8F

Hoehne, M. 2015. Somalia: The changing spectrum of Islam and counterterrorism. *Horn of Africa Bulletin (March-April 2015)*. Life and Peace Institute.

Johnson, J.W. 1996 [1974]. *"Heelloy": Modern Poetry and Songs of the Somali*. London, Haan Publishing.

Johnson, J.W. 2010. The Politics of Poetry in the Horn of Africa: A Case Study in Macro-level and Micro-level Tradition, in M. Hoehne and V. Luling (eds.) *Milk and Peace, Drought and War: Somali Culture, Society and Politics*. London, Hurst Publishing: 221-244.

Kapteijns, L. (with M. O. Ali) 1999. *Women's Voices in a Man's World: Women and the Pastoral Tradition in Northern Somali Orature, c. 1899-1980*. Portsmouth, N.H., Heinemann

Nooshin, L. (ed.) 2009. *Music and the Play of Power in the Middle East, North Africa and Central Asia*. Farnham, Ashgate Publishing Ltd.

Nyairo, W.J. 2005. *"Reading the References": (Inter)textuality in Contemporary Kenyan Popular Music.'* University of the Witwatersrand, unpublished PhD diss.

Ogude, J. 2012. The Invention of Traditional Music in the City: Exploring History and Meaning in Urban Music in Contemporary Kenya. *Research in African Literatures*, 43 (4): 147-1

Omojola, B. 2009. Identity and Nostalgia in Nigerian Music: A study of Victor Olaiya's Highlight. *Ethnomusicology*, 53(2): 249-276.

Samatar, S. 2010. Somalia: A Nation's Literary Death Tops Its Political Demise, in M. Hoehne and V Luling (eds.) *Milk and Peace, Drought and War: Somali Culture, Society and Politics*. London, Hurst Publishing: 205-220.

Warner, M. 2002. Publics and Counter Publics (abbreviated version). *Quarterly Journal of Speech*, 88 (4): 413-425.

Waterman, C.A. 1997. "Our Tradition is a Very Modern Tradition": Popular Music and the Construction of Pan-Yoruba Identity, in K. Barber (ed.) *Readings in African Popular Culture*. Bloomington, Indiana University Press: 48-53.

Woolner, C. 2016. *Hiddo Dhawr*: Singing Love in(to) Somaliland. *Camthropod: The Cambridge Anthropology Podcast*, Episode 5. Division of Social Anthropology, University of Cambridge. Available online at: http://www.socanth. cam. ac.uk/media/listen-and-view/camthropod# episode-5--hiddo-dhawr--singing-love-in-to--somaliland---by-christina-woolner

Dancing to the Marriage Beat(ing): The Gender Debate in a Gĩkũyũ Popular Music Discourse

Maina wa Mũtonya

The current discourse around the husband-bashing women in central Kenya, has elicited popular cultural productions that speak to the gender debate in the Gĩkũyũ community. This chapter looks at recent Gĩkũyũ popular songs that point to the intricate power play in marital relationships. While looking at the theme of love, or lack of it, as has been presented in the music, an art largely dominated by the men, the chapter argues that music has also led to a production of local idioms, stereotypes, and clichés in everyday life of the community. As Karin Barber argues, the functions of such in African popular culture could be treated as the point at which individual experience and shared concerns intersect. It is from this popular culture perspective that the chapter seeks to understand the current domestic strife.

Recent popular productions in the Gĩkũyũ community have made references to the debate in gender relations against the background largely informed by the contemporary social reality of domestic violence within the marriage institution. Although domestic violence is nothing new, highlighted cases of battered husbands, especially in central Kenya have elicited discourses that point to the power politic in a community that is largely believed to be patriarchal. While my chapter will not delve into the sociology of this domestic violence, I will strive to analyse the gender relations as represented in the popular music of the Gĩkũyũ. I will also look into how the music has led to a production of local idioms, stereotypes, and clichés in everyday life of the community.

By looking at the contemporary music of this community, this research is informed by the role of popular culture in the everyday life of a people. As Masolo (2000: 372) notes "[m]ost ... performers do not only entertain; they are also able, and frequently they aim, to raise the awareness level of their audience by arousing in them the imaginative and emotive experiences towards social re-engagement in the form of collective identity."

The performance by the musicians in the gender debate may draw mainly from everyday experiences, but as noted above, this imagined collective identity may arise from the need to rethink, or re-order the prevailing circumstances. As Stokes (1994: 97) aptly argues, "performance doesn't simply convey cultural messages already known, it reorganizes and manipulates everyday experiences of social reality, blurs, elides, ionizes and sometimes subverts common sense categories and markers."

The popular music investigated in this chapter does not just reflect emotions, but plays out "everyday moral dilemmas, posing questions and suggesting answers to our worries, about what we should do" (Street 1997: 9). Barber (1987: 4) notes that in times of rapid social change, the art forms "with their exceptional mobility (whether through technology such as the radio, record and cassette tape, or through physical transportation from place to place by travelling performing groups) will play a crucial role in formulating new ways of looking at things."

Kimani Gecau (1991: 84-5) acknowledges the contribution of popular music in commenting on and analysing the post-independence Kenyan situation and in the collective worldview and consciousness; "popular songs have been a chronicle of the changing social situations and the relations thereof." He adds that most of the songs have commented on the popular subject of the commoditization of all that was previously sacred, e.g., love and sex.

The fact that the music draws from the daily lived experiences of the community signifies that there is need to look at the current social and gender relations, especially within the discourse of husband-bashing in central Kenya.

The discourse around the husband-bashing women in Kenya, and especially in central province has elicited debates in which discussants are quick to make reference to Wangū wa Makeri, the last matriarch of the Gĩkũyũ community. Tensions in gender relations emanate from the myth of origin of the Gĩkũyũ people. Initially, the community was under a matriarchal system, but due to harsh rule of women, men revolted and replaced it with a patriarchal system. But according to Wanjohi, (1997: 28) there was a "compromise after strong opposition from women and the clan titles hitherto retain the female names."

Wanjiku Kabira, in her research on the oral literature has assessed the issues around the politics of gender and control among the Gĩkũyũ people. Important in her research on the representation of women in the oral narratives is how she captures the conflict in the community between the "need to respect the mother and the realization of the low status of women" (1994: 78). This is a paradox that is clearly evident in the contemporary popular music of the community where the mother is revered whereas the wife or girlfriend is rebuked in the songs.

Kabira has captured the portrayal of women in the proverbs of the society too and this is the trend that spreads through the everyday life of the Gĩkũyũ. The woman in the oral literature of the society has been portrayed as "unreliable, disobedient, irresponsible, disloyal, disagreeable, adulterous, cunning, senseless, easily cheated, forgetful, not dependable, evil, trickster, lazy, etc." (1994: 79-80).

As Kabira argues, oral narratives and proverbs in Gĩkũyũ oral literature perpetuate this negative image of women thus contributing to "social gender constructs that call for control of women in society and legitimise male dominance" (1994: 84). It is from this historical background that necessitates a need to comprehend the current discourse of domestic violence that seeks to contradict the oral history of the community.

While this gendered violence (women on men violence) is a phenomenon that cuts across different communities, there has been prominence that has been given to cases happening in Nyeri County, especially in the media. King'ori & Ojiambo (2016) recent research examines the representation of this gender-based violence from Nyeri in the print media. The research came to the conclusion that the narrative of the Nyeri woman as one that is "*angry, violent and dangerous*" (4) whereas the man has been framed as "an alcoholic and helpless victim" (1).

In his study on the causes and consequences of domestic violence against men in Nyeri County, Kubai (2014) came to the conclusion that alcoholism on the part of the man contributes greatly to the violence. Having been rendered irresponsible and useless by drunkenness, the woman in turn has taken over the roles of providing for the family, a role traditionally set for men. A newspaper article on January 2017[1] reported that Nyeri County had recorded an upsurge of domestic violence with most of the victims being men. Again, alcoholism has been quoted as a flashpoint in the domestic violence.

The above is not only peculiar in Nyeri County, but according to the Maendeleo ya Wanaume (A Global Men Empowerment Network),[2] Kenyan men have continually been suffering over the years, and have kept silent, due to the shame associated with the image of a hen-pecked husbands. Research in Nigeria (Adebayo 2014) and India (Kumar 2012) have revealed that this is a global issue, but for the specificities of this research, this comparative sociological study falls beyond the intended scope but also offers new research frontiers this field.

The representation in the Kenyan print media does not vary significantly with the discourse that emanates from the popular music of the Gĩkũyũ people, an art that is largely dominated by the men. Similarly, the oral literature of the Gĩkũyũ community delves into the relationship between men and women and the inherent conflict that was precipitated by the power politic in the traditional days, as has been seen above from Kabira's research.

In the contemporary music of the Gĩkũyũ, artists have continually engaged in the dialogue around the gender constructs. Since most musicians in the community are male, there is a perpetuation of the image of the woman, in the same way as in oral literature, but it is this portrayal that one would want to consider *vis-à-vis* the domestic strife that subverts this patriarchy narrative.

In the early years in the development of popular music of the Gĩkũyũ, the theme of love was the prevailing subject. The relationships presented in the songs followed the accepted girl-boy, wife-husband relationships and the attendant heartaches and disappointments. It was always the case of the overbearing male figure over the subservient woman, in line with the representations in oral narratives and proverbs.

Kamaru's *Ndari ya Mwarimũ* (The Teacher's Lover) talks of a male teacher who is in love with his student, the song itself a critique of the society and the failing moral standards in the years immediately after independence. But altogether, it could still be read as a narrative exploring the theme of love in a male-dominated society.

In his 1969 song, *Andu a Madaraka* (The Independence Generation) Kamaru offers a critique to men who had wasted themselves in alcohol and to the tricks of 'gold diggers, who dated any man for his money' (Mutonya, *et al.* 2010: 83). The woman in the song is represented in the subservient role of the prostitute whose existence is pegged on the social needs of the man, but also as the reason to the failing morality standards amongst the man.

This was a predominant theme in the popular music of the Gĩkũyũ in the 1970s and the 1980s. Alongside this critique of the man was the emergence of the sugar daddy figure in the song; the rich old man who would lure young girls into his den, because of his financial muscle. In fact in the literary field, there was a motif of the sugar daddy lovers [3] in the 70s. But the dialogue was enhanced by Sam Kahiga, the leader of the group The Cousins who released a song *Sugar Mami* which talked about the sugar-mummy phenomenon. In an interview in 1974 in a local newspaper, Kahiga added his voice about the song:

> "Well, it's about the activities of the sugar mummies, you know, these old well-off ladies who go for young men in pursuit of pleasure. So much criticism has been levelled at the sugar daddies that people tend to forget that sugar mummies also exist. I felt that it's high time they were exposed as many of them are corrupting our youth."

Commenting on the song, Nyairo (2016) argues that "its catchy rhythms and sweet harmonies aside, *Sugar Mami* provided bruising social commentary. It confronts a subject that Hollywood has since popularised as 'Cougar Town' — the phenomenon of old well-off women who seduce younger men." The song, done in both Kiswahili and English rightly captures the social imaginary and definitely the kinds of discourses that musicians drew from the everyday experience.

The theme of romance prevailed in the following years. Love songs like Albert Gacheru's *Marirũ*, Peter Kigia's *Gacheri* capturing a man's tears of true love or JB Maina's *Mũirĩtu wa Kabete*, an apologetic man begging for forgiveness for not fulfilling a date, were predominant themes.

It is in the late 1990s that the tone changed. Songs around separations and divorce from the male singers would project a change in the gender politics. For instance, one can sense desperation in Kigia's *Reke Tumanwo*, of a man who cannot stand the cruelty suffered in the marriage from the wife. The singer alludes to the Bible, comparing himself to the suffering of Lazarus in the hands of the rich person. There was a clear recourse to religion, a common leitmotif then, with male artists hiding behind Christianity in an attempt to propagate male dominance that was seemingly in decline.

In another song, *Arũme Twĩmenyerere (Beware Fellow Men)* Kigia captured the complaints, unfulfilled desires, broken promises, separation and loss in a love relationship between a man and a woman. But using Biblical references again, Kigia referred to a tilt in power relations in relationships as represented in Gĩkũyũ music; a turn of events that would be a harbinger of the dynamics of domestic violence today. The musician, representing the male gender tips fellow men on the intricacies of love relationships with *modern* girls:

Arũme rũrũ nĩ rwanyu	Men, this song is for you
Ndĩmũcanũre	Let me enlighten you
Matukũ tũrĩ	These days
Mũndũ ekwendo ehũge	one has to be very careful
To kĩrĩa watũngana nakĩo	It is not everything you come across
ũgaikia kanua	You 'consume'

Kigia is castigating the hypocrisy, difficulties and everyday conflicts in male-female relationships. He compares the women to the Biblical Delilah who conquered the robust Samson. On the other hand though, the song is a condemnation of the craze for material wealth in the wider polity. The musician rejects the girl's overtures to love him forcibly for he is aware that there is a catch:

Arũme twĩmenyerere	Men let's beware
Aa Delilah	of modern day Delilahs
Tondũ ihinda nĩ ikinyu	Because the time has come,
Delilah arũnde Samson	for Delilah to subdue Samson

Kigia's advice to his fellow men:

Rĩmwe nĩ merĩrithagia	Some will come with crocodile tears
Na tũmawara	and a bag of tricks
Menya nĩguo mũtego	Know that that is their trap,
Wao Madelila	these modern Delilahs
Ona arĩra iria	Even when she cries milk, instead of tears,
Reke agakuĩre mbere	just forget about her

Such lyrics are crudely anti-women and gender insensitive. However, there is a historical basis to the gender politics of the Gĩkũyũ community. It is also true that that most of these musicians rely a lot on the past for lyrical inspiration. The Gĩkũyũ community traditionally relegated the women *"to the place of a being lesser than men"* (Muhoro 1997: 107). In the 1920s, *Mũthĩrĩgũ* was a dance to protest against colonial attitude towards female circumcision: "women who failed to be circumcised were given pejorative names which signified their worthlessness" (Muhoro 1997: 108). Advocacy against female genital mutilation in modern days is a clear sign that the practice can be seen to be violating women's rights. Far from being a harsh tradition, it also lowers the status of women.

However, the same traditional music treated women differently on separate circumstances. Men would sing praises of their mothers but at the same time brag as to how "they could not take advice from women who weren't wise enough to teach them some aspects of social life" (Kabira & Mutahi 1988: 21).

This continuous dialogue and interplay in gender and power relations is well manifested in the day-to-day lives and musicians capture this reality aptly. Jane Nyambura, popularly known as Queen Jane in musical circles is well remembered for her stinging lyrics against men. Her song, *Arũme Majini* (Men are Ghosts), she said, was inspired by the increasing number of rape and defilement cases in Kenya 'Everybody knows that men are turning on young girls and abusing them, that is why I composed this song to criticize them', she argues (Muganda 2004).

In most of her songs, she has directly attacked patriarchal hegemony. Some men fans have felt that she has been too harsh in her condemnation of men. But far from the gender debate, her music has been well known for carrying social messages. She not only attacks men, but also wayward women, like the girls who are out to cause mayhem to the family institution.

As Queen Jane castigates the behaviour of men in relationships, especially that of sugar daddies, as in her song *Nĩndarega Kũhikĩra Guka* (I refuse to be married to an old man), male Gĩkũyũ musicians seemed to be offering responses. However, as mentioned above, there was a dialogue that had already been started by Sam Kahiga in the 1970s, a debate that found itself again in the social imaginary of the musicians and their audience in the 1990s, going into the new millennium.

Sam Muraya's famous *Mama Kiwinya* scathingly attacks older women (better known as sugar mummies) who find comfort in young boys as their lovers. Laments a young man in the song:

Wathũkirie mũtwe na kũheaga mbeca	you spoilt me with money
Ndakwĩra ngone aciari akwa ndũngĩtĩkĩra	you never let me visit my parents
Kaĩ wahikirie na ndũgĩtware rũracio	if you married me, pay the dowry
Mama Kiwinya, reke njeracere	Mother of Kiwinya, let me move on
Mĩaka yaku nĩyarega tũikaranie	the relationship can't work because of our age difference.

The same is evident in Joseph Kariuki's *Nyina wa Turera*, where he says that it's wrong for a woman of 40 years to go out with a young boy of 20. The consistent dialogue between musicians across the gender divide encapsulates the day-to-day realities in the society. For Queen Jane, she is unapologetic about her hard-line stance against men; 'the fact that men are among my greatest fans simply means that I am telling the truth' (Muganda 2004).

But much as the above appears as complaints of the man, it also heralds the emergence of the powerful, independent woman in the popular music of the Gĩkũyũ, at a time when the power politic seems to be in favour of the woman. Whereas previous songs would portray the woman in demeaning and negative terms, recent productions have pointed towards a *coup d'état*, where the Gĩkũyũ woman is seen to have regained the control that was last exemplified in Wangũ wa Makeri, the last matriarch of the society.

This power is represented in the stereotype of a Nyeri woman, the all-powerful and conquering female figure. John Ndemethiu's song *Arũme Kwĩna Mbu* (An alarm for men) captures the anxiety of the men in the intricate power/marital relations. This song emanated from the debate that eventually led to the publishing of the Matrimonial Property Act of 2013 that reconsidered the rights and responsibilities in relation to matrimonial property. The song is a literal warning to men of a lurking danger in the battle for gender equity. The song prophesies doom to masculinity especially in the clause that states that "a married woman has the same rights as a married man to acquire, administer, hold, control, use and dispose of property…" The singer seems to question the idea of regulation of matrimonial property on the termination of marriage as envisaged in the current constitutional dispensation.

The stereotype of the Nyeri women is conflated in the metaphor that defines the Gĩkũyũ woman in the popular cultural discourse, social media and other media. In fact, the media has evolved words that have found currency in the everyday parlance of Kenyans. Coinages like *Nyerification*, the "phenomenon where Nyeri women attack assault their male partners by mutilating their genitals" (King'ori & Ojiambo 2016: 7) emphasise this stereotype of the Gĩkũyũ woman but an image that is amplified in the popular music of the community.

In other songs, for example, *Momo*, by Murimi wa Kahalf, the image of the woman is presented in grotesque imagery. Murimi's *Momo* is a man's lament from an overbearing woman, literally (in her physical attributes) and figuratively. The male protagonist in the song complains of "enslavement" to his gigantic spouse whose demands exceed the fuel consumption of an eighteen-wheeler truck:

Ĩno *nĩ momo x2*	This woman is like a Momo[4] truck
Ndamĩikia cabi	Which, when I turn on the ignition key
No kinya ĩkunde *magana*	it's a real fuel guzzler
Yanyua yaigania	and soon after,
Ĩraramaga *ta ngoma anyuĩte kairacĩ*	it roars into life like a wild devil.

The images attributed to the woman not only depict the helplessness of the man, but also point to physical dominance of the woman in the household. This is made all too certain in the video of the same track. Whereas the marital union is supposed to bring bliss, the male protagonist feels out of place in the marriage that only but portends doom. Words like *ngombo* (slave) and *kĩoho* (jail term) for the man describing the travails of the marriage indicate that the male partner is under siege with the attendant emasculation of his ego. The man expresses his disgust at not being able to meet the demands and expectations of the wife, a sense of defeat in a largely patriarchal society. The song ties-in perfectly with the current discourse around the husband-bashing women in Nyeri which has elicited debates, memes and stereotypes in the everyday life of Kenyans.

A different song by Franco wa Subukia's *Mwendwa OCS* (My Police Officer Lover), is a more candid portrayal of the domestic violence experienced these days. His girlfriend is a high ranking police officer, who cocks the gun, ready to shoot, anytime he threatens to leave. The same musician produced a song, *Bibi No. 2* (My second wife) in which he is trying to explain to his first wife the reasons he went for a second wife. The protagonist in the song projects a subdued figure in that he feels remorse for his very actions, but that have been precipitated by an attack of his masculinity from the first wife.

The song, *Kamweretho* by Epha Maina, criticises the traditional *Kamweretho* ceremony in which women return to their parents to shower them with gifts as appreciation of their role in bringing them up. In some circles, *Kamweretho* has been understood as a ceremony for unmarried women to pay bride price for themselves! Musician Epha Maina captures this reality in his song *Kamweretho*, where he finds fault in these all-women gatherings, where the men are conveniently left out.

The issues emanating from these songs resonate with the real experiences of men, in and around Kenya. To paraphrase Barber (1987: 4), it is under conditions of pervasive political, social and economic change that music continues to play a crucial role as a medium of symbolic transaction and a means of forging and defending identities in the community

The problems of the male figure in Kenya, especially in Central Province, an area inhabited by the Gĩkũyũ people has precipitated a legal reaction, where Kenyan men have coalesced together to form an organisation, *Maendeleo ya Wanaume* (A Global Men Empowerment Network) whose main agenda is to address the apparent continuous erosion of masculinity. The group argues that in the fight for gender equity, the counter-hegemony by women has developed structures that disadvantage the boy-child and the men in general.

The lyrics in the music, as well as the formation of this group is a clear pointer that there is an issue that requires further research. Though this chapter shies away from the sociological analysis, it is imperative that a study that is widely interdisciplinary would yield interesting perspectives as relates to the gender dialogue among the Gĩkũyũ; from a historical, cultural, economic, political, literary and popular culture viewpoint.

The textual analysis of the lyrics, placing them within a wider general context of gender discourse amongst the Gĩkũyũ also leads this research into a discussion around the stereotypes and idioms that this theme elicits. While this could be a serious issue, the gender discourse provides a platform in which the experiences, from both real social situations and from the popular music, form a significant part of the repertoire of the everyday life of the Gĩkũyũ people.

The idioms, stereotypes and metaphors emanating from the gender discourse in the Gĩkũyũ music have formed a background which informs the everyday interactions and parlance. It is also that the words that musicians appropriate are products of the everyday discourse but one that also speaks of the way men and women relate in the ever-changing power relations.

Homi Bhabha (1983: 37) argues that 'the stereotype is a form of knowledge and identification that vacillates between what is always in place, already known and something that must be anxiously repeated.

The Gĩkũyũ people have always harped on the different stereotypes of women from Mũrang'a, Kiambu and Nyeri in their narratives; praising the subservient Mũrang'a woman at the expense of her abrasive counterpart from Nyeri. The depiction of the woman in the derisive terms from the male musicians is in itself self-denigrating to the male hegemony, which leads to the exposing of insecurities in the contemporary man.

As stated in the research by King'ori & Ojiambo (2016: 11) above, the term *Nyerification* has been appropriated in levels similar to the Bobbit[5] example from the USA. This serves but to perpetuate the stereotype of the Nyeri woman, and by extension the Gĩkũyũ woman.

Research in Mukurweini district by Kubai, mentioned above underlines the fears of the loss of masculinity.

These fears are also captured in the prevalent motif of the word *"sponsor"* in everyday parlance of the Kenyans, but also a predominant theme in Gĩkũyũ music. The "sponsor" is used in reference to the rich, older man whom young girls are interested in, mostly because they offer a certain form of financial security, above everything else. While the male artist castigates the "sponsor" phenomenon, women artists in the community are embracing this culture, unapologetically.

The sugar daddy motif in the 60s and 70s has returned in recent times, though it has been sanitised by euphemistically regarding this elderly man figure in the relationship as a *sponsor*. In fact, the sponsor, in the modern day idiom doesn't not necessarily refer to an older man, but it is a progression of the *mpango wa kando* (lover) phenomenon, where both men and women are engaged in affairs outside their marriages; but affairs that bring about the financial perspective.

Muthoni wa Wainaina, aka Mzima Mzima's song *Ndĩretha Sponsor* (I am looking for a sponsor) is one of the songs that resonates vividly, not just with the local idiom of sponsor, but also signals a break where female artists talk about the experiences of the woman. This is unlike before, where it is the male artist who initiates and engages in the dialogue on gender relations, of course with the sole exception of Queen Jane.

Niĩ ndĩrenda sponsor	I am looking for a sponsor
Njetherai sponsor	help me get a sponsor
Angĩkorwo wee wĩ sponsor	if you are a sponsor
Ndũgĩcome- come	please make haste to contact me

This new young female artist goes contrary to Queen Jane, whose song we quoted earlier, had strong sentiments against a marriage to an older man, whom she referred to as grandfather. The song *Ndĩrenda Sponsor* by Muthoni neither presents the woman as subservient to the demands of men, nor the powerful female figure as in the songs *Momo* and *Mwendwa OCS* above.

In an interview, Muthoni argues that *macharlie ma thikũ tũrĩ* (contemporary young men) have become specialists in breaking young girls' hearts and have shown zero commitment, especially in the case of a pregnancy to the fiancée. This song lists the advantages of having an older male lover (sponsor) key among them being that younger men are afraid of commitments and are most likely to flee from responsibilities that come with relationships.

The song adds that the '*sponsor ndarĩ hĩndĩ akaumĩria* (the sponsor will never desert you, if he impregnates you) and that the future of a child born with a *sponsor* is always assured. A sponsor, in her song, represents a sense of maturity and financial security. The song could also be read as a bold statement on the liberation of the woman from male dominance, especially as represented in the Gĩkũyũ popular music.

The contemporary woman, as in the song, is one that can make choices unlike the sugar mummy who has been a subject of ridicule and voiceless as seen in the songs above. These songs vilifying the sugar mummy are mainly from the male musicians. However, like the example of Muthoni above, the contemporary woman speaks of herself and she can easily defend her choices of what kind of a man she would want to go out with. This is the message she puts across in her other song *Mūbea* (the priest), where she is breaking tradition and infusing her songs with themes that have never been tackled before, especially by female artists.

This comes across differently from the older woman castigated in earlier songs like *Mama Kiwinya*, mentioned above and the image of the sugar mummy that dominated the soundscape of Gĩkũyũ music in the 1980s, by male artists. The music of Muthoni demands expansive research as well as other young emerging female Gĩkũyũ musicians.

Other idioms and clichés like *Momo, Thiĩ Ũkĩũmaga* and *Kĩhiki Undertsanding* derived from songs by male artists depict women in derisive terms but it is also true that they point to the changing trends in gender and power politics in relationships in the songs. *Kĩhiki Understanding* follows in the same mode as the songs like *Momo* and others, where it is a man's lament in an uncomfortable relationship. He wants to run away from his current predicament and look for a subservient, obedient and understanding woman. It is a song that could be seen as a response from the increasingly independent woman, like Muthoni's song above that is posing a threat to the masculinity.

Even in the search of this understanding spouse, the choice of words itself gravitates towards portraying the image of the woman in negative terms. The neutral word for a bride would be *Mũhiki*. But when this noun is placed in class four (nouns that start with 'Kĩ' prefix) of the Gĩkũyũ language, which presents nouns of lifeless objects or pitiable humans held in disrespect, "scorn or hatred" (Kariuki: 2017), *Kĩhiki* then would assume a denigrating term to the woman.

Other idioms and clichés in the Gĩkũyũ populace emanate from songs, but whose lyrics are deeply embedded in this debate or discourse of gender in everyday life. The song *Thiĩ ũkĩũmaga* and the idiom arising from it presents the diseased body of the woman, but again points to the feeling of emasculation of the man occasioned by the emergence of the powerful, independent woman. The song addresses promiscuity and the HIV scourge, but the male protagonist presents a sense of helplessness in confronting a female cousin whose choices in life go contrary to expectations in the society.

Conclusion

The gender dialogue and the debate therein as gleaned from the lyrics in the songs as well as the resultant stereotypes and local idioms point to a concern in the society, but one that whose underlying theme is that of challenges and changes in both marital and love relationships, based on how men and women relate. The chapter has tried to understand the domestic violence phenomenon from the repertoire that the songs present. The metaphors and messages presented in recent music of the Gĩkũyũ have been analysed in an effort to understand this gender debate. The chapter underscores the relevance in the female musician's attempt to render her voice in this dialogue as we have seen from the examples discussed. It is against this background that power relations in the marriage institution as well as the husband bashing can be understood through music. The research does not in any way ignore the fact that gender-based violence is a reality in Kenya and that women continue to bear the brunt of this violence. It is only for the purview and specificities of the research that the chapter has taken this route. A lot remains to be done especially in relation to marital challenges as expressed in the musical discourse of the Gĩkũyũ people. In the meantime, the marriage beating goes on.

Endnotes

1. Komu, Nicholas (2017) Alarm as wave of love related tragedies hit Nyeri couples. Daily Nation January 5th 2017

2. The organization is largely a reaction to the 1995 Women Beijing Declaration, but it also borrows heavily from the Maendeleo ya Wanawake organization, that was formed during the regime of Arap Moi, to front for the interests of women. At its inception, the female movement was largely political and existed at the whims of the then ruling party, KANU. It is only after the fall of KANU that the women's organization has concentrated on topical issues affecting women, and moved towards being apolitical.

3. One of the popular novels, published in 1975 was Rosemary Owino's *Sugar Daddy Lover* that talked about the seduction of a young school girl by a wealthy businessman from Nairobi.

4. *Momo* is in reference to the huge eighteen-wheeler trucks that you will find around Mlolongo Weigh Bridge along the Mombasa-Nairobi highway according to the musician, in an interview. But in this context, it is a euphemism for both an overweight as well as an abusive woman. The opposite of a *Momo*, according to the musician, is the smaller Vitz Toyota model, a compact car, not known for its fuel consumption and very popular in Kenya. Of course, this is made in reference to smaller women, as contrasted to his *Momo* wife.

5. This derives from a 1993 case where a woman (Lorena Bobbit) chopped off the penis of her husband (John Wayne Bobbit) whom she accused of being abusive but a story whose language "frames the woman as the aggressor and the man as a victim" (King'ori and Ojiambo 2016:11)

Bibliography

Adebayo, A.A. 2014. 'Domestic Violence against Men: Balancing the Gender Issues in Nigeria', *American Journal of Sociological Research* 4(1): 14-19.

Barber, K. 1997. 'Preliminary Notes on Audiences in Africa', in *Africa 67 (3)*.

Barber, K.1987. 'Popular Arts in Africa', *African Studies Review 30(3)*.

Bhabha, H. 1983. 'The Other Question' in *Screen*, 24:6.

Gecau, K. 1991. 'Culture and the Tasks of Development in Africa: Lessons from the Kenyan Experience' in Preben Kaarsholm's (ed) *Cultural Struggle an Development in Southern Africa*. Harare: Baobab.

Kabira, W.M. 1994. 'Gender and the Politics of Control: An Overview of Images of Women in Gĩkũyũ Oral Narratives' in Bukenya, Kabira and Okombo (eds) *Understanding Oral Literature*. Nairobi, Nairobi University Press: 77-92.

Kabira, W.M. & Karega wa Mutahi. 1988. *Gĩkũyũ Oral Literature*. Nairobi: East African Educational Publishers.

Kariuki, E. 2017. *Gĩkũyũ Language online: vocabulary and conversation practice* http://hubpages.com/education/The-Gĩkũyũ-Language (Retrieved January 25th 2017).

Mutonya, M.; M. Wanjohi; S. Kiiru & J. Kariuki. 2010. *Retracing Kikuyu Popular Music*. Ketebul Music, Nairobi Kenya.

King'ori, M. & Ukaiko, B.O. 2016 "Newspaper Framing of Gender-based (Domestic) Violence of women on men from Nyeri County, Kenya" in *Africa Multidisciplinary Journal of Research* 1 (1) pp 4-25.

Komu, N. 2017. 'Alarm As Wave of Love Related Tragedies Hit Nyeri Couples'. *Daily Nation* January 5th.

Kumar, A. 2012. "Domestic Violence against Men in India: A Perspective". *Journal of Human Behavior in the Social Environment* 22 (3): 290–296.

Masolo, D.A. 2000 'Presencing the Past and Remembering the Present: Social Features of Popular Music in Kenya', in Ronald Radano and Philip Bohlman (Ed) *Music and Racial Imagination.* Chicago: University of Chicago Press.

Matrimonial Property Act of 2013.

Muganda, Clay. 2004. ́Queen who's Worthy of the Title ́, in the *Daily Nation,* 12th November.

Muhoro, M. 1997. 'The Song-Narrative Construction of Oral History through the Gĩkũyũ Muthirigu and Mwomboko' in *Fabula: Journal of Folk-Tale Studies.* 38(3 &4).

Nyairo, J. 2013. Kahiga's long wait for recognition *Saturday Nation* July 27.

Mwangi, J. 1974. Sweet Success for the Cousins. *Daily Nation* July 27.

Stokes, M. 1994. *Ethnicity, Identity and Music: The Musical Construction of Place*. Oxford: Berg.

Street, J. 1997. *Politics and Popular Culture*. Cambridge: Polity Press.

Wanjohi, G.J. 1997. *The Wisdom and Philosophy of African Proverbs: The Gĩkũyũ World-View.* Nairobi: Paulines Publications Africa.

Discography

(The songs quoted in the chapter were sourced online)

Joseph Kamaru – *Ndari ya Mwarimu* https://ketebul.bandcamp.com/track/ndari-ya-mwarimu (Retrieved October 6th 2016)

Albert Gacheru – *Mariru* https://www.youtube.com/watch?v=JYuvS3E4zao (Retrieved January 4th 2017)

Peter Kigia – *Gacheri* https://www.youtube.com/watch?v=FgDbjUa8jd8 (Retrieved January 4th 2017)

JB Maina - *Mũirĩtu wa Kabete* https://www.youtube.com/watch?v=dj4Ik8cuUPs&spfreload=10 (Retrieved January 4th 2017)

Peter Kigia - *Reke Tumanwo* https://www.youtube.com/watch?v=GcjXYgf7An4 (Retrieved October 4th 2016)

Queen Jane - *Guka Nindarega* https://www.youtube.com/watch?v=bGQHQZQbrlc (Retrieved October 4th 2016)

Sam Muraya - *Mama Kiwinya* https://www.youtube.com/watch?v=0Ejs5XqjV3s (Retrieved October 6th 2016)

John de Matthew - *Arũme kwĩna mbu* https://www.youtube.com/watch?v=63bXm68h6fI (Retrieved September 28th 2016)

Joseph Kariuki - *Nyina wa Turera* https://www.youtube.com/watch?v=cCTaLcaEnXs(Retrieved October 2nd 2016)

Murimi wa Kahalf- *Momo* https://www.youtube.com/watch?v=_udyS00wGeg (Retrieved September 13th 2016)

Franco wa Subukia - *Wendo wa OCS* https://www.youtube.com/watch?v=wjXLVpJpmwc (Retrieved October 4th 2016)

Franco wa Subukia - *Bibi No. 2* https://www.youtube.com/watch?v=ERgCS_VL_us&spfreload=10 (Retrieved October 6th 2016)

Epha Maina – *Kamweretho* https://www.youtube.com/watch?v=XEE8a-Fj76E (Retrieved October 1st 2016)

Mzima Mzima (Muthoni wa Wainaina) – *Ndirenda Sponsor* https://www.youtube.com/watch?v=Dz24usZVFeo (Retrieved October 6th 2016)

Interview on Utugi TV. The 411 show: Mzima Mzima the sports journalist, musician and deejay https://www.youtube.com/watch?v=_RP1fCZPeyQ&t=1427s&spfreload=10 (Retrieved January 7th 2017)

Jose Gatutura - *Thii Ukiumaga* https://www.youtube.com/watch?v=hyZZyIGEexk (Retrieved January 7th 2017)

Sam Wakiambo - *Kihiki Understanding* https://www.youtube.com/watch?v=isNPcs4mP5Q (Retrieved January 7th 2017)

Joseph Kamaru – *Andu a Madaraka* https://ketebul.bandcamp.com/track/andu-a-madaraka-2 (Retrieved January 7th 2017)

Sam Kahiga – *Sugar Mami* - https://www.youtube.com/watch?v=NzJOGn1Mplc (Retrieved January 26th 2017)

Engendering Music: Changing Trends of Music Performance and Dance in Luo Nyanza

Gordon Onyango Omenya

Just like politics, music also provides major sites where gender and sexuality are culturally negotiated, constructed and contested. This cultural construction of gender thus informs and redefines our conceptions of gender. While the term "gender" can indicate a shift away from identity politics and positions, it more frequently represents an attempt at a more inclusive or nuanced set of identities. McClary (2000) describes music as essentially "a gendered discourse" and the history of musical form as "a heavily gendered legacy", and considers that "classical music—no less than pop—is bound up with issues of gender". In such a cross-contextual field, musical instruments continue to be a site through which gender is affirmed and performed with many individuals drawn to particular instruments on the basis of their affordances in terms of gender and sexuality (Halstead and Rolvsjord 2015). This chapter explores, the changes that have characterized music performance and dance in Luo music and brings forth the engendered changes within a social space that was dominated by men. The chapter argues that, with modernity, urbanization and globalization, Luo music as a popular culture, has transformed and has provided an avenue for both men and women to express themselves and to complement each other in the performance of Luo music.

Keywords: Music, engender, instruments, dance and performance, Luo

Introduction

Halstead and Rolvsjord (2015), argue that issues of gender music and sexual identity have become routinely associated with the instrument through personal and cultural narratives, discourse, instrument design and the performative practices of playing. A myriad of studies, for example, Koskoff (1987); Bowers & Tick (1987); Marcia (1990); Maus (2011) and Whiteley (2000) among many others have advanced this approach by exploring musical roles of women using both ethnographic and historical analysis. Although these studies have explored gender issues in music, especially in the composition of music, they have failed to address the issue of gender dynamics and transformation trends in performance and dance.

However, my research is in tandem with Bjorck's (2011) postulation that:

> [T]he significance of gender in music performance and dance is evident in a number of areas: for the construction of popular music history; the perceived masculine or feminine nature of particular genres/styles; audiences, fandom, and record-collecting; occupation of various roles within the music industry; youth subcultures; and gender stereotyping in song lyrics and music videos (Bjorck's 2011: 84)

This buttresses McClary's (2000) argument of music as essentially "a gendered discourse". It is this gendered contestation and analysis that informs the exploration of the gender dynamics and changing trends in dance and performance of Luo music in Kenya's Nyanza province.

The musical forms have undergone a lot of transformation in the face of powerful influences from the West enhanced by the new wave of urbanization and globalization. The traditional context of performance, institutional roles, and utilitarian objectives are some of the ideas and concepts that inform traditional genres. These are increasingly being eroded by modern and changing trends in the society.

Due to these changes, as Ojaide (2001: 71) argues, "new" idioms and forms of music have evolved. The new musical forms have elements and characteristics that casually resemble the music tradition of the past, but defy the traditional context of performance thereby transforming the traditional music from its traditionalism into modernity. Some traditional music types have, therefore, lost their institutional roles and contextual implications, thus changing their original musicological meaning. Many have compromised their traditional usage hence compromising the context specified and utilitarian foundation of traditional music in the society.

The Luo are among the many Kenyan communities that have been adversely affected by the new developments. Traditionally, the performances of music and dance by the Luo were restricted to specific occasions, events or ceremonies. The music was performed to culturally homogeneous audiences. Performances were also gender specific and also prescribed in terms of age (Ongati 2005). On some occasions, everyone would participate but in other instances, participation was restricted to particular social groups. The context of performance therefore, dictated the content, venue and participants of a particular musical genre in the Luo traditional society. However, we learn that these changes would later allow for the transformation or flexibility of social role. Butler's theory of performative gender envisions social existence in itself as a staging of the self. To claim space on the popular music scene entails being seen and being heard in the strongest sense of the phrase (Bjorck 2011).

For Kirsten (2001: 3), traditional musical performances in many contexts could be seen as microcosms or models for the social structure of the community. Music in its performance also provides new perspectives and ways to study culture and in particular, gender within a cultural context. It is evidently seen, therefore, that changes in these performances offer a window into changing gender relations and identities in both the traditional and contemporary plural space of Luo Nyanza. This is because, we find women sometimes playing roles that were specifically meant for men while performing Luo music. Koskoff (1987) in her research on women and music writes,

> ...what is needed now is a deeper analysis of the relationship between a society's gender structure, what ideologies surround gender, the nature of inter-gender relations, and how all these affect music behavior. Further, we must invert this question and ask how music behavior itself reflects and symbolizes gender behavior (Koskoff 1987: 4).

He further notes that we must not only look at gender roles in society and how they affect musical performances, but also how musical performances reflect society's gender roles. Moisala (1999) on the other hand states that:

> "As we know, music is a specific part of expressive culture. Music marks time, place and space differently than any other spheres of culture. Therefore, music provides a unique site for the performances and negotiation of gender. It allows, or may even require, different gender roles than do other aspects of culture. Music is also a space where we can allow the possibility that gender can be seen in new ways" (Moisala 1999: 3).

We see in Moisala's statement that music is a specific part of expressive culture. If women play important roles in music, it allows them to take on expressive roles within the community. Similarly if art, according to Chernoff (1979: 32) reflects the social realities of its context, then through the study of Luo art of music, one can gain insight into the social realities of the community. Snipe (1998: 25) asserts that, Music, song, dance, and masks tell a story that relates to the daily lives and socio- political realities of the community, substantiating the concept that art is not superfluous in Africa. It is out of this knowledge that this chapter explores the changing trends of gender participation in Luo music brought about by either urbanization or westernization. It examines the evolution and development of Luo music while at the same time it looks at how gender is depicted in this kind of music. Basically, it gives insight into the gender roles during performance, the gendering of the musical instruments, as well as how age, sex, and culture have affected gender participation in Luo Music. Generally, profiles of popular Luo Music show clear patterns of age and gender based genre preferences. Teenagers, young people and even old men and women are a major audience for and consumer of this music.

Engendering Musical Space and Instruments in Luo Music

Among the Luo culture, there was gender division of labour in music performance and dance. Even though there is no embracing term for music, there are many different types of music in Luo society and the performance of any given type of music is very often closely bond up with some specific occasions in the society (Omondi 1980). Musical groups were also formed voluntarily with the primary purpose of music performance and dancing, by invitation at ceremonial occasions. A number of such groups exist. For example, there are groups of girls called *Jobodi* who sing and dance to the accompaniment hand claps and a round metal bar *onge'ngo,* which is beaten on a box drum *sanduk*. There are also groups of men dancers, *jomaranda* and women dancers, *josalu* who specialize in circular dances and wear brightly coloured uniforms. The references to men and women here construct these groups as unitary and with essential voice qualities, obscuring the fact that individual voices vary within these two groups as well as between the groups (Bjorck 2011). There were other performing groups specific to men only called *Ramogi* who paint various parts of their bodies in different colours and wear traditional ceremonial dresses of ostrich feathers, hippo teeth, skins of wild animals such as leopards, while they sing and execute certain acrobatic dances for their spectacular appeal (Omondi 1980: 21).

Ramogi dance performance is more masculine and is mostly done by men. The kind of regalia worn by *Ramogi* dancers during performance also demonstrates some form of brevity and physically fitness associated with masculinity, since this dance goes with acrobatic movements and gestures. The regalia worn while performing this dance and song also require killing of a leopard and a hippo, all fierce and dangerous animals in order to get their skin and teeth respectively for aesthetic purposes. On the other hand, *Jobodi* singers and dancers who are actually females do not need such regalia. Their performance only requires hand clapping and the use of metal bars *Onge'ngo* and skirts made of sisal fibre, locally known as *owallo,* which are easily available. In the words of Esi Sutherland-Addy (2006: 7), we see the feminine aesthetic of clapping being exemplified and how spaces are claimed within the Luo music soundscapes.

More so, there are some gender disparities and exclusion in the performance of Luo Music, in the sense that the basic instruments in Luo music have been gendered in favour of men for example, the men have dominated the playing of *Orutu* and *Thum/ Nyatiti*. According to Ndeda (2005: 51) this exclusion of women is oppression and marginalization which may be structural (repressive cultural customs) or more personalized. It can be expressed externally and internalized by the oppressed. Externalised oppression, according to Ndeda (2005) is manifested through androcentrism, exclusion and subjection. It is important to note that although the men dominated over the playing of these instruments, their songs basically revolved around praising women. They sometimes also employed the use of female voices to express their love for the woman that a particular male musician was singing about. This characteristic thus shows some ambivalence and borrowing of traits which makes these particular male singers to operate within a space which Bhabha (1994) calls an indeterminate or hybrid zone of neither being male or female.

By restricting women from playing Luo music instruments such as *Nyatiti* and *Orutu*, it means that men control the performance. When they are not there to perform, women cannot enjoy dancing leave alone leading in these performances. The third form of oppression is by subjection, which also has cultural forms. Clearly then, oppression has very concrete and damaging forms. These forms of oppression have one thing in common: Men in various categories of life impose them. Hence, all forms of oppression and marginalization can be encompassed under the rubric of patriarchy, literally the rule of fathers or men for the benefit of men (Ndeda 2005: 52). Bringing this discourse to the local scene, the mind of women in the Luo music had been colonized by the Luo culture to believe that only men were allowed to play *Nyatiti* and *Orutu*, to the extent that it was a taboo for a woman to play these instruments. In fact, it was unheard of. The question then is: why this exclusion of women from playing these instruments? I will concur with (Ndeda 2005), that the major reason for this is patriarchy. Although, the precise origins of patriarchy may be difficult to establish, its presence is notable in the persistent male domination current in all spheres of life. While vocalists and instrumentalists are both on display, they engender qualitatively different delineations, with consequences for perceived ability and authenticity. A female vocalist's use of her own body as a source for sound making is in line with patriarchal definitions of femininity as in tune with nature, while a woman instrumentalist, in contrast, assumes the position of controlling an object, a technological position associated with masculinity (Clawson 1993; Green 1997; Lorentzen 2009).

However, furthering the above discourse, I believe that the cultural forms of the Luo people have taken a great deal on the participation of women in Luo music through restriction in handling and playing of certain instruments. For instance, central to the performance of the *Nyatiti* is the man who has to compose a song and perform on the *Nyatiti*. Being a *jathum* was a specialized role in Luo society and the person who may or may not become one was first and foremost determined by sex. Not only were women barred from playing it but they were also forbidden to handle it particularly during their menstrual periods. The belief in women's inherent sexuality, often expressed in terms of menstruation taboos, may, according to Koskoff (1987:7), lead to a separation between women's and men's expressive domains and in some societies to restrictions imposed on certain women's musical activity.

There were only two traditional occasions when a woman could handle a *Nyatiti/thum*. First, if a young girl wished to be married to a *jathum*, she may demonstrate her desire by touching his *thum/Nyatiti* in public. Secondly, if a *jathum* dies, his widow may carry his instrument when lamenting his death. The society believed that if a woman handles a *thum/Nyatiti* at any other time, she became barren while the *thum* she had touched would in turn 'protest' by refusing to sound properly, a state known as *dinruok* (Koskoff 1987; Omondi 1980: 150). This demonstrates that in the past, women's' role in music was closely linked with birth, initiation, marriage and work activities. The first event of birth was a function of womanhood.

Even though performing on the *thum*, which literally translates as *go thum* was men's occupation in the society, not any man could take it up. There were categories of men such as the twin brothers each of whom was barred from being *jothum* (player of *thum/nyatiti*). Then there were other traditional restrictions and beliefs connected with the determination of who may become a *jathum* that further delimited which males could become *jothum*. Could these men then be regarded as 'women'? It therefore points to the fact that concepts as hybridity, which in postcolonial studies we have come to see, have always been intrinsic to African identity formation. In the African context, multiple and hybrid identities are part of the very fabric of the plural society.

Popular culture, dance and gender in Luo Music performance

The Luo, like other African communities are renowned for their love for music. As Osadebey (1949) points out, we sing when we fight; we sing when we work, we sing when we make love, we sing when we hate, we sing when a child is born, we sing when death takes toll. Among the Luo community, this is reflected in the numerous songs, dances and musical instruments that are found in the community. The Luo music contains much teaching about norms and conventions of the community (Odaga 2008). Both socio-cultural events and ceremonies among the Luo are musically oriented. For example, beer parties, funerals, worship, storytelling and healing ceremonies are in most cases accompanied by songs and dances. The art of performance of music was engendered, hereditary and started from childhood (Omondi 1980: 156). It also informed the gender relations and division of labour which mostly characterized Luo musical activities. The process of music making and performance was thus seen to be more patriarchal than matriarchal. This is because the art could only be inherited by a man. That is, from a grandfather, father, maternal or paternal uncle, or any other relative. This inheritance has thus informed the kind of domination that men had in the Luo traditional music arena and the role that they played.

Although it can be argued that Luo women were either marginalized or dominated as far as Luo music is concerned, this domination and marginalization did not deter them from expressing themselves in the society. Digolo (2003) argues that indigenous music forms like *Dodo* and *thum/nyatiti* songs served twofold communicative functions. While they continued as transmitters of indigenous cultural values and beliefs, they were also viewed as a means of propagating essential innovative messages. Among the Luo community, *dodo* songs and dances were exclusively performed by females. Previously *dodo* was a male genre, however, since late 1950s it has been adopted by Luo women as an orature. Henceforth, the *Dodo* has intersected with daily social expression and has provided a window to how Luo women view themselves and their society. During *dodo* dance a suspension rattle, which is called *peke* a relatively recent instrument which is made of bottle tops strung on a rigid metal rod and shaken by hand is used to accompany the women singers (jododo*)* at beer parties. Interestingly too, women performing the *dodo* songs do praise men mostly in their songs. In most recent times, *dodo* songs have been used by women during their merry go round sessions as they raise money and deliberate on issues affecting them.

Luo music goes hand in hand with dancing. It is therefore important to look at the participation of men and women during the *thum/nyatiti* performance. The idea of using girls as regular dancers in *thum* performance as a form of visual entertainment was possibly inspired by a procedure employed in guitar performances, in which young girls sometimes briefly display steps in a practice which was known as *mboko* or *panj* (Omondi 1980: 75). Here we see major changes as women are now getting into men's role as far as dancing and performance of *nyatiti* music is concerned. Certainly, a people's popular artistic creations and heritage provide some leeway to understanding their history, norms, values as well as those things that make them human and unique – their identity. In broad terms, the performing arts are characterized by spontaneous and dynamic interactions between audience and performer within a given space and time.

The dance styles in the Luo traditional music were elegant and graceful. They involved either the movement of one leg in the opposite direction with the waist in step with syncopated beats of the music or the shaking of the shoulders vigorously usually to the tune of the *nyatiti*. Another characteristic in the Luo music was the introduction of a chant in the middle of the performance. The singing stops, the pitch of the instruments goes down and the dance becomes less vigorous as an individual takes performance in self-praise. This is referred to as *Pakruok*. There is also a kind of ululation –*sigalagala* from women that marks the climax of musical performance. The chief function of *pakruok* was to provide entertainment. But also, the heightening of the intensity of the performance also had both aesthetic and emotional functions as well. It was a communication forum in which members of the audience could disseminate knowledge amongst one another. It was also a forum for encouraging and elevating the society's ideals and aspirations while functioning as a corrective measure by condemning the undesirable. The last function of *pakruok* was realized in its being a mechanism of emotional release, such was the case at a funeral, alongside teaching public expression. In this situation, *sigalagala* was the role of women during such performances. It is also noted that even though *pakruok* (self-praise) was open to all, it was men who dominated in this activity, owing to their socio-economic status in the society.

Participation in the *Orutu* song and dance was restricted to middle aged energetic men and women, who danced in pairs, a male and a female holding each other at arm's length. Other members of the clan not involved in the dance were allowed to watch and cheer the dancers, also helping in giving positions to the dancers in case of competition context (Omollo-Ongati 2005: 15). Orutu thus performed traditional, recreational and ritualistic functions. Blacking (1977) observes that music making is a symbolic expression of societal cultural organization, which reflects the value and the past and present ways of life of the human beings who create it. In its traditional context, *Orutu* music served the purpose of music making as advanced by Blacking (1977), being a symbolic expression of the Luo society and performed to express shared values. What, one may ask, are the gender dynamics in this situation? We see the venue of traditional *Orutu* performance being turned into a plural space and so to speak a 'market', where both men and women search for future husbands and wives. Nevertheless, we see women being depicted and used as a commodity for exchange, in the sense that women could easily be exchanged for the purpose of dancing even if not for sale.

Gender and Music

As Moisala (1999: 3) states, music is a specific part of expressive culture. If women play important roles in music, it allows them to take on expressive roles within the community. Traditionally, in the Luo society, just like in West Africa, due to various influences, religious, patriarchal, cultural and colonial, women have been encouraged not to speak out or voice their opinions in many circumstances. Nevertheless, women took prominent roles as singers, dancers and performers. These areas provide important and unique sites for self-expression and exposure. However, within the realm of instrumentation, women are rarely seen or heard. This lack of women instrumentalists in the traditional Luo society is a result of various factors within the culture from which the music emerges. Some important factors affecting musical performances include; ethnicity (the unique history and customs of the people who create the music), the genre (the style, form and context of the music being played), and gender (the roles of men and women in the music and how they are expressed in the performance setting). The purpose of this chapter in this section is to bring to focus the shifting roles for women by looking at changing gender roles in the Luo music.

In order to have a clear assessment of these changing roles, it is also important to bring into focus the functions of the Luo music and see the position of women in these performances. The social functions of the *Thum nyatiti* performance were ritual, social, and psychological ritual functions included marriage and death. In funerals, it was believed that without the performance of *Nyatiti* music the ghost of the dead person would be angry with the living relatives and would take vengeance on them by haunting them. As music often serves as a system in which we represent the world around us, the study of gender relations in musical performances serves as a window into the gender relations within that culture, and the different social roles they fill. Furthermore, when changes in gender roles in music are observed, often they can be traced back to changes in gender roles within the community. Moisala (1999: 2) observes that, cultural changes have affected gender organization and performance of gender in music. Koskoff writes of the important connection between music, gender and social standing in saying,

> Indeed, musical performance provides one of the best contexts for observing and understanding the gender structure of any society. This may be so because in many societies the underlying conceptual frameworks of both gender and musical / social dynamics share an important structural feature; they both rely, to a great degree, on notions of power and control (Koskoff 1987: 10).

Aronson argues that, the boundaries separating women and men's art were clearly defined in the African society. Although there were these distinct roles for men and women, the knowledge of each other's art was apparent. Through boundaries that female (and male) artist imposed, these spheres were kept divided. Nevertheless, it is equally true that women's art could complement those of men; women could affect the arts that men did and, occasionally they could enter art profession that were traditionally dominated by men (Aronson 1992). Looking at the Luo community, and going by the above statement, *Dodo* dance and *Josalu* were purely performed by women. On the other hand, *Orutu* and *nyatiti* were men dominated fields. However, we find that women complemented the men dominated Luo music by participating as dancers, and singers. Later on, with the coming of guitar, which replaced *Nyatiti*, some of the Luo women in contemporary set up are playing guitar and composing songs as well as managing their own music troupes. As Nketia (1992) puts it, just as there were musical roles ascribed to women, so were roles that men could assume in certain contexts. There are situations in which these roles were played spontaneously by men who were not in any kind of associative or organized relationship: for instance, in societies where social life revolved around periodic brewing of millet or banana, beer drinking songs could be performed quite spontaneously.

Among the Luo, love songs were sung by women, take for example the *oigi* lyrics. The *Oigo* were songs sung by young girls on their way to visit the young men they were courting. The girls walked to the hut where they were to be entertained by the men, by the light of the full moon. As they went, they sang these songs, individually or in groups taking it in turns to sing the whole way. Meanwhile, the young men were waiting, straining their ears for the first sounds of the song. When it was heard, one of them announced to the rest, at the top of his voice. The girls came and were welcomed with gifts. And then the evening's entertainment proceeded with the men playing on reed flutes while the girls sang their *oigo* songs (Finnegan 1970: 257). In these songs a special picture of girlhood was represented. For a group of girls, the *oigo* was a means of announcing their presence and differentiating themselves from the older married women; for an individual, it was a way of expressing her idiosyncrasies. Clarke (2003: 4) however, argues that within the hybridized space of urban culture, battles over the interconnected questions of memory, identity and representation were being intensely fought. The emerging fluid cultural identities were thus contested and negotiated in the contemporary urban settings.

Looking at women's roles in communities where musical performance played a key role, Koskoff (1987: 10), argues that, one cannot ignore the representation of women within musical contexts. In this case, it is evident that among the Luo people of Kenya, the roles of women in music were of utmost importance, and by looking at how these roles originated and how they are changing, we can see how they suggest changing roles for women in the Luo society. The relationship between gender behaviors in the community and those in the musical expression of that community seem to be mutually dependent. That is, the music may affect social relations or behaviors of the community and the community's social relations can affect musical expressions. That is why in the *Nyatiti* and *orutu* music performances, men play the instrument while women do the dancing. The importance of the interaction between the two is evident. The issue of gender division can also be seen. Some have termed them "strict" gender divisions, but "distinct" could be a better term, for they are divisions that are undergoing constant change and are allowing for significant flexibility. Changing gender roles in Luo music could suggest that women are beginning to express themselves in more powerful positions within the community. Looking at these instruments, we see masculine and feminine characteristics of the players. *Nyatiti* appears to be a clearly defined masculine instrument, perhaps because of its origin in the oral tradition of the Luo people or perhaps because it is an instrument that requires a certain amount of strength to carry and play with vigor, a reflection of men's self-image as the stronger sex while women were viewed as a weaker sex.

Changing Trends and Gender participation in Music Performance and Dance

It has been stated elsewhere in this chapter that in all spheres of culture, music undergoes constant transformation. Music is also a space where we can allow the possibility that gender can be seen in new ways. Not only can gender be seen or represented in new ways, but gender roles within music can also change. These changes are most often attributed to changing contexts within the community. Addressing changing roles in music among the Mande, Duran (2000: 41) asserts that, "With the growth of urban culture since independence (1960), music has undergone various transformations that have partly been determined by changing contexts. These changing contexts include women's rights movements, education, communication, the influence of technology, as well as the influence of gender roles from outside communities. Besides these influences, music can also be affected by the influence of one musician or family (Kirsten 2001: 23).

African art underwent some transformation during the colonial period. Wole Soyinka (1985) rightly observes this fact when he asserts that an entire people's social organization, artistic and economic patterns were subjugated to strategies for maximum exploitation by outside interests. Nonetheless, the African art forms were affected by the European imports innovation and new inventions. The Europeans intrusion also penetrated music in form, structure and instruments. At the vanguard of these transformations were the missionaries, eager to proselytize and 'civilize', both of which were achieved not only through reading, writing and arithmetic but also through music in church and at schools (Adzeze 2002; Washmann 1971). However, of all the changes that have occurred in Africa throughout history, three in particular have had a great impact on the music of Africa and female roles: the introduction of foreign religions, acculturation from other areas (particularly from Europe and the United States), and urbanization. These three areas overlap to some extent (Stein Hunt 1993: 44).

In the Luo society these changes in musical performances have drawn sharp reactions from two schools of thought: that is the traditionalist and the modernist. The traditionalist school of thought views the developments in traditional Luo music as an 'adulteration of the authentic musical genre'. It is believed that traditional music is facing a serious threat of decline and will eventually be subsumed by the neo-traditional musical forms. This school of thought, therefore, sees a significant change in the traditional Luo musical system and practice hence musical change. The modernist on the other hand, looks at the new developments as a way of preserving the traditional music through performance in 'New' context. It is argued that, traditional music and dances that did not lend themselves to such creative forces and innovations are either extinct or are in the process of fading away (Achieng 2006; Ongati 2005). The modernist therefore views the new developments as a form of innovative continuity, hence an extension of the traditional genre in the contemporary society.

The year 1950 was a turning point for the Luo music, and it was also significant to the changes in gender roles during music performance. During this period, the *dodo* dance, which was previously a male genre, was adopted by Luo women as a folksong (Digolo 2003). As regards the *Thum/nyatiti*, Western culture affected the development of this instrument and its performance styles from two closely related viewpoints that is Christianity and western education. *Thum/nyatiti* was viewed as 'primitive' compared to foreign musical instruments such as the accordion, *kinanda*, the guitar, *gita* and later the gramophone, *thum san*. Christian teaching helped reinforce whatever prejudices existed by outrightly condemning *thum/nyatiti* playing as satanic (Omondi 1980: 70). The same period witnessed the replacement of the *nyatiti*, the string instrument with the guitar, as the Luo started to adopt the *benga* style of music with Luo musicians trying to adapt their traditional dance rhythms to Western instruments, an evidence of some form of hybridization.[1] Luo guitar music developed its compositional practice to be more in line with other Luo genres such as *orutu* and *dodo*.[2] Among the Luo of Kenya, the 'modern traditional' popular musicians have also adapted the *Nyatiti*, an indigenous instrument, into modern compositions. In fact, many studies of Kenyan popular music document the entry of modern instruments such as the acoustic guitar and the accordion and detail the growth of expertise with these instruments through contact with Christian music and military brass bands as well as the effects of cross-cultural contact particularly with musicians from Congo, Malawi and South Africa (Low 1982; Stapleton &

May 1989; Martin 1991). Many of these studies note the influence of traditional instruments on the technique and style of the pioneer guitar players. Indeed, they all mark out the rise of *Benga* style, a variant of traditional Luo dance-music, as the highest point in the development of a modern traditional and unique Kenyan urban music form (Ogude & Nyairo 2007).

The Western influence caused a musical polarization in which the 'civilized' middle-aged people took to the accordion, and the 'civilized' youngsters took to the guitar thus leaving the *thum* to the old the 'primitive' and the 'pagan.' The younger alienated people began to substitute foreign instruments for the *thum/nyatiti* at some events such as funerals. They went to great lengths to deride and discredit the *thum* calling it such names as *thum atielo* 'the instrument of the foot" *thum arin'go* 'the instrument of meat, *thum nyatiti* 'the instrument which merely says *titi* , a derogatory onomatopoeic reference to the sound that were produced by the two highest string of the *thum*. However, *thum nyatiti* was modified with this challenge from Christianity. Further visual appeal in the practice of *go thum* (playing *Nyatiti*) was achieved in dancing, which took place.

As we have seen above, things are changing; some traditional ways are being modified by foreign influence. Women have become involved with the idea of 'liberation' and are taking advantage of the new opportunities open to them. In the words of Stein Hunt (1993: 46), *it certainly seems that the roles of women in Africa are 'modernizing' or 'progressing'*. Currently, among the Luo, there are women singers like Achieng Abura, Princess Jully, and Susan Owiyo who own their own bands and have men playing the reverse roles while they play guitar, compose and sing songs as well as leading the band. In these women-led bands, men have taken other roles initially played by women such as the position of dancers and backing vocalists. It is also worth noting that Princes Jully inherited her band from her late husband. Among the three women mentioned above, Susan Owiyo is a lead guitarist and composer. The context of their performance is both urban and rural with multi-ethnic audience. This adoption of role reversal would seem to signify that these women have stepped out of their circumscribed personae and will not be constrained by them (Esi-Sutherland-Addy 2006: 11). As Aronson (1984: 122), puts it, *this highlights the occurrence previously mentioned of women's knowledge of male dominated fields of work, despite gender restrictions*. It also hints at the influence of family in transcending gender roles. The emergence of women guitarist and leaders of musical groups/band in the Luo society in the opinion of this researcher, is a result of changing roles for women in Luo society. However, this may take time to change.

Makore (2004) in her work 'Women in Music' agrees with the above discourse when she argues that most women have assumed the role of fans rather than that of music makers. However, where they have entered the music world, most of them have been relegated to the positions of backing vocalists. She further laments that, material and ideological constraints have lessened women's full involvement in the creation of music. Nevertheless, A few women have overcome constraints and have succeeded in the music world as creators of music, players of instruments and owners of their own backing groups. What can be asked at this point is that, what are the Luo women just like African women being liberated from? Or what backward state are they emerging from. It seems to me that women have not so much suffered the stifling oppression of men as they have simply played a complementary role as far as gender participation in Luo music is concerned.

It is therefore important to note that western culture opened up the music space for women too. But with the above new developments, the societal ambivalence could not let both men and women go scot-free. The societal principle is that 'good decent girls' are quiet and never make themselves noticeable in public. Making a living through the performing arts has not been seen as a respectable way of making a living for and therefore, within the traditional Luo society, such women were perceived as not morally upright. On the other hand, it was moral for male musicians to engage in playing music (Makore 2004: 49).

> "Women artists be they singers or actresses are often perceived as 'women of the night" or women of the streets; perhaps this is because they exist in these roles in the unmarked territory outside domesticity and also in urban space for historic reasons relating to both colonial and indigenous patriarchy has been officially defined as the territory of men" (Chitauro et al 1994: 11)"

Women artists therefore, have the challenge not only of being treated as serious talented performers; but also they must change the stereotyping messages and images about women that are communicated through forms of popular culture. This is because such messages have enormous influence in shaping the real language of gender and power relations in a culture. Women have to seriously develop a counter discourse. On the other hand, men in music have also been depicted as lazy and womanizers through this societal ambivalence. In spite of the socio-economic advantages a musician read *Jathum* enjoys, the society believes that there is an inherent element of tragedy in the vocation of playing music. A musician can never have a decent home and family, fails to have children, has an unstable marriage and so on. The incidences of social failure among musicians result in their being regarded with ambivalence in the society. Although no causal connection can be established between the apparent social failure of the *jothum* and their being *jothum,* certain socio-cultural rationalizations for their tragic plight seem to make sense.

In the first instance a *jathum* by the nature of his vocation, has to spend many nights away from his own home. This is discouraged in traditional Luo society which believed that while a man is gone, his enemies or wizards got the opportunity to walk freely in his home and deconsecrate or bewitch the home. This aspect of it aside, a *jathum* who spends his nights performing on his instrument has necessarily to spend his days sleeping. Such a way of life does not allow for execution of the occupations such as clearing fields, tilling the land sowing seeds and other tasks, which are part and parcel of the everyday subsistence mode of life and gender roles which the *jathum* is expected to fit. Because he cannot do this, he will therefore appear to be 'lazy'. It is also explained that *a jathum* because of the nature of his vocation, and the resultant socio-economic advantages, is constantly admired and his attention is sought by many women. This makes a *jathum* morally lax, thus contravening the code of moral rectitude in the society and resulting in the lack of success in his marriage or family (Omondi 1980: 242). With the constant absence of *jathum,* the wives of these musicians sometimes have to assume gender roles that are not within their description.

However, much as popular art tends to reinforce gender stereotypes, new technologies and new contexts are giving room for a revision of these. The broadcast media can be mentioned as an arena, which has permitted women artists to engage in forms, which they were traditionally proscribed from performing, at least in public. These developments have given women some liberty thus overstepping the traditional boundaries (Esi-Sutherland-Addy 2006: 13). For instance, among the contemporary Luo women musicians who have gone beyond the opposite binarism of male dominance and gender stereotypes are Achieng Abura, Susan Owiyo and Princess Jully whose songs have not only appealed to Kenyans across the gender divide but have also appealed to the old and the young nationally. These negative stereotypes, based on very limited experience gained widespread acceptance and belief. However, as Bhabha (1994: 66) pointed out, stereotyping depended on a kind of mis-cognition for '*it must always be in excess of what could be empirically proved or otherwise logically construed.*' Therefore, for Bhabha 'the stereotype is not a simplification but a false representation of a given reality'. It is a simplification because it is an arrested, fixated form of representation that, in denying the play of difference (that the negation of other permits) constitutes a problem for the representation of the subject in significations of psychic and social relations. The corollary of stereotypical mode of representation is, for Bhabha, the hybridity's of colonial and postcolonial condition (Zeleza 1997).

With these changing trends, we find that the nature of performance of Luo music as well as gender participation has also changed in terms of context. For instance, *Orutu* music now features in social celebrations of quasi –traditional nature performed in bars, restaurants and nightclubs in rural and urban spaces denoting a change in the context of performance. Other occasions when the music is now performed include parties, national days, political rallies and campaigns. This deprives the music of its original institutional and contextual roles. *Orutu* is now a band music competing with popular guitar bands. The members of the band are mixed in terms of ethnic grouping. It is no longer performer-participant type of music but performer-audience music attended by heterogeneous audiences with no common cultural denominator. This gives the contemporary *orutu* artists a challenging task of searching for modern presentational features that would match the rapid modernizing Kenyan society, since the target population is not Luo any more but an international contemplative audience. This has compromised the sharing of music for social bonding purposes and the spirit of togetherness shared by members of one cultural group. *Orutu* musical performance was an important tool for creating and consolidating Luo community. It was also an important agent in the creation and maintenance of social order. Its utilitarian purpose of fusing the Luo into one unit of an indivisible whole has now been compromised since attendance and participation is free for all, women, men, boys, girls, leaders, children etc. do participate (Omollo Ongati 2005: 17).

The above argument helps us to understand the whole idea about the special link between music and identity. Maina wa Mutonya (2005) argues that, ethnic identity is invoked by individual or social groups in particular circumstances, when it suits their purposes and helps them attain their goals. Music has consistently been used as a means of both recognizing and reifying identity in Kenyan situation. As Bailey (1994) puts it, music is itself a potent symbol of identity. Like language (and attributes of language such as accent and dialect) it is one of those aspects of culture, which can, when the need to assert 'ethnic identity' arises most readily serve this purpose. Its effectiveness may be two-fold; not only does it act as a ready means for the identification of different ethnic or social groups, but it has potent emotional connotations and can be used to negotiate identity in a particularly powerful manner.

Because of the commercialization of music in the contemporary situation, the artists, both men and women have been conditioned to compose music to the taste of their customers. the introduction of Luo nights, which is intended to bring Luos together so that they interact, enjoy old local music played by renowned Luo musicians as they eat traditional foods, has promoted commercial orientation of the art. During this occasion, both Luo women and men musicians entertain revelers consisting normally of a mixture of all people, local and foreign. This is because the event is normally 'hijacked' by people from other ethnic communities as a means of enjoying diverse cultures of the Luo community. Most of the songs played during Luo nights normally have roots in pre-colonial and colonial Luo traditions of praise songs, composed to celebrate love for a girl or to sing one's own praises as well in social commentary (Cohen & Odhiambo 1989; Burton 2002).

Conclusion

This chapter set out to interrogate the process of engendering music and changing trends of performance in Luo music. It has been observed that while looking at these changes, gender roles also came into focus. This is because it is not possible to delink gender roles in music from the societal roles as music always expresses whatever happens in the society. It has been demonstrated that African societies have very unique situations and realities which should be looked into through a very liberal mind devoid of western influence. Looking at this chapter through a gender lens, it has been noted that, traditionally, members of the Luo community played music, and there was gendered division of labour as far as these musical performances were concerned. However, historically, Luo musical instruments had been gendered in favour of men. Women were not allowed to touch, leave alone play these instruments. These instruments for example *nyatiti* were inherited in a patriarchal kind of inheritance, which could not favour women. However, as much as there were songs meant for women such as *dodo*, women also complemented men in some of their musical performances.

The 1950s marked a turning point in gender participation in Luo music in that the introduction of guitar which steadily replaced *nyatiti* revolutionized the participation of women in Luo music. Not only were women able to compose songs but they were also able to play musical instruments which were hitherto a male preserve. However, with all these changes, music has ceased to play the role it traditionally used to play. This is because everything has been commercialized. As a result, women, men, and young children are always found either dancing together in places where Luo music is played or just listening to the music together in public recreational centres. In such situations, people are more concerned with music for its own sake, not attaching it to utilitarian (context) effectiveness. They listen to music and enjoy the music for contemplative reasons not attaching it to its functional meaning and context in the society. Thus, suffice it to say that the traditional role of music has shifted to serve commercial interests. With the societal ambivalence towards musicians in the Luo society, male musicians have been depicted as lazy and without morals since they do not usually have stable families. Women musicians on the other hand have been seen as night workers who have run away from their gender roles of being a mother figure. Nevertheless, both women and men have complemented each other as far as music is concerned in the Luo society. This has produced some hybrid space and traits which may not be easy to identify thereby watering down and transgressing the opposite binarism of male/ female as far as music composition and production is concerned within the Luo society.

Therefore, we can say that, music displayed in a performance setting provides space for new roles to be expressed. Moisala (1999: 15) concurs with this statement, when he says that

> "...the performative nature of music, and its ability to alter our state of consciousness allows for an interesting and possibly radical, if not revolutionary, site in which new kinds of gender performances and gender identities can evolve and which, eventually may transgress the gender boundaries of any society".

Not only do gender roles in society affect gender in music, but gender in music can also have a profound impact on gender roles in society and may even allow for women to transcend gender roles which, at times, can restrict their educational, occupational and musical goals or aspiration (Kirsten 2001).

Endnotes

1 www.answers.com/topic/luo-kenya

2 Ian Eagleson, www. leeds.ac.uk/musicresearch/popuLUs/events/speakers.htm

Bibliography

Adedze, A. 2002. 'African Arts and the Artist: Perspective for the New Milenium'. *Codesria Bulletin Special Issue numbers 3 and 4.*

Aronson, L. 1992. Women in the art 'in Hay M.J (ed) *African Women South of the Sahara.* New York, Longman.

Baily, J. 1994. 'The role of Music in the Creation of an Afghan National Identity, 1923-73' in Martin, Stokes (ed) *Ethnicity, Identity and Music: The Musical Construction of Space.* Oxford: Berg.

Bhabha, H. 1994. *The Location of Culture*, London, Routledge.

Bjorck, C. 2011. Claiming space: Discourse on gender, popular music and social change. Gothenburg, University of Gothenburg, unpublished PhD thesis.

Blacking, J. 1977. 'Some Problems of Theory and Method in the Study of Musical Change' in *Year Book of International Music Council Vol ix P 1-26.*

Bowers, J. & Tick J. 1987. *Women making music: The western art tradition, 1150-1950.* Urbana, Univ. of Illinois Press.

Burton, A. 2002. *The Urban Experience in Eastern Africa,* Nairobi, British Institute in East Africa.

Chernoff, J. 1979. *African Rhythm and African Sensibility*, Chicago. The University of Chicago Press.

Chitauro, M. 1994. Song, story and nation: Women as singers and actress in Zimbabwe in Gunner, L., (ed) *Politics and Performance: Theatre, Poetry and Song in Southern Africa.* Witwatersrand, Witwatersrand University Press.

Clarke, J. 2003. Urban culture: representations and experiences in/ of urban space and culture, *Agenda*, 57:3-10.

Clawson, M. 1993. 'Not just the girl singer: Women and voice in rock bands'. In Fisher S. Davis K. (Eds.), *Negotiating at the Margins: The Gendered Discourse of Power and Resistance.* New Brunswick, N.J, Rutgers University Press.

Clayton, M. Trevor, H. Middleton R. 2011. *The Cultural Study of Music: A Critical Introduction*, London, Routledge,

Cohen, D. & Odhiambo, E.S.A. 1989. *Siaya. The Historical Anthropology of an African Landscape*, Nairobi, Heinemann.

Cusic, S. 2009. *Francesca Caccini at the Medici court: Music and the circulation of power.* Chicago, Univ. of Chicago Press.

Digolo, B. 2003. *Indigenous music and the communication of innovative society concerns: synchronic analysis of dodo and nyatiti songs in Siaya District Kenya.* Nairobi, Kenyatta University, unpublished PhD diss.

Duran, L. 2000. *Women, Music and the 'Mystique of Hunters in Mali the African Diaspora; A Musical Perspective*. New York, Garland Publishing Inc.

Esi, A. 2006. *Perspectives on gender based aesthetics, lecture 111 series*. Paper presented at the Gender Institute, Dakar, 6-29 June.

Esi, A. 2006. *The politics of gender representation in the arts of Africa*. Paper presented at the Gender Institute, Dakar, 6–29 June.

Feldman, M., Gordon B. 2006. *The courtesan's arts: Cross-cultural perspectives*. Oxford, Oxford Univ. Press.

Finnegan, R. 1970. *Oral Literature in Africa,* Oxford, Oxford.

Green, L. 1997. *Music, Gender, Education*. Cambridge, Cambridge University Press.

Halstead, J. & Rolvsjord, R. 2015. The gendering of musical instruments: what is it? Why does it matter to music therapy? *Nordic Journal of Music Therapy*, Vol 26 Issue 1.

Kirsten, M. 2001. *Changing Gender Roles in Sabar Performances: A Reflection of Changing Roles for Women in Senegal*, SERSAS (Southeastern Regional Seminar in Africa Studies) University of Washington.

Koskoff, E. 1987. *An Introduction to Women and Music in Cross-Cultural Perspective*. New York, Greenwood Press.

Koskoff, E. 2000. *Music in Lubavicher life*. Urbana, Univ. of Illinois Press.

Maus, F. 2011. Gender, music and sexuality in Clayton et al (eds.) *The Cultural Study of Music: A Critical Introduction*, London, Routledge,

McClary, S. 2006. Constructions of subjectivity in Schubert's music. Brett, P. Gary C. (ed.) *Queering the pitch: The new gay and lesbian musicology*. New York, Routledge.

Locke, R. & Barr, C. 1997. *Cultivating music in America: Women patrons and activists since 1860*. Berkeley, Univ. of California Press.

Makore, S. 2004. Women in music: some note on Zimbabwe, in Thorsen S. (ed.) *Sounds of Change: Social and Political Features of Music in Africa*. Stockholm, Sida Studies.

Marcia, C. 1990. Gender, professionalism, and the musical canon. *The Journal of Musicology* 8(1): 102-117.

Mbembe, A. 1992. Provisional notes on the postcolony. *Journal of the International African Institute Africa* Vol 62 No 1.

McClary, S. 1991. *Feminine endings: Music, gender and sexuality*. Minneapolis MN, University of Minnesota Press.

Meki, N. 1991. *Musical practice and creativity: an African perspective*. Bayreuth, University of Bayreuth, unpublished PhD diss.

Moisala, P. 1999. Musical gender in performance. *Women and Music Annual* 3: 1-16.

Ndeda, M.A.J., (2005) The Nomiya Luo church: A gender analysis of the dynamic of an African independent church among the Luo of Siaya district' in Ndeda M. Roux E. (ed.) *Gender, Literature and Religion in Africa*. Dakar, CODESRIA.

Nketia, J.H.K. 1992. *The Music of Africa*. London, Victor Golancz Limited.

Odaga, A.B. 2008. *Luo Narratives*. Kisumu, Lake Publishers and Enterprises.

Ogude, J. & Nyairo, J. 2007. *Urban Legends, Colonial Myths: Popular Culture and Literature in East Africa*. New Jersey, Africa World Press.

Ojaide, T. 2001. 'Poetry performance and art: Udfe dance songs of Nigeria's Urhobo people.' *Research in African Literature* Vol 32 No 2: 45-75.

Omollo-Ongati, R. 2005. 'Performance practice of traditional Musical genres in contemporary Kenya: The case of Orutu,' *East African Journal of Music,* Issue No 1.

Oliveros, P. 1990. *Deep listening pieces*. Kingston, NY, Deep Listening Publications.

Omondi, W. 1980. *Traditional lyre music of the Luo people of Kenya*. London, University of London, unpublished PhD diss.

Ongati, R. 2005. 'The concept of aesthetics as applied to and in the musical experience of the Luo,' in Maseno. *Journal of Education, Arts and Science* Vol 5 No1.

Osadebey, D.C. 1949. 'West African voices', *African. Affairs*, 48: 1

Shuker, R. 2005. *Popular music: The key concepts*. London, Routledge.

Soyinka, W. 1985. *The Arts in Africa During the Period of Colonial Rule.* Berkely, University of California Press.

Stapleton, C. &May, C. 1989., *Africa All-Stars: The Pop Music of a Continent*. London, Palladin.

Stein Hunt DL. 1993. 'The changing role of women in African Music.' *UFAHAMU,* Vol xxi, (1-2): 41-49.

Tick, J. 1997. *Ruth Crawford Seeger: A composer's search for American music*. Oxford, Oxford Univ. Press.

wa Mutonya, M. 2005. *Mugithi* performance: popular music, stereotypes and ethnic identity, in Ogude J. Nyairo J (eds.) *East African Popular Culture and Literature, Africa Insight*, Vol 35, No 2: 55-75.

Washmann, K. 1971. *Essays in Music and History in Africa*. Evanston, Northwestern University Press.

Whiteley, S. 2000. *Women and popular music: Sexuality, identity, and subjectivity*. New York, Routledge.

Part IV:

Music and Dance in Life Writing

Representing Performance: Memories of Song, Music and Dance in the Autobiographical Writing of Ngũgĩ and Wainaina

Inge Brinkman

In this contribution I seek to establish in what ways performance is remembered in Kenyan autobiographical writing. It is telling how much attention is being given to performance – song, music, dance and also narrative and speech –, and how strongly performance is considered in aesthetic terms. This is especially noteworthy in view of the tense political situation described in these books. One would expect that there are other, more urgent things to tell than narratives on singing and dancing, but clearly performance is deemed important, and is considered part of the political situation.

Focusing on Ngũgĩ's memoirs, the analysis shows that several authors – notably authors belonging to the political elite and/or with a record of activism – create an oppositional framework. On the one hand, there are the traditional performances – evaluated positively and associated with popular resistance. On the other hand, a missionary musical tradition is presented – in much less positive terms - that destroys this traditional repertoire, reinforced by colonial bans and censorship.

In Mau Mau autobiographies this opposition is less strongly developed, in that local songs do not automatically belong to the resistance repertoire, and church hymns from the missionary realm may be turned into resistance songs. The authors of Mau Mau autobiographies are hesitant to condemn their own Christian upbringing and reason from a much less radical stance. The opposition between "Gikuyu tradition" and missionary Christianity does exist for these authors, but is much less strongly tied to the political realm.

In Wainaina's autobiography, finally, we hardly find such an opposition. Resistance can also be breakdanced, and traditional music may be 'kimay' – the word the protagonist coins to describe chaotic and disconcerting sound. While most authors happily describe the meandering of oral forms and various media into each other, for Wainaina this is a source of confusion and even fear. Only at the very end of his autobiography he evaluates multimodality on more positive terms, as he comes to see in it the possibility to "carry our diversity and complexity in sound."

> "Why don't we listen to crooning and soft drums and strumming pools of water and acoustic guitar meadows? Why not listen to plaintive old folk songs, leather string and goatskin box? The wooden sounds of long ago? Wood rots." (Wainaina 2011: 77)

Introduction

The manifold ways in which African written literatures intertextually and intermedially engage with oral literary traditions have received considerable scholarly attention. In most cases the focus is on contents: we learn about the insertion of proverbs, songs and narratives into writing. At times, form is also discussed, including the employment in written texts of onomatopoeias, repetition, rhyme, and other stylistic elements characteristic of oral genres (there exists a vast body of literature on this, with Eileen Julien, 1992 as a landmark).

Yet, the ways in which performance is represented in written texts from Africa have hardly been discussed; little do we learn as to how African authors write about oral performance (some remarks are made in: Morales, 2003; Samuelson, 2007, but none deals with the representations of performance *per se*). In this contribution I seek to establish in what ways oral performances, especially song, music and dance, are remembered in Kenyan autobiographical writing.

The aim of the contribution is twofold. Firstly I want to offer an analysis of what these authors say about the relations between language, orality, writing, music and dance. This issue leads to more specific questions about language. What terms do the authors use when describing song, music, speech, dance, and performance? At the same time, this issue relates the autobiographies to their broader cultural implications: what is said in these texts about the relations between dance and society, music and history?

The second aim is to establish the relations between memory and performance. How do authors remember oral performances? Do these memories reflect in the narrative structure of their autobiographical writing, and, if so, in what ways? How do author, narrator and protagonist evaluate such performances in the text? What meanings are attributed to them?

These questions will obviously not lead to an analysis of performance as such, but approach music and dance from a meta-level, investigating authors' statements about the role of song, music and dance in their lives. This may help us to assess performance, in this case particularly song, music and dance, as part of Kenya's cultural history, both contemporary and in retrospect.

On Autobiography

Autobiographies, memoirs and diaries pose a problem. They are not literature, they are not history: they are in between. There is a classic notion that as all writing sprouts from the mind of the author, it cannot be but autobiographical, and in that sense all writing adheres to an autobiographical stance. Nevertheless, for analytical purposes it is fruitful to distinguish autobiographical writing as an invitation to a particular reading strategy (Wagner-Egelhaaf 2005: 9) that takes the autobiographical pact as its guiding principle. With the notion of autobiographical pact I follow Lejeune's proposal (1975: 4) in that author, narrator, and protagonist are identical. His famous definition of autobiography reads: "*Retrospective prose narrative written by a real person concerning his own existence, where the focus is his individual life, in particular the story of his personality.*"

A brief exploration of the various forms of autobiographical writing may be in order. The difference between memoir and autobiography is usually placed in the final part of Lejeune's definition: "*in particular the story of his personality*". In memoirs the focus is less on self-realization as a person and more on the author's role in public life. Many publications by political leaders and activists can be said to resort under the rubric "memoir". Yet as the very notion of "personality" has been questioned by various authors especially from postcolonial, postmodern and/or feminist stances (Hunsu 2011), and most of the works under discussion combine attention for public life with descriptions of childhood years, the difference between autobiography and memoir can be said to be merely gradual.

For diaries the term "retrospective" in the definition constitutes the difference: that characteristic of autobiographies hardly holds for diaries. A diary is written nearly simultaneously to the events: events and the author's feelings about them are recorded on a daily basis. We have to bear in mind, however, that published editions of diaries are often heavily edited, rendering the difference between autobiographies and diaries less outspoken. Still, the daily notation characteristic of diaries is not present in autobiographies and the element whereby an older self reflects on a younger self – as in autobiographies – is absent from the diary form.

These three related forms are at once literature and history. Autobiography, memoir and diaries claim a relationship with historical reality that is not characteristic of fictional writing. At the same time – as Ben Yagoda in his history of the memoir pointed out in 2009 – they are not as different from fiction as they themselves suggest. Autobiographical writings constitute constructive and imaginative forms. Far from copying their lives down, the authors create the narrator and the protagonist they write about, even if that narrator and protagonist are identical to themselves.

Autobiographical Writing in Kenya

Nearly all countries know a number of memoir-writings, mostly by political leaders explaining their role in public life. Famous examples in Africa include Nkrumah's *Ghana: the autobiography of Kwame Nkrumah* (1957) and Mandela with *Long walk to freedom* (1994). In Kenya such memoirs are relatively numerous; we can think of Tom Mboya, *Freedom and after* (1963), Oginga Odinga's, *Not yet Uhuru* (1976), Harry Thuku, *Harry Thuku: an autobiography* (1970) and Bildad Kaggia, *Roots of freedom* (1975). Also other public figures, such as Wangari Maathai with her *Unbowed* (2006) may be included.

It is also quite commonplace for authors engaged in writing literary works to publish their memoirs, diaries or autobiographies. On the African continent there are numerous examples: Camara Laye (1953), Wole Soyinka (1981), Buchi Emecheta (1986), Aminata Forna (2003), Zakes Mda (2011), J.M. Coetzee (2011), just to mention a few examples. In the Kenyan case we could mention Ngũgĩ wa Thiong'o (1981, 2011, 2013) and Binyavanga Wainaina (2011).

For politicians and writers to publish their memoirs is hence not that exceptional, although for Kenya the number of such memoirs is relatively high. What is unique about the Kenyan case, is the spate of autobiographical writings dealing particularly with one period in Kenya's history, namely the Mau Mau memoirs. In South Africa we have rather some people writing about resistance to the *apartheid* system. Yet also in this case most of the authors are public figures, and outside South Africa, we find no example comparable to the Kenyan one on the continent. The publishing of Mau Mau memoirs experienced a boom in the 1960s and 1970s, and trickles on until this very day, with a total of more than thirty memoirs, diaries and autobiographies.

We have autobiographical writings dealing with life in the colonial camps, such as J.M. Kariuki, *Mau Mau detainee* (1963) and Gakaara's diary (1988). There are Mau Mau memoirs on life in the forests, for example Barnett and Njama (1966) and Waruhiu Itote (1979). Civilian experiences in an Emergency village are described by Charity Waciuma (1969), one of the first published autobiographies in English by an African woman. Some of these books on Mau Mau were written by the leadership, but quite some also by rank-and-file or civilians. Indeed these memoirs together form a unique body of literature in Africa's literary history.

Despite the number and the particularity of Kenyan autobiographical writing, relatively little attention has been given to them. Even if life writing is the most practiced genre in Kenya, literary analyses are mostly devoted to the novel (Peterson 2012). The most important work dealing with autobiography in Kenya largely discusses it as historical source for the interpretation of political history (Clough 1997). Even if this theme is framed in narrative terms (Atieno-Odhiambo & Lonsdale 2003), relations between autobiography and the wider political context are regarded as the most important feature of these autobiographies. While such an approach holds water, an approach that does justice to the form that these narratives take and their cultural implications is equally valid. Many authors of Kenyan autobiographical writing detail the role that music, dance, songs, narratives and other oral forms played not only in their childhood, but in their lives on the whole. If we were to limit our analysis to political history, we would miss out on such features that apparently matter enough for these author to write about.

With over forty publications, it would be beyond the scope of this chapter to discuss all Kenyan autobiographical writings in their relation to music and dance performance. In two publications – namely Ngũgĩ wa Thiong'o, *Dreams in a time of war: a childhood memoir* (2011) and Binyavanga Wainaina, *One day I will write about this place* (2011) – music plays a particularly important role, as it is in many ways constitutive of the narrative. These two publications will form the basis of this chapter, while being framed in the wider context of Kenyan autobiographical writing.

The Mau Mau autobiographies mostly stem from authors who were adults during the war and/or were written quite soon after Kenya's independence (in most cases in the 1960s and 1970s), whereas Ngũgĩ's book dates from 2011. Other autobiographies from the activist realm, such as Koigi wa Wamwere's (2002) and Wangari Maathai's (2008 [2006]) works are also of a comparatively recent date. Binyavanga Wainaina's book (2011) not only is of a recent date, it also was written by an author of a different generation than Ngũgĩ and the authors of the Mau Mau memoirs, with a gap of more than thirty years in their date of birth. It would be interesting to frame Wainaina's work in reference to other authors of his generation. Being a young autobiographer, however, Wainaina's *One day I will write about this place* is exceptional; so far no other authors of his generation wrote their memoirs. It would be beyond the scope of this chapter to also draw in fiction and other works that intertextually anchor Wainaina's autobiography in relation to Kenya's wider literary history.

Apart from the generation gap and the date of publishing, representations of the politics and aesthetics of music and dance may also be related to the issue of audience. The earliest examples of Mau Mau memoirs may have addressed colonial discourse on Mau Mau, but the bulk of these memoirs speak to each other and a Kenyan audience. Ngũgĩ and Wainaina may relate to a wider international readership, while Wainaina's urban, middle class upbringing in a globalized context in any way brought in a more international musical experience. These remarks in literary history and context are tentative: in the first instance this chapter aims at a textual approach.

Writing in Multimodality

"The choice and arrangements of the words, the cadence, I can't pick any one thing that makes it so beautiful and long-lived in my memory. I realize that even written words can carry the music I loved in stories, particularly the choric melody. And yet this is not a story; it is a descriptive statement. It does not carry an illustration. It is a picture in itself and yet more than a picture and a description. It is music. Written words can also sing." (Ngũgĩ wa Thiong'o 2011: 65).

With these words the most famous author from Eastern Africa, Ngũgĩ wa Thiong'o, wrote about the time when he learnt to read as a young boy. Deliberately blurring the boundaries between the literary, the visual and the musical, this quote indicates an ensemble of aesthetics that informs the performance of oral story-telling and singing, the practice of reading, and the creation of visual arts.

"Music" is a word often taken for granted, but the role that music and dance play in people's lives and even its very definition is not easy to establish. The performance of genres that are usually conceived of as "textual" may by African audiences regarded as "music". As Ruth Finnegan points out: "Where language ends and music begins is a moot point for example, perhaps differently construed in different traditions" (Finnegan 2007: 203-217, quote 212). Likewise David Coplan proposed the word "*auriture*" to indicate that the boundaries between text-driven performance and rhythmic, melodious song is a matter of definition. When asking for explanation of some words of a song, Coplan (1994: 8-9) was told: "*If you want to understand my song, mister, just listen to the music*".

The quote from Ngũgĩ suggests that "music" and "text" may be fluid categories, not always easily distinguishable. This also shows in other autobiographies from Kenya. Ngũgĩ makes a similar statement in his follow-up memoir *In the house of the interpreter (2013: 38)* when music is shown to be "*the gateway to literature, particularly poetry*" while also ascribed aspects of "*soundless motion*". Another example comes from the former Mau Mau guerrilla Joram Wamweya who has a camp guard "sing" at them as they escape through the barbed wire in the 1950s: "Eiyu! Rudi!' ('*Come back!*'), *he sang as he went at us.* 'Eiyu! Rudi!', *shooting at us*" (1971: 88), and he refers to the Mau Mau oath as "*chanting*" (1971: 52).

In many memoirs, speech and language itself are also attributed strong performative qualities. Kenyatta told the famous journalist Henry Muoria (1994: 11, for another example: Wamweya 1971: 119): "*The power of the spoken word is so great that even the Bible recognizes that fact.*" Binyavanga Wainaina (2011: 188) also describes language use in performative terms: "*A Jamaican accent smudges the seams of his Sheng. His voice has the rich musical undertones of a Luo.*" When discussing a church collection, people are said to throw money "*in the moving dancing collection baskets. A crescendo is reached, after we have given money, and people are writhing and shouting in the heat. Words are flowing from their lips, like porridge, in no language I know, but in a clear coherent pitch. Each person has his or her own tongue.*" Movement and tongue together form one sound, while at the same time "*each individual lives inside his or her own sound*" (Wainaina 2011: 58).

The multimodality in the foregoing examples does not lie in the combination of various modes, but in the fluidity of the boundaries between them. Rhythm, music, singing, chanting, speech, and writing are not neatly bounded, but meander into each other. For Wainaina (2011: 25-26) this intermediality or multimodality forms a constant source of discomfort, and he finds out a new word to describe it: "*kimay*" ("*This is my new word, my secret*"):

> "*Kimay is the talking jazz trumpet [...] Kimay is yodeling Gikuyu women [...]. I can speak English. I can speak Swahili. Kimay is any language that I cannot speak, but I hear every day in Nakuru: Ki-kuyu, Ki-Kamba, Ki-Ganda, Ki-sii, Gujarati, Ki-Nyarwanda, (Ki)Ru-fumbira,* Ki-May*. There are so many, I get dizzy.* Ki-May *is the accordion, the fiddle, the bagpipe, the trumpet. All those spongy sounds. [...] Most of all I fear accordions.*"

Only at the end of the memoir he begins to attach meaning to this meandering of modes into each other. As he watches a documentary on 1960s Kenyan *benga* music, he suddenly realises "*Here it is, the source of all* kimay *[...] Any good* benga *guitarist can mimic the architecture and musical rhythms and verbal sounds of any Kenyan language. Stripped down, that is the intent of benga. Kimay is people talking without words, exact languages, the guitar sounds of Kenya speaking Kenya's languages.*" (Wainaina 2011: 253).

Ngũgĩ (2011: 115-116) describes different, oppositional sets of performativity that internally form wholes: "*The difference lay in intangibles. When I think back on Kamandũra* [a missionary school], *what pops up are images of church, silent prayer, and individual achievement; in Manguo* [an independent school], *images of performance, public spectacle, and a sense of community.*" He juxtaposes as contrasting the "*slow, mournful, almost tired*" melodies of the missionary hymns to the hymns sung during the church service at the African-independent school, sung "*with zest and rhythm*", accompanied by drums and cymbals.

For Ngũgĩ these are clearly distinguishable contexts – in contents and form – and he associates with the African independent school and resistance context as opposed to the colonial, missionary context. For Wainaina there are no such neatly bordered contexts: "*The music sounds like, like chaos*" (Wainaina 2011: 24) as "*We are mixed-up people*" (Wainaina 2011: 21).

Remembering Childhood Performance

> "It is a sunny day, but for some reason what comes to mind is the song we used to sing to welcome rain" (Ngũgĩ 2011: 248)

Music – especially songs – appear in all sorts of occasions in Kenyan autobiographical writing. The authors pay much attention to describing their memories of music and song, and sometimes also of dance. Music and dance can certainly serve as mnemonic devices, invoking the past through associations of rhythm rather than verbally. As Laura Fair (2001: 260) writes about coastal *taarab* music: "*Elderly men and women who lived through these times frequently draw on Siti's songs as mnemonics of memory, triggers that allow them to see and hear the struggles and debates of the times.*" It is clear, however, that the references to music and dance in Kenyan autobiographical writing surpass the functionalist idea of mnemonics. Given the charged political context about which the authors write, it is noteworthy how much attention they give to song, music, dance and other performative genres. Oginga Odinga (1976: 9-10), for example, renders his childhood memories of songs with full details. For a high-ranking politician there is apparently nothing childish or irrelevant about this – to the contrary, songs and music are worthy of detailed description. Thus in his chapter "*At the feet of the village elders*", he refers to story-tellers and harpists as "*the sources of education in the village*" and he quotes one of the songs he heard as a child at length.

Ngũgĩ (2011: 30-31) also elaborates on his childhood memories of oral story-telling and singing, and likewise does so in a particularly positive manner. Oral performance is rendered in full musical detail in his *Dreams in a time of war*. A strong example is the description of his mother telling a tale of a man asking for the way to a medicine-man Ndiro in a musical manner: "*He describes the medicine man in terms of his gait, dance steps, and the rhythmic jingles around his ankles that sound his name, Ndiro.*" The narrative thus revolves around sound and movement, both within and without the narrative, as the children mimic the narratives' protagonist, "*stepping on the ground and calling out "Ndiro" in unison*". Such vivid description is also encountered in Maathai's autobiography. She recounts how her aunt Nyakweya, a "great story-teller", when she told stories, *"would sing and imitate the movements of the characters."* (Maathai 2006: 51).

In these autobiographies the performances are not only detailed, they are also evaluated in positive terms. Of course, not all is bliss: in Ngũgĩ's book, for example, some children would take away the walking sticks of their lame and blind half-sister if she did not want to tell a story (Ngũgĩ 2011: 124). Yet, overall the image is one of a near to idyllic traditional African authenticity. The oppositional framework that Ngũgĩ creates, begins here: as little children they are firmly embedded in local traditions of story-telling, singing and music; a homestead experience hardly disrupted by the wider context of missionaries and colonialism. It is only when going to school that the protagonist realises that there are forces at work that try to counter these local popular cultures. This scheme of opposition is also created in Wangari Maathai's autobiography (2006: 50) when she writes that stories like Cinderella and Little Red Riding Hood meant little to her, while stressing that the Gikuyu stories that she was told as a child did make sense.

Authors of the Mau Mau memoirs dwell less on their childhood memories of song, dance and other performances of oral literatures, focusing on their role in the Mau Mau period. If they do write about their childhood experience of performance, they also maintain an opposition between "tradition" and "Christianity", yet this is much less strongly framed in favour of "tradition" than with authors like Ngũgĩ and Maathai. Thus Joram Wamweya (1971: 4) remembers getting nightmares from some of the stories he was told by his grandmother. Most of the authors do evaluate traditional performance positively, but this positive evaluation is not necessarily related to a negative assessment of Christianity and colonialism. Charity Waciuma (1969: 10, 65) recalls listening to her grandfather's stories as *"fun"*, and sings *"all sorts of songs, but not hymns"* on the way to church (*"hymns after all, are only meant to be sung during the service"*, she comments). Joram Wamweya also recounts how he hears *"the sound of boys and girls singing sweetly together"* on moonlit nights. After having made some enquiries, he and his brother visit a dance that also involves some *"heathen rituals"* (Wamweya 1971: 5). Belonging to a Christian family, they realize that they are not supposed to attend the dance at all. While the authors of the Mau Mau memoirs are opposed to colonialism, most of them have a Christian background, and describe their childhood in Christian families without idealising "tradition" or condemning Christian missionaries. J.M. Kariuki (1963: 3, 5), for example, describes the element of performance in his childhood in a rather enumerative, matter-of-fact way:

> "Up till the age of seven I led the normal life of a Kikuyu small boy of those days, herding the cattle and goats, learning Kikuyu customs and traditions from my grandparents, spying on the dances of my elders, stealing sugar-cane and maize and being thoroughly spoilt by my elder sisters and their lady-friends."

Somewhat later, the protagonist goes to school; *"we were taught singing, dancing, drawing, counting and scripture, in which we learned the catechism. It was not really a good school but my three years of discovery and development were a vital part of my life."* Both the experiences as "a Kikuyu small boy" and as a schoolboy are rendered without much detail, and the missionary education is not evaluated as morally less defendable than the "Kikuyu customs and traditions" or posing a threat to them.

Wainaina's book is again very different. While the other authors discuss "traditional" as different from "Christian", Wainaina does not uphold any such opposition. His childhood memories of music are not always positive. Only in one instance does he refer to childhood memories music in innocent and warm terms: *"Mum is shelling and humming, and our bodies all hum smoothly with her"* (Wainaina 2011: 27). The narrator's childhood memories do not relate to "tradition" in a framework of living authentic popular culture as with Ngũgĩ. Tradition is a funny and bewildering thing for Binyavanga Wainaina as a child. When Kenyatta has died, for example, he watches television with his sister Ciru:

> "If goat tripe could sing, this is what it would sound like, boiling goat tripe singing on television, singing for Kenyatta. Jimmy is in his room listening to Top of the tops on BBC Radio. […] Television voice: 'This delegation from Nyanza Province is playing a nyatiti. They have come to sing for the late President Kenyatta. A nyatiti is a traditional Luo musical instrument.' Matiti. Ciru giggles. I giggle. Titi. Titties." (Wainaina 2011: 23-24).

Traditional performance is associated with goat tripes, the children create a joke out of the "strange" word *nyatiti*, and the experience is contrasted to "Top of the pops *on BBC radio*".

At best, the performance of "traditional songs" is presented as folkloristic: interesting in a way, yet remote from the experience of the protagonist and his schoolmates:

> "Sometimes we practice traditional songs for the interschool music festival. We try to make sure we do not shake our bodies too much. […] At practice, the conductor, our music teacher Mr. Dondo, keeps us in do-re-mi-fa key with his mouth organ before we start. Don't move like a villager, he likes to say. We often do not know the meaning of the traditional songs we are singing, but we learn the words well." (Wainaina 2011: 34-35).

To conclude, the childhood memories of music and dance in Ngũgĩ's book are positively evaluated and tied to village life and local popular traditional culture. This element can also be found in autobiographies by politicians, and political activists like Wangari Maathai. The authors of most of the Mau Mau memoirs perceive a difference, an opposition even between "tradition" and "Christianity", but their evaluation of these is much less outspoken and less tied to the political realm. For Binyavanga Wainaina, finally, childhood memories of performance are not per se positive: traditional performance is presented as alienating, only appearing on television or at school.

Political Meanings: A Tradition of Popular Resistance?

> "They would sing a song over and over and then move to other songs. I was merely the trigger." (Ngũgĩ 2011: 136)

Singing, music and dance are clearly not only pastime to the protagonists: performance has meanings beyond pure form and – apart from its educational and recreational functions – is often strongly related to politics. Ngũgĩ wa Thiong'o describes how he became a singer himself, triggering people's resistance songs. After changing from the missionary to the Gikuyu independent school, he notices how performance accompanies all activities in his new environment (Ngũgĩ 2011: 122). The establishment of the new independent schools leads to the creation of a corpus of new songs, gradually spreading beyond the school confines and being sung at social gatherings *"in homes or in the open air"* (Ngũgĩ 2011: 123-124). As the political conflicts in the region rise in the course of the 1940s, songs are made that ever stronger relate to local political leaders, to land evictions, and to resistance against colonialism. The young Ngũgĩ learns many of the songs and soon becomes one of the performers at such social gatherings. As he quotes a song in Gikuyu, translating it into English:

Njamba īrīa nene Kenyatta	Kenyatta our great hero
Rīu nī oimire Rūraya	Has now returned from Europe.
Jomo nī oimīte na thome	He came back through the main gate (Mombasa).
Ningī Jomo mūthigani witū	Jomo has been our eyes.
	(Ngũgĩ 2011: 122-128, 135-136 (quote 136)).

The transition from member of the audience as a child to song performer as adolescent is presented as seamless. For Ngũgĩ the homestead performance and the singing of protest songs at gatherings form a continuum. The scenario is only disturbed by the colonial authorities: *"Mau Mau songs and all references to Waiyaki, Kenyatta, or Mbiyū were criminalized. This abruptly ended my career as a troubadour"* (Ngũgĩ 2011: 156). Once again Ngũgĩ creates a strong opposition between a local tradition of popular performance related to resistance, and colonial forces that disrupt this tradition and try to undermine it.

A similar oppositional framework can be found in Koigi wa Wamwere's memoir. Here also, song is mentioned as a means of resistance that the colonial authorities try to curb and control. Yet, this tradition of resistance through song continues: *"Can I sing you a short song"*, the young Koigi is asked by a Mau Mau fighter, followed by a Mau Mau hymn (Koigi wa Wamwere 2002: 105-107).

Apart from the colonial legislation in terms of bans and censorship, several authors also refer to the slower processes of cultural change that undermined local traditions. Thus in Wangari Maathai's *Unbowed* (2006: 11) we find Gikuyu culture destroyed by missionary enterprise: *"The athomi [readers, meaning those trained in missionary schools] culture brought with European ways and led to profound changes in the way Kikuyus dressed and adorned themselves, the kinds of food they ate, the songs they sang, and the dances they performed […] Dancing and non-Christian festivities and initiation rites were discouraged or even demonized and banned by missionaries and converts."* Another author who discusses the steady disappearance of performance in the context of colonial domination is Henry Muoria (1994: 33-34). He first specifies all the *"great dances"* that were performed on occasions like circumcision and also functioned as a meeting-place for young people. He subsequently explains that, as the dances were performed with dignity, *"the whites"* did not like them and that all these dances *"disappeared under influence of education and evil propaganda."*

Several authors who had participated in Mau Mau describe their encounter with the legal prohibition of political songs and dances as well as the continued attempts of people to circumvent such laws. Thus H.K. Wachanga (1975: xxxiii-xxxiv) starts his book with a story on how dancing functioned as an act of resistance. Colonial censorship not only targeted writings, like books, pamphlets and periodicals, but also dance performance. As of 1940 no authorisations for holding dances were meted out, but the political movement of the Forty Group *"defied the Government and organized dances on river banks and in the valleys."* During one such dance, a local headman tried to intervene, but the dancers attacked him and the accompanying Tribal Police, and managed to chase them away. When a larger government force eventually returned, all dancers had already disappeared. Wachanga decided to commemorate this event in a song, lauding the attackers for *"Hitting the bastard and knocking him down"*. Henceforth the dancers were left in peace. Such narratives portray the protagonist and the political groupings as heroically resisting colonial intrusion in local life; in this sense they resemble Ngũgĩ's and Koigi's representation of colonialism and resistance.

In the Mau Mau autobiographies, the importance of resistance songs is stressed and several authors detail the context of the performance and offer the lyrics of such songs. Wachanga (1975:

xxvii, 70-71, 86-88), for example, himself a composer, repeatedly refers to songs that were created to commemorate historical events. Rather than to tell about the past then, history is sung about:

> "Blend with ours your voices
> In our triumphant song
> Glory, praise and honour
> Unto Jomo the King."

Wachanga (1975: 88) also relates to the Christian context in which performance takes place: "*After we finished singing that song, I opened the Holy Bible to Zephania 3:18-20 and read the following words,*" after which the Bible text is given.

Yet, while for Ngũgĩ and Koigi singing is unequivocally related to a tradition of popular resistance, this is much less strongly developed in the Mau Mau memoirs. In the Mau Mau memoirs song is not uniformly tied to resistance. Wachanga (1975: 160) for example also describes a prostitutes' song in the detainee camp he was held, rendering the lyrics in full. Also in Gakaara's diary we find performances that are carried out without any reference to resistance. And Joram Wamweya (1971: 123) relates how he began to sing after he had been left behind by his co-fugitives and managed to board a train on his own: "*I began to sing aloud so that should they hear me, they would know that now they were the trailers. I sang* Muomboko. *When we approached the next station, I stopped singing and returned under the car.*" Not only the singing itself is remembered, it is also specified what type of song the protagonists used to challenge his co-fugitives with. The song, however, is not sung to perform an anti-colonial act, but serves as a means to communicate.

For Wainaina (2011: 86), resistance is not necessarily embedded in a local tradition of popular resistance at all. He relates to a school protest in mixed and global terms: "[We] *run around the school, breakdancing and shouting and singing South African songs.*" Furthermore performance can also be used in a high-political sense that is far removed from the popular resistance model that Ngũgĩ employs. The protagonist describes choirs practising political praise songs ("*Rule, Moi, rule*") and stadium performance for the President: "*…rows and columns of citizens, in clear straight lines, in crisp uniforms, Boy Scouts and policemen, the navy, the army, and ten thousand schoolchildren in new uniforms. Then there are the tribes- each one in a costume, here to tell the president we sing and dance for you.*" (Wainaina 2011: 45-46, 50). The relation between politics and performance is for Wainaina hence not restricted to traditions of popular resistance; it can equally entail a legitimizing project on the part of established political rulers. Yet the protagonist is also suspicious of the model that activists like Ngũgĩ stand for:

> "Ngũgĩ wa Thiong'o is a writer and playwright, a Kenyan playwright, and people say he says that women should not perm their hair or wear lipstick. I have permed my hair. I like it. [...] I don't like Moi, but if those people take over the government, what music will we listen to? Nyatiti?" (Wainaina 2011: 88).

This section argued that especially authors from the political elite and/or with a record of activism describe a valuable local popular tradition that is undermined by colonial legislation in the form of bans and censorship, as well as through a slower process of cultural change related to Christian missionaries. Performance takes the form of popular resistance against this process of undermining. For Mau Mau bibliographers the opposition between local popular resistance versus colonial-missionary destruction is less clear in that performances of resistance songs often take place in a Christian framework, and examples of songs are given that do not at all relate to popular resistance. In Wainaina's autobiography the politics of performance extend beyond resistance and also may include the legitimisation of power structures.

Aesthetics in Troubled Times

> "In the dark times
> Will there also be singing?
> Yes, there will be singing
> About the dark times"
> (Ngũgĩ, quoting Bertold Brecht 2011: 1)

As indicated, music and dance are hardly ever described in a matter-of-fact tone, but in most cases receive a positive description and are regarded in terms of beauty. Thus as we saw most of the authors remember the songs and dances of their childhood well.

Singing can bring solace in difficult situations. Charity Waciuma in her *Daughter of Mumbi* (1969: 126) describes singing in detail. After she and her family are forcibly moved, she nostalgically relates to her former home: "*This other one is a prison. Strange that the Home Guard cannot understand* when *we sing how we wish we have wings like angels and over the high prison walls we would fly; we would fly back to the arms of our beloved and then be willing to die.*"

The performances during Mau Mau are described not only in detail, but also in terms of worthiness. Gakaara wa Wanjaũ (1988: 117), for example, emphasizes the role of dance and music in the detention camp he was during the Emergency:

> "After the lecture there were cultural dances in the open field. We watched detainees performing for others. Mahuti wa Gĩcuhĩ had organised the most beautiful performance; his group performed the mũcũng'wa dance. The dancers were resplendent in colourful cloth; they wore strings of beads of cowrie shells collected from the sea shore; on their ankles they wore rattles made of tins containing pebbles which thundered in the rhythm of their energetic steps."

The prisoners strongly feel the need to engage in artistic expression and use much creativity to continue performing their repertoire: "*Some danced the* mwomboko *to the improvised music of one piece of metal beaten against another*" (Gakaara 1988: 165). In the degrading and dehumanising environment of the camp, the prisoners seek to establish their dignity through performance.

These aesthetics can bind people over all sorts of barriers. Thus Gakaara (1988: 32) writes how the prison guards start being involved in the prisoners' song because of rhythm of the "sweet song":

> "We marched to the beach in style, in line formation, two people abreast, singing our song "To be isolated on an island in detention is an unforgettable experience". [...] Then we marched back in formation to the rhythm of our sweet song; to the show tune, some of us whistled in the manner of recorded music. The beat was so good that the warders, walking on either side of our formation, could not help joyfully marching with us to the rhythm of our song."

Apart from the aesthetic evaluation – that can be gathered from the positive markers like "sweet song", the beat that was "so good", the "joyful" marching of the warders – and the ironic title of the song, the quote also shows that the music transforms the positions that the detainees and the warders normally have towards each other. Through the song, the warders "could not help" step out of their role, and the prisoners and their guards for this short moment become one group, like in the shouting "in unison" of Ngũgĩ mentioned earlier.

Gakaara (1988: 132) also has a scene in which a traditional dance is held, whereby *"the camp officer, the sergeant, the camp personnel and their wives all came to watch and they enjoyed the performances tremendously."* In this case also, the usual barriers between prisoners and personnel are to some extent overcome, although hierarchy is maintained through the dancers-spectators relation. It would be inconceivable to have the military and the personnel perform for the prisoners.

A similar process of overcoming barriers is described by Wangari Maathai (2006: 272):

> "When we were confronted with a tense situation, we would sing about the need to protect the forest, and dance. This was a way to disarm the armed men in front of us-and it worked. We could see their frowns and scowls vanish and their faces soften. We were only women singing and dancing, after all, and those things didn't pose a threat. As far as they were concerned, we could sing and dance all day! What they didn't know is that the singing and dancing made us feel strong. It also ensured that nobody got hurt."

In these cases it concerns processes of momentary unification, nearly as in carnival. But performance can also be meant as a more enduring process over ethnic boundaries: Thus Wamweya (1971: 102) writes about an encounter of the runaways with "Wakamba":

> "We ate our porridge and told the Wakamba that we would sing them a Kamba song. Muroki Karuga began singing and because of its great charm, the two Akamba on hearing the words kept on saying: 'Ai!-Ai!-Ai!' We told the men that the song was composed by two young Kamba men who had decided to join hands with the Agikuyu in the fight for freedom, until Kenya's independence was won."

In a very different way, Wainaina (2011: 52) also suggests that music can overcome barriers: *"Music makes whole worlds, out of unwhole lives."* Yet this assessment always has an undertone of irony. When the experience is finally genuine, the protagonist is drunk: he ends up in a village bar, with a local chief and a *dombolo* song starts: *"I have struggled to get this dance right for years. I just can't get my hips to roll in circles as they should. Until tonight. The booze is helping, I think… My body finds the rhythmic map quickly."* […] *"If you ask me now, I'll tell you this is everything that matters. So this is why we move like this? We affirm a common purpose: any doubts about others' motives must fade if we are all pieces of one movement."* (Wainaina 2011: 140 and 141). As indicated before, Wainaina does not always describe music and dance with positive markers; movement, sound and music can be a source of disconcertment, fear even.

Conclusion

This analysis has shown that several authors – notably authors belonging to the political elite and/or with a record of activism – create an oppositional framework. On the one hand, there are the traditional performances – evaluated positively and associated with popular resistance. On the other hand, a missionary musical tradition is presented – in much less positive terms - that destroys this traditional repertoire, reinforced by colonial bans and censorship. For these authors, performance is directly related to the wider history of missionary and colonial control, and childhood memories of performance are wrought into a single narrative of oppression and resistance.

In Mau Mau autobiographies this opposition is less strongly developed, in that local songs do not automatically belong to the resistance repertoire, and church hymns from the missionary realm may be turned into resistance songs. These authors are hesitant to condemn their own Christian upbringing and reason from a much less radical stance. The opposition between "Gikuyu tradition" and missionary Christianity does exist for these authors, but is much less strongly tied to the political realm. Their autobiographies stress the Mau Mau struggle as anti-colonial, but the memory of performance is only partly related to this: other performances – not connected to resistance – are also described.

In Wainaina's autobiography, finally, we hardly find such an opposition. Resistance can also be breakdanced, and traditional music may be *kimay* – the word for chaotic and disconcerting sound. While most authors happily describe the meandering of oral forms into each other, for Wainaina this is a source of confusion and even fear. Wainaina is also much less positive about performance than the other writers.

Whatever assessment is presented, it is telling how much attention is being given to performance – song, music, dance and also narrative and speech – and how strongly performance is considered in aesthetic terms. This is especially noteworthy in view of the tense political situation described in these books. One would expect that there are other, more urgent things to tell than singing and dancing, but clearly oral performance is deemed important, and forms part of the situation.

Generally speaking, performance is described in positive terms, and the markers to describe music with are often situated in the aesthetic realm. The notable exception is Binyavanga Wainaina's autobiography. Sound and music are the crucial elements around which the narrative in *One day I will write about this place* is structured, but the assessment is often not positive at all. The protagonist views the intermedial character of Kenya's music as chaotic, and experiences anxiety and fear when listening to it.

Yet, in the final analysis even he – despite all his discomfort and irony – sees possibilities in *kimay*, as he writes on the very last page of his autobiography:

> "Right at the beginning, in our first popular Independence music, before the flag was up, Kenyans had already found a coherent platform to carry our diversity and complexity in sound." (Wainaina 2011: 253).

Bibliography

Atieno Odhiambo, E.S. & Lonsdale, J. (eds) 2003. *Mau Mau and Nationhood, Arms, Authority and Narration.* Oxford, James Currey; Nairobi, EAEP; Athens, Ohio University Press.

Barnett, D. & Njama, K. 1966. *Mau Mau from Within: Autobiography and Analysis of Kenya's Peasant Revolt.* New York, Monthly Review Press.

Clough, M.S. 1997. *Mau Mau Memoirs: History, Memory and Politics.* Boulder, Lynne Rienner.

Coetzee, J. M. 2011. *Scenes from Provincial Life.* London, Vintage Publishing.

Coplan, D.B. 1994. *In the Time of Cannibals. The Word Music of the South Africa's Basotho Migrants.* Chicago, University of Chicago Press.

Emecheta, B. 1986. *Head Above Water.* London, Fontana.

Fair, L. 2001. Voice, authority, and memory: the Kiswahili recordings of Siti binti Saadi, in White, L., Miescher, S.F. & Cohen, D.W. (eds.) *African Words, African Voices. Critical Practices in Oral History*. Bloomington, Indianapolis, Indiana University Press: 246-263.

Finnegan, R. 2007. *The Oral and Beyond. Doing Things with Words in Africa*. Chicago, University of Chicago Press.

Forna, A. 2003. *The Devil that Danced on the Water*. New York, Grove Press.

Gakaara wa Wanjaũ, 1988. *Mau Mau Author in Detention*. Nairobi, Heinemann.

Gatheru, M. 1964. *Child of Two Worlds*. Frederick A. Praeger, New York.

Hunsu, F. 2011. Critical directions in African autobiography. *Marang* 21: 119-134.

Itote, W. 1979. *Mau Mau General*. Nairobi, East African Publishing House.

Julien, E. 1992. *African Novels and the Question of Orality*. Bloomington, Indianapolis, Indiana University Press.

Kaggia, B. 1975. *Roots of Freedom, 1921-1963: The Autobiography of Bildad Kaggia*. Nairobi, East African Publishing House.

Kariuki, J.M. 1963. *"Mau Mau" Detainee*. Oxford, Oxford University Press.

Koigi wa Wamwere. 2002. *I Refuse to Die: my Journey for Freedom*. New York, Seven Stories Press.

Laye, C. 1953. *L'Enfant Noir*. Paris, Plon.

Lejeune, Ph. 1989. *On Autobiography*. Minneapolis, University of Minnesota Press.

Maathai, W. 2008 [2006]. *Unbowed: a Memoir*. New York, Penguin.

Mandela, N. 1994. *Long Walk to Freedom*. London, Little Brown.

Mboya, T. 1963. *Freedom and After*. London, Deutsch.

Mda, Z. 2011. *Sometimes there is a Void: Memoirs of an Outsider*. London, Penguin.

Morales, D.M. 2003. The pervasive force of music in African, Caribbean, and African American drama. *Research in African Literatures* 34 (2): 145-154.

Muoria, H. 1994. *I, the Gikuyu and the White Fury*. Nairobi: East African Educational Publishers.

Neubauer, C. 1983. One voice speaking for many: The Mau Mau Movement and Kenyan Autobiography. *Journal of Modern African Studies* 21 (1): 113-131.

Thiong'o, Ngũgĩ wa. 1981. *Detained: a Writer's Prison Diary*. Nairobi, *Heinemann*.

Thiong'o, Ngũgĩ wa. 2011. *Dreams in a Time of War: a Childhood Memoir*. London, Vintage Books.

Thiong'o, Ngũgĩ wa. 2013. *In the House of the Interpreter*. Nairobi, East African Educational Publishers.

Thiong'o, Ngũgĩ wa. 2016. *Birth of a Dream Weaver: A Writer's Awakening* London, Vintage Books.

Nkrumah, K. 1957. *Ghana: the Autobiography of Kwame Nkrumah*. New York, Nelson.

Odinga, O. 1976 [1967]. *Not yet Uhuru*. Nairobi, East African Educational Publishers.

Obiechina, E. 1975. *Culture, Tradition and Society in the West African Novel.* Cambridge, Cambridge University Press, esp Chapter: Nature, Music and Art. 42-81.

Olney, J. 1973. *Tell me Africa: an Approach to African Literature.* Princeton, Princeton University Press.

Peterson, D.R. 2012. *Ethnic Patriotism and the East African Revival.* Cambridge, Cambridge University Press.

Peterson, D. R. 2006. Casting characters: autobiography and political imagination in Central Kenya. *Research in African Literatures* 37 (3): 176-192.

Pugliese, C. 1986. The life-story in Kenya: a bibliography (1920-1984). *Africa* (Rome) 41 (3): 440-446.

Samuelson, M. 2007. Yvonne Vera's *Bulawayo*: modernity, (im)mobility, music, and memory. *Research in African Literatures* 38 (2): 22-35.

Soyinka, W. *Aké: The Years of Childhood.* New York, Random House.

Thuku, H. 1970. *Harry Thuku: an Autobiography.* Nairobi, Oxford University Press.

Wachanga, H.K. 1975. *The swords of Kirinyaga. The fight for land and freedom.* Nairobi, Kenya Literature Bureau.

Waciuma, C. 1969. *Daughter of Mumbi.* Nairobi, East African Publishing House.

Wagner-Egelhaaf, M. 2005. *Autobiographie.* Stuttgart, Metzler.

Wainaina, B. 2011. *One day I Will Write about this Place.* Minneapolis, Graywolf Press.

Wamweya, J. 1971. *Freedom Fighter.* Nairobi: East Africa Publishing House.

Yagoda, B. 2009. *Memoir: a History.* New York, Riverhead Books.

Index

A

Abdi Aden Haad 53–62
African residential estates 32, 33, 35, 43
    Kaloleni 34–35, 37, 39, 42–43
    Makongeni 32, 34–35, 39
    Muthurwa 34–36, 39, 42–43
    Ziwani 37, 42
Aga Galgallo 66, 70, 73
Alcohol
    alcoholic victims 92
    Alcoholism and domestic violence 92–93
    consumption 19, 21
Anthropology 9
    British 9
    of dance and cultural studies 9
Autobiography 120–134. *See also* diary and memoirs
    difference between 121
    in Kenya 122–123

B

Ballroom 32–33, 35, 37–40
BBC radio 127
Black Atlantic 48, 49
Branchements 48
Brinkman, Inge 120

C

Change 103–104, 107–117
Christian 20
    Churches 21
    missionaries/missions 20–21
Colonial Choreography 16–27
Colony
    British colonial administration 16–23, 27
    British Somaliland 50
    colonialism 22, 26
    Colony Music and Drama Officer 24
    Italian Somaliland 50
    Kenya Colony 17–28
    settlement/settler colonialism 17–20, 22, 24
Competitive festivals 23, 27
Culture studies 10–11
Cuud (oud) 76–77, 81–82, 84–86

D

Dance 120–134
Dance and performance 103
Dansi 38, 40
Diary. *See* Autobiography
Djibouti 48–61
Domestic violence 91
    gendered violence 92
    within the marriage institution 91–94

E

Electoral politics 66
Engender 103, 105–107, 115
Ethnic
    and cultural boundaries 10
    and national identities 11
    competing interests 8
Ethnicity 66–67, 109
Everyday experience 8
    and social conventions 11
    music and dance as part of 8

F

folklore
    folklorisation 24–25
Folklore 22, 24
    heritagisation 21

G

Gadamojji 65, 69–72
Gada system 63–66
Gender 103–117
    and control among the Gĩkũyũ 92
    and power relations 95
    constructs 92–93
    debate 91, 95, 99
    dialogue 97, 99
    discourse amongst the Gĩkũyũ 97
    divide 95
    equity 96–97
    in everyday life 99

insensitive 94
politics 94
relations 91–92, 98
Gender roles 104–105, 109–116
Genres 103–105, 107, 109, 111
Gonda dance 20

H

Haaraan 76, 79
Hargeysa 51, 56, 76–81, 84–87
Hargeysa Brothers 51
Heritage dance 16–17, 23–27
Heritage preservation 76–77, 80–81, 84, 86–87
Hiddo Dhawr 76–78, 80–87
Humanities
  music and dance in the 11
  thematic concerns of 9
Husband
  bashing 91–92, 96, 99
  battered 91
  hen-pecked 93
  penis chopped off 100
Hybrid 106–107, 110–111, 115

I

Identity 63–72, 103, 107–108, 110, 116–117
  and performance levels 8
  and politics 63
  construction of state, national and ethnic 10–11
  creation for community members 10
Idioms 85, 91, 99
  gada terms 67
Instruments 103, 105–108, 110–112, 117
Interdisciplinary
  barriers 9
  labels 9
  perspective to music and dance 11
Isukuti dance 20, 25

K

Kamaru, Joseph 93, 101–102
Kenedid, A. Hassan 48
Kenya 121–135
  autobiography, diary and memoirs 122–123
Kiiru, Kahithe 8, 16
Kochore, Hassan H. 63

L

Labor 33, 41–43
Local-national lens 64
Love
  and sex 92
  in a male-dominated society 93
  related tragedies 100
  songs 94
  theme of 91, 93
Love songs 76–77, 80, 84, 86–88
Luo 103–115

M

Maendeleo ya Wanaume 93, 97
Maendeleo ya Wanawake 100
Marriage
  affairs outside 98
  beating 91, 99
  cruelty in 94
  institution 91, 99
  termination of 96
Marsabit Boran 64–66, 69, 72
Mau Mau 120–134
  songs 128–129
Memoirs. *See* autobiography
Memory 120–134
  childhood 125
Modern identity 40
Mpango wa kando 98
Multimodality 123–124
Music 103–117, 120–134
  as therapy 83, 85
  identity and politics 63
Music and dance 8–11
  adjectives used 8
  and socio-political realities 8
  cultural expressions 9
  genres 10
  study of 8–10
  within social and cultural studies 8
Musicians 36, 38–42
  Daudi Kabaka 42
  David Amunga 36
  Eduard Masengo 36
  Fadhili Williams 41–42
  Fundi Konde 36, 42
  Gabriel Omolo 42
  George Mukabi 36, 42
  Jean-Bosco Mwenda 36

John Mwale 36, 42
Music producers
  Ally Sykes 40
  Charles Worrod 40
  Peter Colmore 40
Mūthīrīgū songs 21
Mūtonya, Maina wa 8

N

Nairobi sound 33, 36–39, 43
Narrative. *See* performance
Nation
  building and creation of national identity 9
  post-colonial 8
National Front United 51
Native 17–27
  Commissioner 21
  Council 19
  dances (ngoma) 16–27
  reserve 20–21
  stadiums 23–24
Native affairs 17–18, 22
Ngũgĩ wa Thiong'o 122, 123
  memoirs 120–134
Ng'weno, Bettina 32
Nostalgia 66, 72, 84–85
Nyeri
  Nyerification 97
  woman 92, 96–97
Nyeri County 92–93

O

Oral literature 126
  and politics of gender and control 92–93
  representation of women 92–93
Orchestration 17–27
  orchestrated cultural diversity 25

P

Pan-Somalism 48, 55
Performance 8, 120–134. *See also* music and dance
  and African independent school 125–127
  and colonial legislation 128
  and esthetics 130–131
  as resistance 127–130
  missions 125–127
  of local politics and national identities, 11
  of music and everyday experiences 8
  of music and in Uganda 9
Political meanings of performance 127–130
Popular culture 103, 107, 113, 118
Popular music 103–104, 111, 116, 118
Post-war 50, 76–77, 80, 87
Prohibition
  of dances 16, 19–21, 24, 27
Public space 51, 77, 79, 84–85

R

Radio 35, 39–41
  Kenya Broadcasting Service 41
  Railway Showboat 39–42
Railway 39–43
Railways 34–35
Railway strike 41
Representation 25–27
  self-representation 26

S

Sahra Halgan 80–81, 83–87
Siyaad Barre, General 52
Social halls 33–42
  Bahati 34
  Tobacco Village 34–35
Social sciences
  inclusion of music and/or dance in 10
  relevance of music and dance studies in 11
  thematic concerns of contemporary humanities 9
Socio-political change 64, 66, 72
Somaliland 76–85, 87
Somaliland National League 51
Somali National Movement 78, 80–81, 87
Speech and language as performance 124
Sponsor
  as a form of financial security 98
  in everyday parlance 98
  Ndīretha song 98
  older male lover 98
Staging 16–27
Stereotypes 99, 114–115, 118
  as a form of knowledge and identification 97
  idioms and clichés 91, 99
  in the everyday life of Kenyans 96
  metaphors emanating from the gender discourse 97
  of a Nyeri woman 96–97
  of the Gĩkũyũ woman 96

of women from Mũrang'a, Kiambu and Nyeri 97
Sugar daddy
  in songs 93
  lovers 93
  motif in the 60s and 70s 98
Sugar Daddy Lover - novel 100
Sugar mummy 98
  Cougar Town 93
  image of 99
  older women lovers 95
  Sugar Mami song 93
Symbolism 63–65, 72
Syncretize 64

T

Taarab 64
Thum nyatiti 109, 111–113
Thum Nyatiti 105–107
Tom Mboya 42–43
Tourism, cultural 24–27
tourismification 26
Traditional as opposed to Christian 126–127
Traditional music
  and dance expressions 10
  eroticization of traditional ngoma 10
  genres 10
Trends 103–104, 110, 114

W

Wainaina, Binyavanga
  kimay 120, 124–125, 132
  memoirs 120–134
Wangari Maathai 127
Wife
  and husband relationships 93
  cruel 94
  expectations of the 96
  first 96–97
  second 96
Woolner, Christina J. 76

www.ingramcontent.com/pod-product-compliance
Lightning Source LLC
Chambersburg PA
CBHW060420300426
44111CB00018B/2919